Lecture Notes in Computer Science

Commenced Publication in 1973
Founding and Former Series Editors:
Gerhard Goos, Juris Hartmanis, and Jan van Leeuwen

Editorial Board

Gary T. Leavens   Peter O'Hearn
Sriram K. Rajamani (Eds.)

Verified Software: Theories, Tools, Experiments

Third International Conference, VSTTE 2010
Edinburgh, UK, August 16-19, 2010
Proceedings

 Springer

Volume Editors

Gary T. Leavens
University of Central Florida, School of Electrical Engineering
and Computer Science, 439C Harris Center, Building 116
4000 Central Florida Boulevard, Orlando, FL 32816-2362, USA
E-mail: leavens@eecs.ucf.edu

Peter O'Hearn
Queen Mary, University of London
School of Electronic Engineering and Computer Science
Mile End Road, London E1 4NS, UK
E-mail: ohearn@eecs.qmul.ac.uk

Sriram K. Rajamani
Microsoft Research India, "Scientia" - 196/36 2nd Main
Sadashivnagar, Bangalore 560 080, India
E-mail: sriram@microsoft.com

Library of Congress Control Number: 2010931860

CR Subject Classification (1998): D.2, F.3, D.3, D.1, C.2, F.4

LNCS Sublibrary: SL 2 – Programming and Software Engineering

ISSN   0302-9743
ISBN-10   3-642-15056-X Springer Berlin Heidelberg New York
ISBN-13   978-3-642-15056-2 Springer Berlin Heidelberg New York

Typesetting: Camera-ready by author, data conversion by Scientific Publishing Services, Chennai, India
Printed on acid-free paper   06/3180

Preface

Verified Software: Theories, Tools and Experiments, VSTTE 2010, was held in Edinburgh, Scotland during August 16-19, 2010. This conference is part of the Verified Software Initiative (VSI), which is a 15-year international project that focuses on the scientific and technical challenges of producing verified software. Previous VSTTE conferences were held in Zurich, Switzerland (in 2005) and Toronto, Canada (in 2008).

The goal of VSTTE 2010 was to advance the state of the art in the science and technology of software verification through the interaction of theory development, tool evolution, and experimental validation. The accepted papers represent work on verification techniques, specification languages, formal calculi, verification tools, solutions to challenge problems, software design methods, reusable components, refinement methodologies, and requirements modeling. Several of the accepted papers also presented case studies, either in response to published challenge problems or problems of practical interest. Many of the papers were also concerned with concurrent programs.

As specified in the call for papers, authors submitted 15-page papers electronically. The EasyChair system handled submissions and was used to manage the reviewing of papers and subsequent discussion. This system aided the Program Committee in avoiding conflicts of interest during the reviewing and discussion process. There was electronic discussion among the Program Committee members about the merits of each submission, moderated by the Program Committee Co-chairs.

This year the conference received 32 submissions, of which 11 were accepted, for an acceptance rate of about 34%. Seven of the accepted papers were co-authored by members of the Program Committee.

We were pleased to have invited talks by Tom Ball, Gerwin Klein, and Matthew Parkinson. The authors of these invited talks also graciously consented to the publication of accompanying invited papers in this volume.

We thank the VSTTE organizers, in particular the conference chair, Andrew Ireland, for providing essential support and encouragement. We also thank the authors of all submitted papers. But most of all, we thank the Program Committee for their hard work in reviewing the papers and making decisions about the program.

June 2010

Gary T. Leavens
Peter O'Hearn
Sriram K. Rajmani

Organization

VSTTE 2010 was organized by Andrew Ireland and hosted by Heriot-Watt University.

Steering Committee

Tony Hoare	Microsoft Research, Cambridge, UK
Jay Misra	University of Texas, Austin, USA
Natarajan Shankar	SRI, Palo Alto, USA
Jim Woodcock	York University, York, UK

Organizing Committee

Conference Chair:	Andrew Ireland (Heriot-Watt University, UK)
Program Co-chairs:	Gary T. Leavens (University of Central Florida, USA)
	Peter O'Hearn (Queen Mary, University of London, UK)
	Sriram K. Rajamani (Microsoft Research, India)
Local Arrangements Chair:	Ewen Maclean (Heriot-Watt University, UK)
Publicity Chair:	Gudmund Grov (University of Edinburgh, UK)
Workshops General Chair:	Peter Müller (ETH Zurich, Switzerland)
Theory Workshops Chairs:	David Naumann (Stevens Institute of Tech., USA)
	Hongseok Yang (Queen Mary, University of London, UK)
Tools & Experiments Workshops Chairs:	Rajeev Joshi (NASA JPL, USA)
	Tiziana Margaria (University of Potsdam, Germany)

Program Committee

In addition to the three Co-chairs, the Program Committee consisted of the following dedicated computer scientists.

Ahmed Bouajjani	Xavier Leroy	Zhong Shao
Leo Freitas	David Naumann	Aaron Stump
Philippa Gardner	Matthew Parkinson	Serdar Tasiran
John Hatcliff	Wolfgang Paul	Willem Visser
Ranjit Jhala	Shaz Qadeer	Chin Wei-Ngan
Joseph Kiniry	Andrey Rybalchenko	Stephanie Weirich
Rustan Leino	Augusto Sampaio	Greta Yorsh

Subreviewers

We thank the following subreviewers who assisted the Program Committee in evaluating submitted papers.

David Costanzo
Thomas Dinsdale-Young
Mike Dodds
Sophia Drossopolou
Constantin Enea
Fintan Fairmichael
Xinyu Feng

Alexey Gotsman
Mark Hillebrand
Neelakantan
  Krishnaswami
Sidney Nogueira
Rodrigo Ramos
Stan Rosenberg

Ali Sezgin
Alexander Summers
Nikhil Swamy
Alexander Vaynberg
John Wickerson

Sponsoring Institutions

We thank the following sponsors of VSTTE for their generous support.

The US National Science Foundation (NSF)
The UK Engineering and Physical Sciences Research Council (EPSRC)
Microsoft Research
The Scottish Informatics and Computer Science Alliance (SICSA)
Altran Praxis
Software Systems Engineering Institute (SSEI)
Formal Methods Europe (FME)
Contemplate Ltd.
Heriot-Watt Working with Industry

Table of Contents

Invited Talk

Verification Techniques

Verification of Low-Level Code

Invited Talk

Requirements and Specifications

Verification Techniques

Invited Talk

Locality in Reasoning

Towards Scalable Modular Checking of User-Defined Properties

Thomas Ball[1], Brian Hackett[2], Shuvendu K. Lahiri[1]
Shaz Qadeer[1], and Julien Vanegue[1]

[1] Microsoft
[2] Stanford University

Abstract. Theorem-prover based modular checkers have the potential to perform scalable and precise checking of user-defined properties by combining path-sensitive intraprocedural reasoning with user-defined procedure abstractions. However, such tools have seldom been deployed on large software applications of industrial relevance due to the annotation burden required to provide the procedure abstractions.

In this work, we present two case studies of applying a modular checker HAVOC to check properties on large modules in the Microsoft Windows operating system. The first detailed case study describes checking the synchronization protocol of a core Microsoft Windows component with more than 300 thousand lines of code and 1500 procedures. The effort found 45 serious bugs in the component with modest annotation effort and low false alarms; most of these bugs have since been fixed by the developers of the module. The second case study reports preliminary user experience in using the tool for checking security related properties in several Windows components. We describe our experience in using a modular checker to create various property checkers for finding errors in a well-tested applications of this scale, and our design decisions to find them with low false alarms, modest annotation burden and high coverage.

1 Introduction

Developing and maintaining systems software such as operating systems kernels and device drivers is a challenging task. They consist of modules often exceeding several hundred thousand to millions of lines of code written in low-level languages such as C and C++. In many cases, these modules evolve over several decades where the original architects or developers have long ago departed. Such software may become fragile through the accumulation of new features, performance tuning and bug fixes, often done in an ad-hoc manner. Given the astronomical number of paths in any real program, testing can only cover a relatively very small fraction of the paths in a module. Bugs found in the field often occur in these rarely exercised paths.

Static analysis tools provide an attractive alternative to testing by helping find defects without requiring concrete inputs. However, the applicability of completely automatic static tools is limited due to several factors:

- First, most static analysis tools check *generic* properties of code such as buffer overrun, null dereference or absence of data-races. These checkers are not *extensible*,

G.T. Leavens, P. O'Hearn, and S.K. Rajamani (Eds.): VSTTE 2010, LNCS 6217, pp. 1–24, 2010.

i.e., they cannot be easily augmented to create a checker for a new user-defined property — testing still remains the only way to check such properties.

- Second, most scalable static analysis tools are based on specific abstract domains or dataflow facts. These tools generate numerous false alarms when the property being checked depends on system-specific invariants that fall outside the scope of the analysis. This happens particularly when the property depends on the heap — even when the property being checked is a generic property as above.
- Finally, more extensible tools (such as those based on predicate abstraction) have scalability problems to large modules because they try to automatically find a proof of the property by searching an unbounded space of proofs. They rely on various automated refinement strategies which are not robust enough to generate all non-trivial invariants for large modules.

Contract-based modular checkers such as ESC/Java [17], Spec# [4], HAVOC [5] and VCC [9] have the potential to perform scalable checking of user-defined properties. These checkers share the following strengths:

1. They provide the operational semantics of the underlying programs irrespective of the property being checked. This is in stark contrast to static analyzers based on data-flow analysis or abstract interpretation, which require defining abstract semantics for each new property.
2. They use a theorem prover to perform precise intraprocedural analysis for loop-free and call-free programs, in the presence of contracts for loop and called procedures.
3. They provide an extensible contract language to specify the properties of interest, and contracts. The use of theorem provers allow rich contracts to be specified, when required, to remove false alarms.
4. Generic interprocedural contract inference techniques (e.g. Houdini [16]) exist to infer contracts to relieve the user from manually annotating the entire module. By allowing the user to provide a restricted space of procedure abstractions (contracts) to search for proofs, the approach allows the user to aid the analysis to find proofs in a scalable fashion.
5. Finally, the presence of contracts provide *incremental* checking across changes to procedures without reanalyzing the entire module, and the contracts can serve as valuable documentation for maintaining these large codebases.

In spite of the potential benefits offered by modular checkers, such tools have been seldom deployed successfully on large software applications of industrial relevance. We believe this is due to the following limitations:

1. The annotation burden for checking a property on such a large code-base can be substantial, and can often be several times the size of the source code. Although contract inference has been proposed to relieve the user burden, previous work in ESC/Java [16,15] does not allow for inferring user-defined contracts. We provide one particular way for inferring a class of contracts from module invariants [21], but it has not been shown to scale to modules considered in this work.
2. The problem of capturing the side-effect of each procedure and aliasing between pointers can be difficult. Various ownership and encapsulation methodologies have

been proposed [4], but they impose restrictions on the heap manipulation that are often not satisfied by low-level systems code.

3. Finally, there is a lack of good case studies illustrating the feasibility of using such a tool on real-world software to provide value in discovering hard-to-find bugs, with modest investment of user effort.

In this paper, we present a feasibility study of using contract-based modular checkers for cost-effective checking of user-defined properties on large modules of industrial relevance. We first describe our experience with applying the modular checker HAVOC [5,20] on a core component COMP of the Windows kernel — the name of the module and the code fragments have been modified for proprietary reasons. The code base has more than 300 thousand lines of C code and has evolved over two decades. The module has over 1500 procedures, with some of the procedures being a few thousand lines long — a result of the various feature additions over successive versions. For this component, we specified and checked properties related to the synchronization protocol governing the management of its main heap allocated data structures. The correctness checking of the protocol was decomposed into checking for correct reference counting, proper lock usage, absence of data races and ensuring that objects are not accessed after being reclaimed (teardown race). Verification of these properties required expressing many system-specific intermediate invariants (see Section 2) that are beyond the capabilities of existing static analysis tools. The highlights of the effort that was conducted over a period of two months were:

1. We found 45 bugs in the COMP module that were confirmed by the developers and many of them have been fixed at the time of writing. Most of these bugs appear along error recovery paths indicating the mature and well-tested nature of the code and signifying the ability of modular checkers to detect subtle corner cases.
2. The checking required modest annotation effort of about 250 contracts for specifying the properties and operating system model, 600 contracts for procedure contracts. The contract inference generated around 3000 simple contracts, a bulk of the required annotation effort, to relieve the need for annotating such a large code base. This corresponds to roughly one manual contract per 500 lines of code, or one per 2.5 procedures.
3. The tool currently reports 125 warnings, including the 45 confirmed bugs, when the checker runs on the annotated code base. The extra warnings are violations of intermediate contracts that can be reduced with additional contracts.

Next, we report on preliminary user experience in using the tool for checking security related properties in several other Windows components. Various property checkers have been constructed using HAVOC to check for correct validation of user pointers, and restricted class of exploitable buffer overrun problems. The tool has been deployed on more than 1.3 million lines of code across three or four large components each measuring several hundred thousand lines of code. The effort has yielded around 15 security vulnerabilities that have been already patched.

We describe the challenges faced in using a modular checker for finding errors in well-tested applications of this scale, and our design decisions to find them with low false alarms, modest contract burden and high coverage. Our decisions allowed us to

```
typedef struct _LIST_ENTRY{
  struct _LIST_ENTRY *Flink, *Blink;
} LIST_ENTRY, *PLIST_ENTRY;

typedef struct _NODEA{
  PERESOURCE Resource;                #define CONTAINING_RECORD(addr, type, field)\
  LIST_ENTRY NodeBQueue;                  ((type *)((PCHAR)(addr) -              \
  ...                                         (PCHAR)(&((type *)0)->field))) \
} NODEA, *PNODEA;
                                      //helper macros
typedef struct _NODEB{                #define ENCL_NODEA(x)                      \
  PNODEA     ParentA;                     CONTAINING_RECORD(x, NODEA, NodeBQueue) \
  ULONG State;                        #define ENCL_NODEB(x)                      \
  LIST_ENTRY NodeALinks;                  CONTAINING_RECORD(x, NODEB, NodeALinks) \
  ...
} NODEB, *PNODEB;
```

Fig. 1. Data structures and macros used in the example

achieve an order of magnitude less false alarms compared to previous case studies using modular checkers [16], while working on C modules almost an order more complex than these previous case studies. We believe that the studies also contribute by identifying areas of further research to improve the applicability of these modular checkers in the hands of a user.

2   Overview

In this section, we use the example of checking data-race freedom on the main data structures of COMP to illustrate some of complexities of checking properties of systems software with low-false alarms. In particular, we show that precise checking of even a generic property such as data-race freedom often requires:

- contracts involving pointer arithmetic and aliasing,
- conditional contracts, and
- type invariants to capture aliasing relationships.

Such requirements are clearly beyond the capabilities of existing automated software analysis tools that scale to such large components. This justifies the use of modular checkers that involve the users to decompose the problem using domain-specific knowledge.

We first describe high-level details of the data structure and the synchronization protocol, some procedures manipulating these structures, and finally the contracts to check the absence of data-races.

2.1   Data Structures

Figure 1 describes a few types for the heap-allocated data structures in COMP. The type LIST_ENTRY is the generic type for (circular) doubly-linked lists in most of Windows source code. It contains two fields Flink and Blink to obtain the *forward* and *backward* successors of a LIST_ENTRY node respectively in a linked list. An object of type NODEA contains a list of children objects of type NODEB using the field

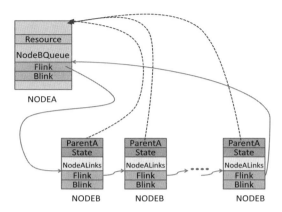

Fig. 2. The list of NODEB children of a NODEA

NodeBQueue. Figure 2 describes the shape of the children list for any NODEA object. Each child NODEB node also maintains pointers to its *parent* NODEA object with the ParentA field.

The macro CONTAINING_RECORD (defined in Figure 1) takes a pointer addr to an internal field field of a structure of type type and returns the pointer to the enclosing structure by performing pointer arithmetic. The helper macros ENCL_NODEA and ENCL_NODEB uses the CONTAINING_RECORD macro to obtain pointers to enclosing NODEA and NODEB structures respectively, given a pointer to their LIST_ENTRY fields. The CONTAINING_RECORD macro is frequently used and is a major source of pointer arithmetic.

Since these objects can be accessed from multiple threads, one needs a synchronization mechanism to ensure the absence of data-races on the fields of these objects. Each NODEA structure maintains a field Resource, which is a pointer to an ERESOURCE structure that implements a reader-writer lock. The lock not only protects accesses to the fields in the NODEA structure but additionally also protects the fields NodeALinks, ParentA and State in all of its NODEB children.

2.2 Procedures

Figure 3 describes three procedures that manipulate the NODEA and NODEB objects. Contracts are denoted by __requires, __ensures and __loop_inv. ClearChild takes a NODEA object NodeA and clears a mask StateMask from the State field of any NODEB child that has this mask set. It uses the procedure FindChild in a loop to find all the children that have the StateMask set and then clears the mask on the child by calling ClearState. Finally, the procedure FindChild iterates over the children for a NODEA object and returns either the first child that has the mask set, or NULL if no such child exists.

To encode the data-race freedom property on the fields of NODEA and NODEB objects, we introduce assertions that each access (read or write) to a field is guarded by the Resource lock in the appropriate NODEA object. The three procedures clearly

```
#define __resA(x)          __resource(''NODEA_RES'',x)
#define __resrA_held(x)     __resA(x) > 0

VOID ClearChild(PNODEA NodeA, ULONG StateMask) {
  AcquireNodeAExcl(NodeA);
  PNODEB NodeB;
  FindChild(NodeA, StateMask, &NodeB);

  __loop_inv(NodeB != NULL ==> NodeB->ParentA == NodeA)
  while (NodeB != NULL) {
     ClearState(NodeB, StateMask);
     FindChild(NodeA, StateMask, &NodeB);
  }
  ReleaseNodeA(NodeA);
}


__requires(__resrA_held(NodeA))
__ensures(*PNodeB != NULL ==> (*PNodeB)->ParentA == NodeA)
VOID FindChild(PNODEA NodeA, ULONG StateMask, PNODEB* PNodeB) {
  PLIST_ENTRY Entry = NodeA->NodeBQueue.Flink;

  __loop_inv(Entry != &NodeA->NodeBQueue ==> ENCL_NODEB(Entry)->ParentA == NodeA)
  while (Entry != &NodeA->NodeBQueue) {
     PNODEB NodeB = ENCL_NODEB(Entry);
     if (NodeB->State & StateMask != 0) {
        *PNodeB = NodeB; return;
     }
     Entry = Entry->FLink;
  }
  *PNodeB = NULL; return;
}


__requires(__resrA_held(NodeB->ParentA))
VOID ClearState(PNODEB NodeB, ULONG StateMask) {
   NodeB->State &= ~StateMask;
}
```

Fig. 3. Procedures and contracts for data-race freedom

satisfy data-race freedom since the lock on the NODEA object is acquired by a call to AcquireNodeAExcl before any of the operations.

2.3   Contracts

Now, let us look at the contracts required by HAVOC to verify the absence of the data-race in the program. The procedure ClearState has a *precondition* (an assertion inside __requires) that the Resource field of the NodeB->ParentA is held at entry; this ensures that the access to NodeB->State is properly protected. The __resrA_held(x) macro expands to __resource("NODEA_RES", x > 0), which checks the value of a *ghost field* "NODEA_RES" inside x. The integer valued ghost field "NODEA_RES" tracks the state of the re-entrant Resource lock in a NODEA object — a positive value denotes that the Resource is acquired. For brevity, we skip the contracts for AcquireNodeAExcl and ReleaseNodeA, which increments and decrements the value of the ghost field, respectively.

The procedure FindChild has a similar precondition on the NodeA parameter. The procedure also has a *postcondition* (an assertion inside __ensures) that captures the child-parent relationship between the out parameters PNodeB and NodeA.

```
#define FIRST_CHILD(x)     x->NodeBQueue.Flink
#define NEXT_NODE(x)       x->NodeALinks.Flink

__type_invariant(PNODEA x){
    ENCL_NODEA(FIRST_CHILD(x)) != x  ==>
    ENCL_NODEB(FIRST_CHILD(x))->ParentA == x
)

__type_invariant(PNODEB y){
    NEXT_NODE(y) != &(y->ParentA->NodeBQueue) ==>
    y->ParentA == ENCL_NODEB(NEXT_NODE(y))->ParentA
)
```

Fig. 4. Type invariants for NODEA and NODEB types

Let us inspect the contracts on `ClearChild`. We need a *loop invariant* (an assertion inside `__loop_inv`) to ensure the precondition of `ClearState` inside the loop. The loop invariant states that `NodeB` is a child of `NodeA` when it is not `NULL`. The postcondition of `FindChild` ensures that the loop invariant holds at the entry of the loop and also is preserved by an arbitrary iteration of the loop.

Finally, consider the loop invariant in procedure `FindChild`: the loop invariant is required for both proving the postcondition of the procedure, as well as to prove the absence of a data-race on `NodeB->State` inside the loop. This loop invariant does not follow directly from the contracts on the procedure and the loop body.

To prove this loop invariant, we specify two *type invariants* for NODEA and NODEB objects using the `__type_invariant` annotation in Figure 4. The type invariant on any NODEA object x states that if the children list of x is non-empty then the parent field `ParentA` of the first child points back to x. The type invariant for any NODEB object y states that if the next object in the list is not the head of the circular list, then the next NODEB object in the list has the same parent as y. The two type invariants capture important shape information of the data structures and together imply that all the NODEB objects in the children list of `NodeA` point to `NodeA`.

3   Background on HAVOC

In this section, we provide some background on HAVOC, including the contract language, the modular checker and an interprocedural contract inference. In addition to the details of HAVOC described in earlier works [5,6], we describe the main additions to the tool for this paper. This includes adding support for *resources* and *type invariants* in contracts, and the instrumentation techniques.

3.1   Contracts

Our contracts are similar in spirit to those found in ESC/Java [17] for Java programs, but are designed for verifying systems programs written in C. We provide an overview of the subset of contracts that are used in this work. Throughout this paper, we use the terms "contracts" and "annotations" interchangeably, although the former is primarily used to express an assertion. More details of the contract language are described in the HAVOC user manual[1].

Procedure contracts and loop invariants. Procedure contracts consist of preconditions, postconditions and modifies clauses. The `__requires` contract specifies a precondition that holds at the entry to a procedure. This assertion is assumed when analyzing the body of the procedure and checked at all call-sites of the procedure. The `__ensures` contract specifies a postcondition that holds at exit from the procedure. The `__modifies` contract specifies a set of locations that are possibly modified by the procedure; it generates a postcondition that *all other* locations in the heap remain unchanged. The postconditions are checked when analyzing the body of the procedure, and assumed at all call-sites for the procedure.

The `__loop_inv` contract specifies a loop invariant — an assertion that holds every time control reaches the head of the loop. The assertion should hold at entry to the loop, and should be preserved across an arbitrary iteration of the loop.

Contract expressions. A novel feature of our contract language is that it allows most call-free and side-effect free C expressions in the assertions. The assertions can refer to user defined macros, thereby allowing complex assertions to be constructed from simpler ones. We allow reference to the return value of a procedure with the `__return` keyword. The postconditions may also refer to the state at the entry to the procedure using the `__old` keyword as follows:

```
__ensures  (__return == __old(*x) + 1)
__modifies (x)
int Foo (int *x) {*x = *x + 1; return *x;}
```

Resources. In addition to the C program expressions, we allow the contracts to refer to "ghost fields" (called *resources*) of objects. Resources are auxiliary fields in data structures meant only for the purpose of specification and manipulated exclusively through contracts. We allow the user to use `__resource(name, expr)` to refer to the value of the ghost field `name` in `expr`. The contract

$$\_\_modifies\_resource(name, expr)$$

specifies that the resource `name` is possibly modified at `expr`. Consider the following contract on the procedure `ReleaseNodeA` that releases the `Resource` field of a `NODEA` object:

```
#define __resrA(x)  __resource(''NODEA_RES'', x)
#define __modA(x)   __modifies_resource(''NODEA_RES'', x)

#define __releasesA(x)                               \
    __requires (__resrA(x) > 0)                       \
    __ensures  (__resrA(x) == __old(__resrA(x)) - 1)\
    __modA(x)                                         \

__releasesA(NodeA)
void ReleaseNodeA (NODEA NodeA);
```

Type invariants. Figure 4 illustrates type invariants for the NODEA and NODEB types, using the `__type_invariant` contract. Type invariants specify assertions that hold

---

[1] Available at http://research.microsoft.com/projects/havoc/

for all objects of a given type. Such invariants typically hold at all control locations except for a handful of procedures where an object is being initialized or being torn down, or may be broken locally inside a basic block (e.g. when an NODEB object is added as a child for NODEA). The user has the flexibility to specify the control locations where he or she expects the invariants to be temporarily violated.

3.2   Modular Checker

In this section, we provide a brief overview of the checker for verifying an annotated procedure. Interested readers can find more details in other works [5]. The main enabling techniques in the checker are:

Accurate memory model for C. HAVOC provides a faithful operational semantics for C programs accounting for the low-level operations in systems code. It treats every C pointer expression (including addresses of stack allocated variables, heap locations, and values stored in variables and the heap) uniformly as integers. The heap is modeled as a mutable map or an array Mem mapping integers to integers. A structure corresponds to a sequence of pointers and each field corresponds to a compile-time offset within the structure. A pointer dereference *e corresponds to a lookup of Mem at the address e and an update *x = y is translated as an update to Mem at address x with value y. Contract expressions are translated in a similar fashion.

Given an annotated C program, the tool translates the annotated source into an annotated BoogiePL [12] program, a simple intermediate language with precise operational semantics and support for contracts. The resulting program consists of scalars and maps, and all the complexities of C (pointer arithmetic, & operations, casts etc.) have been compiled away at this stage. Example of the translation can be found in earlier work [6].

Precise verification conditions. HAVOC uses the Boogie [4] verifier on the generated BoogiePL file to construct a logical formula called the *verification condition* (VC). The VC is a formula whose validity implies that the program does not go wrong by failing one of the assertions or the contracts. Moreover, it ensures that the VC generated for a loop-free and call-free program is unsatisfiable *if and only if* the program does not go wrong by failing any assertion or contract present in the code. This is in sharp contrast to most other static analysis tools that lose precision at merge points.

Scalable checking using SMT solvers. The validity of the VC is checked using a state-of-the-art *Satisfiability Modulo Theories* (SMT) solver Z3 [11]. SMT solvers are extensions of the Boolean Satisfiability (SAT) solvers that handle different *logical theories* such as equality with uninterpreted functions, arithmetic and arrays. These solvers leverage the advances in SAT solving with powerful implementation of theory specific algorithms. These tools can scale to large verification conditions by leveraging conflict-driven learning, smart backtracking and efficient theory reasoning. The modular analysis with efficient SMT solvers provides a scalable and relatively precise checker for realistic procedures up to a few thousand lines large.

3.3 Interprocedural Contract Inference

HAVOC, like any other procedure-modular checker, requires contracts for called procedures. We have implemented a contract inference algorithm in HAVOC based on the
Houdini [16] algorithm in ESC/Java. The algorithm takes as input a partially annotated module along with a finite set of *candidate contracts* for each procedure in the
module, and outputs a subset of the candidates that are valid contracts for the module.
The candidate contracts are specified by providing an expression inside __c_requires,
__c_ensures and __c_loop_inv contracts. For example, the candidate contracts on a
procedure Foo are shown below:

```
__c_requires (x != NULL)
__c_ensures  (__return > __old(*x))
int Foo (int *x) {*x = *x + 1; return *x;}
```

The Houdini algorithm performs a fixed point algorithm as follows: Initially, the contract for each procedure is the union of the user-provided contracts and the set of candidate contracts. At any iteration, it removes a candidate contract that can be violated
during a modular checking of a procedure. The algorithm terminates when the set of
candidate contracts does not change.

3.4 Instrumentation

HAVOC also provides different ways for instrumenting the source code with additional
contracts (either candidate or normal ones), to relieve the user of manually annotating
large modules with similar assertions. The two principle mechanisms of instrumentation are:

- *Access-instrumentation*: The user can direct the tool to add any assertion at every
  (read, write or both) access to either (i) a global variable, (ii) all objects of a given
  type, or (iii) fields of objects of a given type.
- *Function-instrumentation*: The user can also direct the tool to add a contract (possibly a candidate contract) to every procedure with a parameter of a given type.

These instrumentations are extremely useful to define properties and thereafter populate
candidate contracts of a given kind. For example, to specify that any access to a field
x->f of an object x of given type T is always protected by a lock x->lock, we use
the *access-instrumentation* feature to add an assertion x->lock being held before any
access to x->f. On the other hand, one can use the *function-instrumentation* feature to
populate a class of candidate contracts on all the procedures in a module. For instance,
we can add a candidate precondition that the lock x->ParentA->Resource is acquired, for any procedure that has a parameter x (to be substituted with the formal
parameter) of type NODEB. Note that in the original implementation in ESC/Java, the
Houdini algorithm was used with a fixed set of candidate contracts — namely for checking non-null assertions, index-out-of-bound errors etc. on parameters and return values.
The ability to add user-defined candidate contracts is extremely crucial for allowing the
user to leverage the contract inference while checking user-defined properties.

4   Challenges and Design Decisions

In this section, we describe the challenges we faced in applying HAVOC to well-tested codebases of this complexity. We also outline the design decisions that have enabled us to find serious bugs with relatively low false alarms, modest annotation effort and high coverage (particularly on COMP).

4.1   Aliasing

Checking properties that depend on the heap can be difficult because of indirect accesses by pointers; this is because different pointer expressions can evaluate to the same heap location. The problem affects modular checkers as it is not natural to express aliasing constraints as procedure contracts, and may require substantial annotation burden. Finally, the problem is worse for C programs where the addresses of any two fields &x->f and &y->g can be aliased, due to the lack of type safety. This results in numerous false alarms while checking properties that depend on the heap. We introduce two sources of *justifiable assumptions* that allow us to check the desired properties by separating concerns about type-safety of the program as explicit assumptions.

- **Field safety.** We assume that the addresses of two different *word-type* fields (fields that are not nested structures or unions) can never alias, i.e., &x->f and &y->g cannot be equal, whenever f and g are distinct fields. This assumption is mostly maintained with the exception of cases where the program exploits *structural subtyping* whereby two structures with identical layout of types are considered equivalent, even though the field names might differ. The user only needs to specify these exceptions to the tool using additional contracts.
- **Type assumptions.** Many aliasing and non-aliasing constraints can be captured by type invariants similar to the ones shown in Figure 4. These invariants are established after object initialization and are violated at very few places temporarily. The type invariants are currently assumed but not asserted, and help to reduce false positives significantly when dealing with unbounded sets of objects in lists.

Although, both field-safety and the type invariants can be verified in HAVOC [6,20,21], they require reasoning with quantifiers and the annotation overhead can be fairly high. Discharging these obligations would improve the confidence in the results of the property checking.

4.2   Modifies Clauses

Modifies clauses are used to specify the side-effect of a procedure on the globals and the heap. Specifying a precise set of modified locations for the heap and the resources may require significant annotation burden. On one hand, using coarse-grained modifies information may result in invalidating relevant facts at call sites needed for checking a property; on the other hand, the checker would complain if the specified locations do not contain the locations that are actually modified. Various ownership and encapsulation methodologies have been proposed [4], but they impose restrictions on the heap manipulation that are often not satisfied by low-level systems code. For soundness, these methodologies impose additional assertions in the program that might require substantial annotation overhead to discharge.

We have found the two following strategies to achieve a low annotation overhead without sacrificing significant coverage.

Property state modifies: To keep the annotation burden low for checking, we decided to make the modifies clauses for the heap unchecked, i.e., they are assumed at the call sites, but not checked as postconditions. However, for the resources in the property, we require the user to specify sound modifies clauses. Although this introduces unsoundness in our checking and may suppress real bugs, we found it to be pragmatic tradeoff based on the following observation: most of the pointer fields in the program that point to other objects in the heap and define the *shape* of data structures are immutable with very few exceptions. For instance, the ParentA in a NODEB object is set after initialization and remains immutable afterwards. A quick grep revealed that the ParentA field in a NODEB object is read at least in 1100 places in the source, however it is written to at only 8 places, mostly in the creation path. For fields like ReferenceCount in NODEA objects that form part of a property, we maintain a resource to track the value of this field, and thereby support sound modifies clauses.

OUT parameter modifies: Making the modifies clause *free* for fields in the heap almost allowed us to avoid specifying modifies clauses for the fields in the heap. However, we found the need for specifying modifies clauses for *out* parameters of a procedure to avoid the following situation that is quite common in systems code:

```
void Bar(.., PSCB *LocalScb);

void Foo(...){
        PSCB LocalScb = NULL;
        ....
        Bar(..., &LocalScb);
        ...
        if (LocalScb){...}
        ...
}
```

If we do not provide a modifies clause for Bar to indicate that the heap has changed at the location &LocalScb, the checker would assume the code inside the **then**-branch of "if(LocalScb)" is unreachable, and therefore be unsound. To avoid this, we used the contract inference to infer modifies clauses for the parameters that are used as out parameters.

4.3   Interactive Contract Inference

The typical use of the contract inference engine was to infer a set of simple contracts that would hold for a large number of procedures, possibly with a few exceptions. The inference relieves the user by finding the exception set without having to manually inspect the complex call graph. For example, for checking data-race freedom, we inferred the set of procedures where the lock Resource in a NODEA object is held. This can be achieved by creating candidate contracts about this lock being held on all procedures that have either a NODEA or a NODEB as a parameter or return value.

However, the precision of the inference crucially depends on the existing contracts. These contracts could have been manually specified or inferred previously. An attempt

```
void CreateChild(PNODEA NodeA, ATTRIBUTE attr,...){
  PNODEB NodeB;
  AcquireNodeAExcl(NodeA);
  CreateNodeB(NodeA, &NodeB,..);
  Initialize1(NodeB, attr,...);
  ...
}

__ensures((*PNodeB)->ParentA == NodeA)
void  CreateNodeB(PNODEA NodeA, PNODEB *PNodeB,..);

void Initialize1(PNODEB NodeB, ..){

  <modify ParentA, State fields in NodeB >
  Initialize2(NodeB, ...);
}

void Initialize2(PNODEB NodeB,..){
  <modify ParentA, State fields in NodeB>
  Initialize3(NodeB, ...);
}
```

Fig. 5. Procedure calls chains

to infer contracts without being cognizant of other constraints on the module can lead to significant loss of precision. Consider the Figure 5, where the procedure CreateChild creates a child of NodeA in CreateNodeB and then initializes different parts of the child object and other data structures through several layers of deeply nested calls. Suppose we are interested in inferring the procedures where the Resource in an NODEA object is held, to check for data-race freedom. Unless the contract on CreateNodeB is already specified, the inference engine fails to discover that NodeB->ParentA-> Resource is held at entry to all the InitializeX procedures. The contract on CreateNodeB is more difficult to infer since it involves two objects PNodeB and NodeA.

Therefore, the process of adding manual contracts and applying inference was coupled with the feedback from each step driving the other.

4.4 Exceptions

COMP (and several other modules in Windows) uses *Structured Exception Handling* (SEH) to deal with flow of control due to software and hardware exceptions. In SEH, the program can use either __try/__except blocks to implement an exception handler, or __try/__finally blocks to deal with cleanup along both normal and exceptional paths.

```
__try{                          __try{
   //guarded code                  //guarded code
} __except (expr) {             } __finally{
   //exception handler             //termination code
   //code                       }
}
```

To model exceptions, we introduced a resource variable __thrown to denote whether a procedure call raises an exception. The variable is reset to FALSE at entry to any procedure, is set to TRUE whenever a kernel procedure that could raise an exception (e.g. KeRaiseStatus or ExAllocatePoolWithTag) returns with an exception, and

is reset to FALSE once the exception is caught by an exception handler in __except.
We introduced a new contract macro:

```
#define __may_throw(WHEN)    __ensures(!WHEN ==> !__thrown)
```

A procedure with a __may_throw(WHEN) contract denotes that the procedure *does not*
raise an exception if the condition WHEN does not hold at exit from the procedure.
This allows specifying __may_throw(TRUE) on one extreme to indicate that any call
to the procedure may throw an exception, and __may_throw(FALSE) on the other
extreme to indicate that the procedure *never* raises an exception. Every procedure in the
module also has a default modifies clause saying that __thrown can be modified by the
procedure.

The presence of exceptions increases the number of paths through a procedure, since
any called procedure can potentially throw an exception and jump to the exit. Our initial
attempt at ignoring the exceptional paths revealed very few bugs, signifying the well-
tested nature and the maturity of the codebase.

To circumvent the problem, we used the inference engine to infer the set of procedures in this module that do not raise an exception. We first annotated the kernel procedures like KeRaiseStatus with __may_throw(WHEN) to denote the constrains on
its inputs WHEN under which the procedure may throw an exception. Next, we added a
candidate contract __may_throw(FALSE) to each procedur. The interprocedural inference algorithm removes __may_throw(FALSE) from procedures that may potentially
raise an exception. The set of procedures on which __may_throw(FALSE) is inferred
denotes the procedures that never throw an exception. To improve the precision of inference, we had to manually add contracts for internal procedures that could raise an
exception only under certain conditions.

5   Property Checking on COMP

5.1   COMP

In this section, we briefly describe the core driver COMP from the Windows®operating
system, and the synchronization protocol that was checked. For the sake of security,
we keep the component and the names of the procedures anonymous. The component
has around 300 thousand lines of code, excluding the sources for the kernel procedures.
There are more than 1500 procedures present in the module. The code for the component has evolved over almost two decades, and each new generation inherits a lot
of the code from the previous versions. Some of the procedures in the module have
up to 4,000 lines of code, signifying the complexity and the legacy nature of the code
base. COMP also heavily employs the Microsoft *Structured Exception Handling* (SEH)
mechanism for C/C++ to deal with flow of control due to exceptions (discussed more
in Section 4.4).

We first provide a brief description of the synchronization protocol governing the
management of the main heap-allocated structures in COMP. We will focus on four
main type of objects: NODE that is the root type which can contain multiple instances
of NODEA, NODEB and NODEC types.

Each NODE has an ERESOURCE field NodeResource and a mutex NodeMutex for synchronization. The ERESOURCE structure implements a reader-writer lock in Windows that can be recursively acquired. The NodeResource acts as a global lock for access to any NODEA, NODEB and NODEC objects within a given NODE (i.e. it is sufficient to acquire this lock to access any field in the NODEA, NODEB and NODEC objects).

Each NODEA object has a list of NODEB children (as described in Section 2) and a list of NODEC children. Each NODEA has a ERESOURCE field Resource that protects most of its fields and the fields of its children NODEB and NODEC objects; each NODEA also has a mutex NodeAMutex that protects a set of other fields in each NODEA and its NODEB and NODEC children.

Each NODEA also has an integer field ReferenceCount that signifies the number of threads that have a handle on a particular NODEA object — a positive value of ReferenceCount on an NODEA object indicates that some thread has a handle on the object and therefore can't be freed.

There is a global list ExclusiveNodeAList of all the NODEA objects for which the Resource has been acquired. A call to the procedure ReleaseNodeAResources releases the Resource field of any NODEA on the ExclusiveNodeAList.

5.2   Properties

COMP has a synchronization protocol governing the creation, usage and reclamation of the objects in a multi-threaded setting. The synchronization is implemented by a combination of reference counting, locks and other counters in these objects, and is specific to this module. The integrity of the protocol depends on several properties whose violations can lead to serious bugs:

1. Ref-count usage. We checked that for every execution path, the increments and decrements of the ReferenceCount field of a NODEA object are balanced. Decrementing the count without first incrementing could lead to freeing objects in use and a net increment in this field would correspond to a resource leak, as the NODEA object will not be reclaimed.

2. Lock usage. We check for the violation of the locking protocol for the various locks in NODE and NODEA objects. For a mutex field, we check that the lock is acquired and released in alternation; for a reader-writer lock which can be acquired recursively, we check that each release is preceded by an acquire.

3. Data race freedom. This is roughly the property that we described in Section 2, except that we monitor reads and writes for the other fields in these objects too. Since the NodeResource in a NODE object acts a global lock, we need the Resource field in a NODEA object be held only when the global NodeResource lock is not held.

4. Teardown race freedom. We check for races between one thread freeing a NODEA object, and another thread accessing the same object. Any thread freeing a NODEA object must hold that NODEA's Resource exclusive, hold the parent NODE's NodeMutex, and ensure that NODEA's ReferenceCount is zero. Conversely, any thread accessing a NODEA must *either* hold the NODEA's Resource shared or exclusive, hold the parent

Annotations	LOC
Property	250
Manual	600
Inferred	3000
Total	3850

Property	# of bugs
Ref-count	14
Lock usage	12
Data races	13
Teardown	6
Total	45

Fig. 6. Annotation overhead and bugs

NODE's NodeMutex, or have incremented the ReferenceCount field. These rules ensure mutual exclusion between threads freeing and accessing NODEA objects, and any rule violation could lead to a teardown race. This is a domain-specific property which requires the user to define the property.

5.3 Results

In this section, we describe our experience with applying HAVOC on COMP. Figure 6 summarizes the annotation effort and the distribution of the 45 bugs found for the four properties listed above. The "Property" annotations are specifications written to describe the property and also to specify the behavior of kernel procedures. The "Manual" annotations correspond to procedure contracts, loop invariants and type invariants for this module. Finally, the "Inferred" annotations are a set of contracts that are automatically generated by the contract inference described in Section 3.3.

Currently, our checker runs on the annotated code for COMP, and generates 125 warnings over the approximately 1500 procedures in 93 minutes — this corresponds to roughly 3.7 seconds spent analyzing each procedure on average. Most of the runtime (roughly 70%) is spent in a non-optimized implementation for converting C programs into BoogiePL programs, which can be significantly improved. Further, each source file (roughly 60 of them in COMP) in the module can be analyzed separately, and hence the process can be easily parallelized to reduce the runtime.

Out of the 125 warnings, roughly one third of the warnings correspond to confirmed violations of the four properties listed above. This is a fairly low false positive rate, given that we have not invested in various domain-specific filters to suppress the unlikely bugs.

In the following sections, we discuss details of a few bugs, the breakup of the manual annotations and the inferred annotations, and the assumptions that might lead to missed bugs.

5.4 Bugs Found

In this section, we describe two representative bugs from the set of 45 violations to the different properties. An interesting nature of most of the bugs is that they appear along exceptional paths — paths where some procedure raises an exception. This suggests the maturity and well-tested nature of the code as well as the fact that HAVOC can find these subtle corner cases. Besides, some of these synchronization bugs are hard to reproduce in a dynamic setting; the developers of the codebase suspected a leak in the ReferenceCount field but had been unable to reproduce it.

```
...
__try{
   ...
   NodeA = CreateNodeA(Context, ..);

   if (!AcquireExclNodeA(Context, NodeA, NULL, ACQUIRE_DONT_WAIT )) {

       NodeA->ReferenceCount += 1;
       ...
       AcquireExclNodeA(Context, NodeA, NULL, 0 );
       ...
       NodeA->ReferenceCount -= 1;
   }
   ...
} __finally {
   ...
}
...
```

Fig. 7. Reference count leak

```
...
if (!AcquireExclNodeA(Context, NodeA, NULL, ACQUIRE_DONT_WAIT)) {
    ...
    AcquireExclNodeA(Context, NodeA, NULL, 0);
    ...
}

SetFlag(NodeA->NodeAState, NODEA_STATE_REPAIRED);
...
PerformSomeTask(Context, ...);
...
if (FlagOn( ChangeContext.Flags, ... )) {
    UpdateNodeAAndNodeB(Context, NodeA, ChangeContext.Flags);
}
...
```

Fig. 8. Data race on NODEA object

Reference count leak. Figure 7 illustrates an example of a bug that leads to a violation of the Ref-count usage property. In the example, an object NodeA of type NODEA is created in CreateNodeA and then an attempt is made to acquire the Resource in NodeA using the procedure AcquireExclNodeA. This procedure has the behavior that it can return immediately or perform a blocking wait on the Resource depending on whether the flag ACQUIRE_DONT_WAIT is specified or not. Hence, if the first non-blocking acquire fails in the if statement, then it tries a blocking acquire. Before doing that, it increments the ReferenceCount field to indicate a handle on this NODEA object; the field is decremented once the Resource is acquired. However, if AcquireExclNodeA throws an exception, then the __finally block does not decrement the ReferenceCount field, and hence this NODEA object will always have a spurious handle and will never be reclaimed.

Data-race. Figure 8 illustrates an example of data-race on the fields of NODEA object. The procedure first acquires the Resource lock of an object NodeA in the first if block. The fields of NodeA are modified in the SetFlag macro and in the UpdateNodeAAndNodeB procedure. The access in SetFlag is protected by the Resource lock. However, the procedure PerformSomeTask calls the procedure

`ReleaseNodeAResources` transitively with a deeply nested call chain, which might release the `Resource` lock in any `NODEA` object. This means that the `Resource` lock is not held at entry to `UpdateNodeAAndNodeB`, although the procedure expects this lock to be held at entry to modify the fields of `NodeA`.

5.5 Manual Contracts

We classify the main source of manual contracts in this section. In addition to the aliasing constraints and type invariants described in Section 2, we also annotated a variety of interesting conditional specifications and loop invariants.

Conditional specifications. Consider procedure `AcquireExclNodeA` that was present in the two bugs described in Section 5.4 and its contract:

```
__acquire_nodeA_excl(NodeA, !__thrown && __return != FALSE)
__ensures(!FlagOn(Flags, ACQUIRE_DONT_WAIT) && !__thrown
                    ==> __return != FALSE)
BOOLEAN AcquireExclNodeA (PCONTEXT Context,
                          PNODEA NodeA, PNODEB NodeB, ULONG Flags);
```

Recall (from Section 4.4) that `__thrown`indicates whether a procedure has a normal return or an exceptional return. The first annotation (an annotation macro composed of `__requires`, `__ensures` and `__modifies`) describes the condition under which the `Resource` field of `NodeA` parameter is acquired. The second annotation specifies that if `ACQUIRE_DONT_WAIT` flag is not set, and the procedure does not throw an exception, then the return value is never `FALSE`.

Loop invariants. We also specified loop invariants when the property being checked depends on state modified inside a loop. The procedure `ClearChild` in Figure 3 provides an example of such a loop invariant. But a more common form of loop invariant arises due to the following code pattern:

```
BOOLEAN TryAcquireNodeA(PNODEA NodeA,..)
{
    BOOLEAN AcquiredFlag = FALSE;
    ...
    __try{
        ...
        __loop_inv(AcquiredFlag == FALSE)
        while (true) {
            CallMightRaise1();
            if (..){
                AcquireNodeAExcl(NodeA);
                AcquiredFlag = TRUE;
                CallMightRaise2();
                return TRUE;
            }
        }
    } __finally {
        ...
        if (AcquiredFlag)
            ReleaseNodeA(NodeA);
        ...
        return FALSE;
    }
}
```

The callers of `TryAcquireNodeA` expect that the procedure acquires the resource of `NodeA` at normal exit. However, in the absence of the loop invariant, the checker

Contracts type	# of inferred annot
May throw	914
`NodeResource` held	107
`NodeMutex` not held	674
`NODEAResource` held	360
`NODEAResource` release all	210
OUT parameter modified	271
Parameter flag set	331
Total	2867

Fig. 9. Distribution of inferred contracts

would report a false warning where the `ReleaseNodeA` tries to release a resource without first acquiring it. This happens because in the absence of the loop invariant, the checker will report a path where the value of `AcquiredFlag` is `TRUE` at the loop head, the procedure `CallMightRaise1` throws an exception and control reaches the `__finally` block.

5.6   Inferred Contracts

HAVOC's automatic inference capability generated a majority of the simple contracts (around 3000 of them) and was crucial to the automation of the tool for such a complex codebase (i.e. only 600 manually written contracts on around 1500 functions analyzed by the tool).

Figure 9 summarizes the main classes of contracts that were generated using the automated inference mechanism. In addition to the inference about `__may_throw` contracts and modifies clauses for the out parameters of a procedure, we employed the inference engine to infer a certain type-state property on some objects of type `NODEA` or `NODEB` on the procedures in the module.

1. **May throw:** as described in Section 4.4, this denotes the set of procedures that do not raise an exception.
2. `NodeResource` **held:** infers a set of procedures where the lock `NodeResource` on the global `NODE` object is held at entry to ensure data-race freedom.
3. `NodeMutex` **not held:** infers a set of procedures where the `NodeMutex` field of the global `NODE` is not held at entry. Since most procedures acquire and release this lock locally inside a procedure, this contract is useful for proving that locks are not acquired twice.
4. `NODEAResource` **held:** infers that the `Resource` field for an `NODEA` parameter or the `Resource` field for the parent of an `NODEB` or `NODEC` object is held at entry to a set of procedures. This along with `NodeResource` ensures absence of data-races.
5. `NODEAResource` **release all:** infers the set of procedures that could release the `Resource` of any `NODEA` object by a transitive call to `Release-NodeAResources`.

6. **OUT parameter modified:** adds a __modifies(x) contract for an out parameter x that is modified inside a procedure, as described in Section 4.2.
7. **Parameter flag set:** infers a set of procedures where a certain field of a parameter is set to TRUE on entry to the procedures. The parameter captures the state of computations that span multiple procedures and is threaded through the nested procedure calls. The parameter Context in Figures 7 and Figure 8 is an example of such a parameter.

5.7   Assumptions

HAVOC provides a set of options that allows the user to introduce a class of *explicit* assumptions into the verification, which can be enumerated and discharged later with more contracts or a separate analysis. This allows the user of the tool to control the degree of unsoundness in the verification, and to recover from them using more contracts. This is in contrast to most other static analysis tools that bake these assumptions into the analysis and there is no way to recover from them. There are three main sources of such assumptions in our current analysis: (1) field safety, (2) type invariant assumptions and (3) free modifies for the heap fields. The first two sources were discussed in Section 4.1 and the third in Section 4.2.

Of the three options, we believe that both field safety and the type invariants hold for the module with very few exceptions and separate the proof of the high-level properties from the proofs of type-safety and type/shape invariants. Eliminating the free modifies clauses for the heap fields are the assumptions that we would like to eliminate to increase the confidence in the checking.

5.8   False Warnings

As mentioned earlier, the tool generates a total of 125 warnings, and roughly one third of the warnings correspond to confirmed violations of the four properties listed above. Unlike typical static analyzers, the remaining warnings are not violation of the properties being checked. Instead, most of these warnings are violations of intermediate procedure contracts which were used to discharge the properties of interest.

Of course, the soundness of a modular proof can be compromised by the presence of even a single warning. However, for large code bases, it is very difficult to verify *every* contract. To obtain a balance, we require that the remaining warnings are not violations of automatically generated assertions (for the property), but rather violation of user-specified contracts. The rationale being that user provided contracts are a result of understanding the code, and have a good chance of being true (although they may not be inductive). However, proving these contracts require adding contracts on other fields of these structures, or devising a new template for contracts (e.g. checking which fields of an object are non-null).

6   Security Audit

In this section, we briefly describe preliminary experience of applying HAVOC for checking security vulnerabilities in some of the modules in Microsoft Windows. In spite of extensive testing and the application of customized static analysis on these components, these components still have bugs that make them vulnerable to malicious attacks. Careful code audit is essential to safeguard the systems against such attacks, but manual inspection is expensive and error-prone.

HAVOC has been deployed to check several properties whose violation can often lead to exploitable attacks:

- *ProbeBeforeUse*: any pointer that can be passed by a user application (*user* pointers) to the kernel APIs must undergo a call to a procedure *Probe* before it is dereferenced.
- *UserDerefInTry*: any dereference of a user pointer must happen inside a __try block,
- *ProbeInTry*: any call to *Probe* should happen inside a __try block to correctly deal with cases when a user passes illegal pointers,
- *Alloc0*: ensure that the non-null buffer returned by calling *malloc* with a size of zero is handled safely. Although it is legal to call allocation procedures with a size of zero, such allocations often lead to buffer overruns without proper safeguard [23].

Although the properties are simple, it is non-trivial to ensure the absence of these bugs primarily due to deep call chains and the presence of deeply nested pointers. For example, to check either the *ProbeBeforeUse* or *UserDerefInTry*, one needs to know whether any pointer that is dereferenced in the program can alias with one of the pointers that are reachable from the globals or parameters to the entry functions of the module. There can be several thousand dereferences in a large module and validating each of them (especially those in deeply nested procedures) can be challenging. On the other hand, the *Alloc0* property requires arithmetic reasoning as the allocation size could be 0 because of an overflow.

The properties were specified quite easily by adding suitable contracts to *Probe* and *malloc* procedures. We have analyzed several modules (with more than a million lines across all of them) for various subset of these properties. We have created various inference for interprocedural reasoning including (a) propagation of information about the pointers that have undergone a call to *Probe*, (b) the procedures that are always called from within a __try block, etc. Details of the inference and results are outside the scope of this article, since this is a work in progress. In addition, the user had to provide some annotations (in the order of a few hundred currently) manually. The effort has lead to the discovery of four vulnerabilities related to *ProbeBeforeUse* and around ten vulnerabilities related to *Alloc0*, all of which have been patched. The tool allows the auditor to only inspect around 2-3% (for modules with around 3000 procedures) of all procedures for warnings for the *ProbeBeforeUse* properties and around 10% of the allocation sites for the *Alloc0* sites. We are working to further reduce these false alarms with better inference, loop invariants etc. However, the ability for the user to construct these property checkers and guide the inference to use the domain knowledge has provided value in focusing the time of an auditor on the more problematic procedures.

7 Related Work

There is a rich literature on static analysis tools for finding various defects in software programs. We discuss some of these tools in this section, to perform a qualitative analysis of the strengths and weaknesses of using these tools for our case study.

Contract-based checkers. HAVOC is closely based on the principles of ESC/Java [17] tool for Java programs and Spec# [4] tool for C# programs. The main difference lies in our intent to analyze systems program written in C, that requires support for low-level operations in both the source and the contract language. Secondly, although ESC/Java was applied to real life Java programs to demonstrate the usefulness of contract inference [16,17], the tool did not allow the user to create customizable inference for particular contracts. These tools have not been applied to real progams of the scale considered in this paper to find bugs in a cost-effective manner with low annotation overhead.

SAL in an annotation language for documenting buffer related properties for C programs and espX is a checker for the language [18]. This is one of the few examples of annotation based checker for a specific property. The language is not extensible, and does not allow specifying new user-defined properties.

Dedicated property checkers. A majority of the numerous static analysis tools developed for systems software in the last decade fall in this category — we highlight only a representative sample for the different properties that scale to several thousand lines of code. Examples of data-race checkers include Relay [24], LOCKSMITH [22], RacerX [13]. CALYSTO [2] finds null dereference bugs in C programs by using SAT solvers. The ASTREÉ analyzer [8] uses abstract interpretation [7] to prove the absence of certain runtime errors such as buffer overruns, integer overflows in embedded safety-critical software. Most of these tools do not require user annotations, use novel algorithms based on data-flow analysis, often with the intent of finding bugs at the cost of unsound assumptions.

Extensible property checkers. Tools such as SLAM [3], BLAST [19] and ESP [10] are examples of software model checkers that check a property by exhaustively analyzing models of C programs. Their property languages allow specifying simple state-machines over the typestate of objects, and can express simple lock usage properties. These tools are most suited for checking properties on global variables, and lose precision and soundness when dealing with low-level operations and relationships between objects in the heap. Our case study shows the need for both in checking the synchronization protocol.

Meta-level compilation [14] provides compiler extensions to encode patterns of violations for system-specific properties in a state-machine language *metal*, which are checked at compile time. The technique finds serious errors in systems code, but does not attempt to maintain soundness or guarantees about the absence of such bugs. These tools are suitable for describing bug patterns in a code, but once again are poorly suited for describing detailed properties of the heap (for example the absence of teardown race).

Saturn [1] uses a logic programming framework to specify static analysis. Saturn also uses a concrete operational semantics similar to HAVOC. While HAVOC's meta-theory is fixed and based on contracts, the meta-theory of Saturn may be extended by analyses expressed in a logic programming language. The ability to add inference rules adds flexibility in analysis design but comes at two different costs. First, extending Saturn requires an expert analysis designer whereas extending HAVOC could be done by a programmer simply by the use of contracts. Second, the meta-theory behind the analyses is usually not proved correct and could therefore introduce unexpected unsoundness into the system.

8 Conclusions

In this work, we have demonstrated the feasibility of applying contract-based checkers for scalable user-defined property checking, and the challenges involved in scaling such an approach to large code bases with modest annotation overhead, low false alarms, without sacrificing a lot of coverage. Our work points out several immediate directions of future work that would improve the usability of modular checkers such as HAVOC in the hand of a user: better inference of conditional contracts can relieve a lot of annotation burden, inference of modifies clauses will allow us to remove unsoundness issues related to the unchecked modifies clauses, and finally, we need easy-to-use annotations for specifying invariants at the level of types.

References

1. Aiken, A., Bugrara, S., Dillig, I., Dillig, T., Hackett, B., Hawkins, P.: An overview of the Saturn project. In: Workshop on Program Analysis for Software Tools and Engineering (PASTE 2007), pp. 43–48 (2007)
2. Babic, D., Hu, A.J.: Structural abstraction of software verification conditions. In: Damm, W., Hermanns, H. (eds.) CAV 2007. LNCS, vol. 4590, pp. 366–378. Springer, Heidelberg (2007)
3. Ball, T., Majumdar, R., Millstein, T., Rajamani, S.K.: Automatic predicate abstraction of C programs. In: Programming Language Design and Implementation (PLDI 2001), pp. 203–213 (2001)
4. Barnett, M., Leino, K.R.M., Schulte, W.: The Spec# programming system: An overview. In: Barthe, G., Burdy, L., Huisman, M., Lanet, J.-L., Muntean, T. (eds.) CASSIS 2004. LNCS, vol. 3362, pp. 49–69. Springer, Heidelberg (2005)
5. Chatterjee, S., Lahiri, S.K., Qadeer, S., Rakamarić, Z.: A reachability predicate for analyzing low-level software. In: Grumberg, O., Huth, M. (eds.) TACAS 2007. LNCS, vol. 4424, pp. 19–33. Springer, Heidelberg (2007)
6. Condit, J., Hackett, B., Lahiri, S.K., Qadeer, S.: Unifying type checking and property checking for low-level code. In: Principles of Programming Languages (POPL 2009), pp. 302–314 (2009)
7. Cousot, P., Cousot, R.: Abstract interpretation: A Unified Lattice Model for the Static Analysis of Programs by Construction or Approximation of Fixpoints. In: Principles of Programming Languages (POPL 1977), pp. 238–252 (1977)
8. Cousot, P., Cousot, R., Feret, J., Mauborgne, L., Miné, A., Monniaux, D., Rival, X.: The ASTRÉE Analyzer. In: Sagiv, M. (ed.) ESOP 2005. LNCS, vol. 3444, pp. 21–30. Springer, Heidelberg (2005)

9. Dahlweid, M., Moskal, M., Santen, T., Tobies, S., Schulte, W.: Vcc: Contract-based modular verification of concurrent c. In: International Conference on Software Engineering (ICSE 2009), Companion Volume, pp. 429–430 (2009)
10. Das, M., Lerner, S., Seigle, M.: ESP: Path-Sensitive Program Verification in Polynomial Time. In: Programming Language Design and Implementation (PLDI 2002), pp. 57–68 (2002)
11. de Moura, L., Bjorner, N.: Efficient Incremental E-matching for SMT Solvers. In: Pfenning, F. (ed.) CADE 2007. LNCS (LNAI), vol. 4603, pp. 183–198. Springer, Heidelberg (2007)
12. DeLine, R., Leino, K.R.M.: BoogiePL: A typed procedural language for checking object-oriented programs. Technical Report MSR-TR-2005-70, Microsoft Research (2005)
13. Engler, D.R., Ashcraft, K.: RacerX: effective, static detection of race conditions and deadlocks. In: Symposium on Operating Systems Principles (SOSP 2003), pp. 237–252 (2003)
14. Engler, D.R., Chelf, B., Chou, A., Hallem, S.: Checking system rules using system-specific, programmer-written compiler extensions. In: Operating Systems Design And Implementation (OSDI 2000), pp. 1–16 (2000)
15. Flanagan, C., Freund, S.N.: Type-based race detection for java. In: PLDI, pp. 219–232 (2000)
16. Flanagan, C., Leino, K.R.M.: Houdini, an annotation assistant for ESC/Java. In: Oliveira, J.N., Zave, P. (eds.) FME 2001. LNCS, vol. 2021, pp. 500–517. Springer, Heidelberg (2001)
17. Flanagan, C., Leino, K.R.M., Lillibridge, M., Nelson, G., Saxe, J.B., Stata, R.: Extended static checking for Java. In: Programming Language Design and Implementation (PLDI 2002), pp. 234–245 (2002)
18. Hackett, B., Das, M., Wang, D., Yang, Z.: Modular checking for buffer overflows in the large. In: International Conference on Software Engineering (ICSE 2006), pp. 232–241 (2006)
19. Henzinger, T.A., Jhala, R., Majumdar, R., Sutre, G.: Lazy abstraction. In: Principles of Programming Languages (POPL 2002), pp. 58–70 (2002)
20. Lahiri, S.K., Qadeer, S.: Back to the future: revisiting precise program verification using SMT solvers. In: Principles of Programming Languages (POPL 2008), pp. 171–182 (2008)
21. Lahiri, S.K., Qadeer, S., Galeotti, J.P., Voung, J.W., Wies, T.: Intra-module inference. In: Bouajjani, A., Maler, O. (eds.) CAV 2009. LNCS, vol. 5643, pp. 493–508. Springer, Heidelberg (2009)
22. Pratikakis, P., Foster, J.S., Hicks, M.W.: LOCKSMITH: context-sensitive correlation analysis for race detection. In: Programming Language Design and Implementation (PLDI 2006), pp. 320–331 (2006)
23. Vanegue, J.: Zero-sized heap allocations vulnerability analysis
24. Voung, J.W., Jhala, R., Lerner, S.: RELAY: static race detection on millions of lines of code. In: Foundations of Software Engineering (FSE 2007), pp. 205–214 (2007)

Tressa: Claiming the Future[*]

Ali Sezgin[1], Serdar Tasiran[1], and Shaz Qadeer[2]

[1] Koc University, Istanbul, Turkey
{asezgin,stasiran}@ku.edu.tr
[2] Microsoft Research, Redmond, WA, USA
qadeer@microsoft.com

Abstract. Unlike sequential programs, concurrent programs have to account for interference on shared variables. Static verification of a desired property for such programs crucially depends on precisely asserting the conditions for interference. In a static proof system, in addition to program variables, auxiliary (history) variables summarizing the past of the program execution are used in these assertions. Capable of expressing reachability only, assertions (and history variables) are not as useful in the proofs of programs using optimistic concurrency. Pessimistic implementations which allow access to shared data only after synchronization (e.g. locks) guarantee exclusivity; optimistic concurrency implementations which check for interference after shared data is accessed abandon exclusivity in favor of performance.

In this paper, we propose a new construct, tressa, to express properties, including interference, about the future of an execution. A tressa claim states a condition for reverse reachability from an end state of the program, much like an assert claim states a condition for forward reachability from the initial state of the program. As assertions employ history variables, tressa claims employ prophecy variables, originally introduced for refinement proofs. Being the temporal dual of history variables, prophecy variables summarize the future of the program execution. We present the proof rules and the notion of correctness of a program for two-way reasoning in a static setting: forward in time for assert claims, backward in time for tressa claims. We have incorporated our proof rules into the QED verifier and have used our implementation to verify a small but sophisticated algorithm. Our experience shows that the proof steps and annotations follow closely the intuition of the programmer, making the proof itself a natural extension of implementation.

1 Introduction

The main challenge in proving a concurrent program is reasoning about interactions among threads on the shared memory. In a proof based on validating assertions that specify a program's desired behavior, one has to consider all possible

[*] This research was supported by a career grant (104E058) from the Scientific and Technical Research Council of Turkey, the Turkish Academy of Sciences Distinguished Young Scientist Award (TUBA-GEBIP), and a research gift from the Software Reliability Research group at Microsoft Research, Redmond, WA.

G.T. Leavens, P. O'Hearn, and S.K. Rajamani (Eds.): VSTTE 2010, LNCS 6217, pp. 25–39, 2010.
© Springer-Verlag Berlin Heidelberg 2010

interleavings of conflicting operations. Most existing methods verify programs at the finest level of granularity of atomic actions: only actions guaranteed to be executed without interruption by the runtime are considered to be atomic. At this level of granularity, there are a large number of possible interleavings. Proving at this level requires one to consider concurrency- and data-related properties at the same time and this results in complicated proofs.

A static verification method called QED alleviates this complexity [1]. A proof in QED consists of rewriting the input program iteratively using abstraction and reduction so that, in the limit, one arrives at a program that can be verified by sequential reasoning methods.

Reduction, due to [2], creates coarse-grained atomic statements from fine-grained ones. Whether statements can be thus combined depends on their *mover types*. For instance, a statement is right-mover if commuting to the right of any concurrent statement in any execution does not affect the property being verified. QED is a static verification tool which determines the mover type of each statement via a local check based on pair-wise comparison of all possible statements. Local checks necessarily abstract away all execution dependent information including control flow and synchronization mechanisms. Thus, deciding solely using local checks, QED will tag a statement accessing a shared variable as non-mover regardless of that access being lock protected or not. This is where abstraction comes into picture.

In QED, there are two kinds of abstraction. The first kind is to replace the statement with a less deterministic one, if the particular statement is of no consequence to the property being verified. The second kind, which will be our main concern in this paper, is to confine the local checks, via assertions, to only pairs of statements that *can* execute concurrently. For instance, annotating each access to a lock-protected shared variable with an assertion expressing a condition on the owner of the lock will effectively declare all these accesses non-concurrent (at a given time, at most one can execute) making them both (right and left) movers.

For implementations based on optimistic concurrency, our experience with QED suggests that expressing facts about concurrency control mechanisms in the form of assertions over history variables is unnatural and counter-intuitive. Correct operation of optimistic concurrency, used in the implementation of non-blocking data structures or Software Transactional Memories (STM's) [3], do not depend on exclusive access to shared variables. The idea is to carry out computation *as if* no interference will occur and then, prior to *committing*, check whether this assumption is correct. If it is, then simply commit; if not, *roll-back* any visible global change and, optionally, re-start. In this case, what is needed is not a claim about reachability from an initial state which an assertion provides, but a claim about the possibility of reaching a state from the current state. The desired property is of the form: Either there will be no interference until the commit point and each shared access satisfies some condition φ, or interference occurs before reaching the commit point. We would like to make use of the condition φ in a static proof but the truth of φ cannot be decided based on the execution prefix; its truth is a function of the execution suffix.

In this paper, we propose a new construct, tressa, which enables the specification of properties about the rest of the program execution. A tressa claim will typically express what the user believes will happen in case interference does (or does not) occur. QED can then make use of the absence or presence of interference in the rest of the execution following a statement in order to decide that statement's mover type. For instance, imagine a procedure which optimistically reads a shared variable g, does some computation, reads g again and if no update has occurred to g in between, it commits. Optimistic read means that concurrent threads can update g, so claiming non-interference using assertions is not possible. However, in any execution where this procedure runs without interference, the first read of g is a right-mover. That is precisely what a tressa claim will capture.

We incorporate prophecy variables into our static proof system. Frequently, the desired property that needs to be asserted for a statement depends on the particular code path or execution prefix reaching that statement. History variables aid the user in capturing this kind of execution specific information. Prophecy variables serve a similar purpose for tressa claims. Annotating actions with prophecy variables allows information about the rest of the execution to be used in tressa claims which in turn aid in deciding the mover types of actions.

We present the proof rules and the notion of correctness of a program for two-way reasoning in a static setting: forward in time for assert claims, backward in time for tressa claims. Building on our initial work [1], we reformulate simulation and mover definitions such that they are now valid for both forward and backward reasoning. Even though the interaction between the two is non-trivial, the formalization is intuitive and accessible. We demonstrate how to prove the atomicity of a representative optimistic concurrency implementation.

Related Work. A variety of techniques have been proposed for static verification of concurrent programs (e.g., [4,5,6,7]). Reduction as a means to reduce the complexity in reasoning for concurrent programs was introduced by Lipton [2] and has been the topic of recent work on concurrent program verification (e.g.[8,9,10]). Prophecy variables were introduced in [11] and were used to define refinement mappings between a specification and its implementation in cases where the mapping between abstract and concrete states depends on the rest of the execution. Subsequent work on prophecy variables were almost exclusively on refinement checking (e.g., [12,13]). In the context of program verification, backward reasoning (or simulation) has been used as an alternative to prophecy variables with the same goal of establishing a mapping between states [14,12,15]. The only work on prophecy variables in static verification we know of is by Marcus and Pnueli [16]. In the context of a static method for proving refinement between two transition systems, the authors present two sound ways of augmenting a sequential program with assignments that involve temporal logic formulas with future operators. Their soundness condition for annotating programs with auxiliary variables is, as expected, similar to ours. In contrast, our proof system targets concurrent software and the verification of claims (in the form of assert and tressa statements) rather than refinement, and uses atomicity as a key reasoning tool. To the best of our knowledge, this is the first work that proposes the use of a construct, tressa, enabling backwards reasoning in reduction based static verification.

Roadmap. In Sec. 2, we formalize the framework, describing the programming language syntax and semantics. In Sec. 3, we develop our proof system by redefining the notions of correctness, simulation, mover checks to accommodate tressa claims. We formalize prophecy variables by giving a new proof rule. We also prove that these modifications do not affect the soundness of our proof system. In Sec. 4, we show in detail how to reason and use prophecy variables and tressa annotations in the proof of implementations using optimistic concurrency. We finish with concluding remarks.

2   Preliminaries

In this section, we will introduce a simple programming language and define the relevant terminology.

2.1   Syntax

Let e range over arithmetic and logical expressions, p range over logical expressions and x be a variable. A *simple* statement is either an assignment (x := e), a non-deterministic assignment (havoc x), an assertion (assert p), a tressa claim (tressa p), an assumption (assume p) or a no-op (skip). We assume that each variable is either *global* or *local*. An assignment can contain at most one global variable. That is, if x is a local variable, e can have at most one occurrence of a global variable; if x is a global variable, then no global variable can appear in e. A statement is either a simple statement, or statements, s_1, s_2, combined by sequential composition ($s_1 ; s_2$), conditional branching (if(*) $\{s_1\}$ else$\{s_2\}$), looping (while(*) $\{s_1\}$). A statement can also be an *atomic* statement (atomic$\{s\}$), where s is a statement not containing a loop. As a syntactic restriction, nested use of atomic is not allowed. By definition, each simple statement is also an atomic statement. We will omit atomic when it encloses only a simple statement to avoid cluttering.

A *program* is a set of statements, each of which is called a *proc-statement*. For a given program $\mathcal{P}$, let $\mathcal{S}_\mathcal{P}$, $Simple(\mathcal{P})$ and $Atoms(\mathcal{P})$ denote the sets containing all statements, all simple statements and all atomic statements in $\mathcal{P}$, respectively.

In the sample codes given in this paper, we make use of the following syntactic sugar:

$$\text{while}(e)\ \{s\} \triangleq \text{while}(*)\ \{\text{assume}\ e; s\}\ \text{assume}\ !e;$$

The formal treatment given in this paper can easily be extended to a programming language allowing a parallel operator and (non-recursive) procedure calls. Their omission is solely to make the presentation simpler.

$$\boxed{\{\sigma\}\,t : s\,\{\sigma'\},\ t \in Tid}$$

$$\frac{|\sigma(\mathsf{err})| = 1 \quad \mathrm{x} \notin gV(\mathcal{P})}{\{\sigma\}\ t : \mathrm{x} := e\ \{\sigma[(t,\mathrm{x}) \mapsto [\![e]\!](\sigma[\mathtt{tid} \mapsto t])]\}} \qquad \frac{|\sigma(\mathsf{err})| = 1 \quad k \in dom(x)}{\{\sigma\}\ t : \mathsf{havoc}\,\mathrm{x}\ \{\sigma[\mathrm{x} \mapsto k]\}}$$

$$\frac{|\sigma(\mathsf{err})| = 1 \quad \mathrm{g} \in gV(\mathcal{P})}{\{\sigma\}\ t : \mathrm{g} := e\ \{\sigma[(\mathrm{g}) \mapsto [\![e]\!](\sigma[\mathtt{tid} \mapsto t])]\}} \qquad \frac{|\sigma(\mathsf{err})| = 1}{\{\sigma\}\ t : \mathsf{skip}\ \{\sigma\}}$$

$$\frac{s \in \{\mathsf{assume}\,p, \mathsf{assert}\,p, \mathsf{tressa}\,p\} \quad |\sigma(\mathsf{err})| = 1 \quad t.\sigma \vDash p}{\{\sigma\}\ t : s\ \{\sigma\}} \qquad \frac{\sigma(\mathsf{err}) = 1 \quad t.\sigma \nvDash p}{\{\sigma\}\ t : \mathsf{assert}\,p\ \{\sigma[\mathsf{err} \mapsto 2]\}}$$

$$\frac{\sigma(\mathsf{err}) = -2 \quad t.\sigma \nvDash p}{\{\sigma\}\ t : \mathsf{tressa}\,p\ \{\sigma[\mathsf{err} \mapsto -1]\}} \qquad \frac{|\sigma(\mathsf{err})| = 2 \quad s \in \mathcal{S}_{\mathcal{P}}}{\{\sigma\}\ t : s\ \{\sigma\}}$$

Fig. 1. Rules for updating valuations

2.2   Semantics

Valuations. For a program $\mathcal{P}$, let $Var(\mathcal{P})$ denote the set of variables declared in $\mathcal{P}$. For any variable x, let $dom(x)$ denote the set of its admissible values. Let Tid be a finite set of thread identifiers. $Var(\mathcal{P})$ is assumed to contain distinguished global variables tid ($dom(tid) = Tid$), err ($dom(\mathsf{err}) = \{-2, -1, 1, 2\}$), all of which are undeclared in $\mathcal{P}$. Let $gV(\mathcal{P}) \subseteq Var(\mathcal{P})$ be the set of global variables.

A *valuation* σ is a mapping from $Tid \times Var$ to a set of values. Intuitively, $\sigma(t, x)$ gives the value of the variable x as seen by thread t. We require for all $t, u \in Tid$, $g \in gV(\mathcal{P})$, $\sigma(t, g) = \sigma(u, g)$. For simplicity, we let $(t.\sigma)(x) \triangleq \sigma(t, x)$, refer to $t.\sigma$ as a valuation and $\sigma(g) \triangleq \sigma(t, g)$ whenever g is a global variable. The notation $[\![e]\!]\sigma$ denotes the value of the expression e for the valuation σ under the standard interpretation of arithmetic and logical operators. A valuation σ is said to satisfy a boolean expression p, written $\sigma \vDash p$, if $[\![p]\!]\sigma$ evaluates to true. Otherwise, σ is said to violate p, written $\sigma \nvDash p$. For a function f, let $f[x \mapsto v]$ be the same as f except $f(x) = v$, and let $|\cdot|$ denote absolute value.

Let s be a statement in which while does not occur, t be a thread identifier and σ, σ' be valuations. The small step execution semantics are given in terms of triples $\{\sigma\}\,t : s\,\{\sigma'\}$, called *valuation updates*, whose rules are given in Fig. 1.

Intuitively, a valuation update $\{\sigma\}\,t : s\,\{\sigma'\}$ defines the effect of executing s on the values of the variables as seen by thread t represented by the valuations σ and σ'. The only interesting cases are for the assert and tressa instructions when the valuation does not satisfy the claim. In both cases, the update is allowed only if $\sigma'(\mathsf{err}) = \sigma(\mathsf{err}) + 1$. We will see below the effect of the value of err on the rest[1] of the execution.

---

[1] Rest refers to the suffix for err $= 1$; it refers to the prefix for err $= -1$.

$$\boxed{\dashrightarrow \ :\subseteq \mathcal{S}_{\mathcal{P}}^* \times Atoms(\mathcal{P}) \times \mathcal{S}_{\mathcal{P}}^*}$$

$$\frac{a \in Atoms(\mathcal{P})}{a\gamma \stackrel{a}{\dashrightarrow} \gamma} \qquad\qquad \frac{s = s_1; s_2 \quad s_1 \stackrel{a}{\dashrightarrow} s_1'}{s\gamma \stackrel{a}{\dashrightarrow} s_1' s_2 \gamma} \qquad\qquad \frac{s = \mathsf{while}(*)\{s_1\}}{s\gamma \stackrel{\mathsf{skip}}{\dashrightarrow} \gamma}$$

$$\frac{s_1 \stackrel{a}{\dashrightarrow} s_1'}{s = \mathsf{while}(*)\{s_1\}} \qquad \frac{s = \mathsf{if}(*)\{s_1\}\,\mathsf{else}\{s_2\}}{s\gamma \stackrel{\mathsf{skip}}{\dashrightarrow} s_1 \gamma} \qquad \frac{s = \mathsf{if}(*)\{s_1\}\,\mathsf{else}\{s_2\}}{s\gamma \stackrel{\mathsf{skip}}{\dashrightarrow} s_2 \gamma}$$
$$\frac{}{s\gamma \stackrel{a}{\dashrightarrow} s_1' s \gamma}$$

Fig. 2. Control Flow

Program States. A program state is a pair (σ, Δ). The first component σ is a valuation for $Var(\mathcal{P})$. The second component Δ is a mapping from Tid to a string over statements, $\mathcal{S}_{\mathcal{P}}$. Intuitively, $\Delta(t) = d$ means that thread t is yet to execute the (not necessarily atomic) statements in d. For instance, for ε representing the empty string, s representing a proc-statement, $\Delta(t) = s$ means that t has not started executing the procedure s, whereas $\Delta(t) = \varepsilon$ means that t has finished its execution.

A program state (σ, Δ) is *initial* if for all $t \in Tid$, $\Delta(t) = b$ such that b is a proc-statement for some procedure in $Proc$. A program state (σ, Δ) is *final* if for all $t \in Tid$, $\Delta(t) = \varepsilon$.

Program Executions. Let γ be a string over $\mathcal{S}_{\mathcal{P}}$ and s be a statement. The evaluation order of a statement is given in Fig. 2. Intuitively, $s \stackrel{a}{\dashrightarrow} s'$ means that a is an atomic statement that can be executed next in statement s where s' represents the remaining part to execute.

Program execution is formalized over a labeled transition system defined as:

$$\frac{s \in Atoms(\mathcal{P}) \quad \{\sigma\}\, t : s\, \{\sigma'\} \quad \gamma \stackrel{s}{\dashrightarrow} \gamma' \quad \Delta(t) = \gamma \quad \Delta' = \Delta[t \mapsto \gamma']}{(\sigma, \Delta) \xrightarrow{(s,t)} (\sigma', \Delta')}$$

Intuitively, there is a transition from $q = (\sigma, \Delta)$ to $r = (\sigma', \Delta')$ with label (s, t) whenever s is an atomic statement that can be executed by t at q and the valuations at r are updated according to the statement s (local variables of threads different from t remain unchanged).

A *trace* is a sequence of labels, $l = \langle l_1 \dots l_k \rangle$. It moves a state q_0 to q_k, written $q_0 \stackrel{l}{\to} q_k$, if there is a sequence of states $\langle q_i \rangle_{0 < i \leq k}$, a *run* of P over l, such that for all $0 < i \leq k$, $q_{i-1} \stackrel{l_i}{\to} q_i$.

An atomic statement s preserves a predicate p over $gV(\mathcal{P})$, written as $p \rightleftarrows s$, if for any valuation $\sigma \vDash p$, $\{\sigma\}\, t : s\, \{\sigma'\}$ implies $\sigma' \vDash p$. If all the atomic statements of program $\mathcal{P}$ preserve a predicate p over $gV(\mathcal{P})$, p is an *invariant* of $\mathcal{P}$, written $p \rightleftarrows \mathcal{P}$. We let $\mathcal{I}$ range over invariants. A state (σ, Δ) is in $\mathcal{I}$ if $\sigma \vDash \mathcal{I}$. For program $\mathcal{P}$, $\mathcal{P}[x \mapsto y]$ is the same as $\mathcal{P}$ except the statement x is replaced with the statement y. The addition of a new global variable a into program $\mathcal{P}$ is written as $gV \mapsto gV \cup \{a\}$. For atomic statements $s = \mathsf{atomic}\{s_1\}$, $\tilde{s} = \mathsf{atomic}\{s_2\}$, let $s \circ \tilde{s} = \mathsf{atomic}\{s_1; s_2\}$.

3   The Proof System

In this Section, we will formalize our proof system.

Correctness. A program's correctness is a property of its terminating runs. Unlike standard definitions which only consider assertions, our notion of correctness has to take into account both assert and tressa claims.

Definition 1 (Failing Runs). *Let* $\langle (\sigma_i, \Delta_i) \rangle_{0 \leq i \leq k}$ *be a run of program* $\mathcal{P}$. *It is* failing *if* (σ_0, Δ_0) *is an initial state,* (σ_k, Δ_k) *is a final state and* $\sigma_k(\mathsf{err}) = \sigma_0(\mathsf{err}) + 1$. *It is* forward *(*backward, resp.*) failing if it is failing and* $\sigma_0(\mathsf{err}) = 1$ *(*$\sigma_0(\mathsf{err}) = -2$, resp.*).*

Intuitively, a run starting from an initial state and ending at a final state is forward failing if some state does not satisfy the assert claim of the statement executed at that state. Similarly, a run is backward failing if some state does not satisfy the tressa claim of the statement executed right before reaching that state. A program is *failing* for an invariant $\mathcal{I}$, if it contains a failing run starting from a state in $\mathcal{I}$; the program is *safe* for $\mathcal{I}$, otherwise.

Remark. Assume that $\mathcal{P}$ has a forward failing run. Then, $\mathcal{P}$ must have a run $(\sigma_0, \Delta_0) \xrightarrow{l_1} (\sigma_j, \Delta_j) \xrightarrow{l_2} (\sigma_k, \Delta_k)$ such that (σ_0, Δ_0) is initial, (σ_k, Δ_k) is final, $\sigma_i(\mathsf{err}) = 1$ for all $0 \leq i < j$, and $\sigma_i(\mathsf{err}) = 2$ for all $j \leq i \leq k$. This is because every forward failing run necessarily has a prefix where each state has err assigned to 1, the prefix ends at a state which assigns 2 to err and by the definition of valuation updates, it is always possible to extend any run whose end state has err $= 2$ to a run ending at a final state. The prefix up to and including q_j is a *visible* execution of the program whereas the suffix is invisible because the effects of statements on the values of variables are ignored altogether. The visible execution is the *witness* to the violation of an assertion in s_j. This *canonical* form of a forward failing run coincides with the intuitive interpretation of an assertion: Any execution of the program should not reach a state where an assertion of a possible transition out of that state evaluates to false.

Now, consider the dual case for tressa claims. Following the argument above, if a $\mathcal{P}$ has a backward failing run, then it must have a run $(\sigma_0, \Delta_0) \xrightarrow{l_1} (\sigma_j, \Delta_j) \xrightarrow{l_2} (\sigma_k, \Delta_k)$ such that (σ_0, Δ_0) is initial, (σ_k, Δ_k) is final, $\sigma_i(\mathsf{err}) = -2$ for all $0 \leq i \leq j$ and $\sigma_i(\mathsf{err}) = -1$ for all $j < i \leq k$. It is possible to view this run as an invisible prefix followed by a visible suffix separated by a state which violates the tressa claim of the last transition of the prefix. However, referring to the duality, we prefer the following interpretation: Any backward execution of the program should not reach a state where the tressa of a possible transition out of that state evaluates to false. Equivalently, a tressa claim stands for backward reachability from a final state (and does not necessarily claim anything about forward reachability).

Abstraction. Our proof system is based on the concepts of abstraction and reduction. We start with abstraction which in turn is formalized via a relation over pairs of atomic statements, called simulation.

Definition 2 (Simulation). *Let s_1, s_2 be two atomic statements and p be a predicate. Then, s_2 simulates s_1 with respect to p, written $p \vdash s_1 \preceq s_2$, if for any t and for any $t.\sigma_1, t.\sigma_1' \vDash p$ with $\{\sigma_1\} t : s_1 \{\sigma_1'\}$, one of the following holds:*

- EXACT: $\{\sigma_1\} t : s_2 \{\sigma_1'\}$,
- *there exist σ_2, σ_2' with $t.\sigma_2, t.\sigma_2' \vDash p$ such that*
    - FAIL-F: $\sigma_2'(\mathsf{err}) = 2$ *and* $\{\sigma_1[\mathsf{err} \mapsto 1]\} t : s_2 \{\sigma_2'\}$,
    - FAIL-B: $\sigma_2(\mathsf{err}) = -2$ *and* $\{\sigma_2\} t : s_2 \{\sigma_1'[\mathsf{err} \mapsto -1]\}$.

Intuitively, s_2 simulates s_1 if s_2 makes the same transition as s_1 (EXACT), or for s_1 making a transition from q to q', an assert claim of s_2 fails at q (FAIL-F) and a tressa claim of s_2 fails at q' (FAIL-B). In the case where the program does not contain any tressa claims, only EXACT or FAIL-F needs to hold. Similarly, when the program does not contain any assert claims, only EXACT or FAIL-B is required to hold. We have the following lemma relating failing runs to simulation.

Lemma 1. *Let s_1, s_2 be atomic statements and $\mathcal{I}$ be a predicate such that $\mathcal{I} \vdash s_1 \preceq s_2$. If $\mathcal{P}$ is failing for $\mathcal{I}$, then so is the program $\mathcal{P}[s_1 \mapsto s_2]$.*

Proof. Let some run $q = \langle (\sigma_i, \Delta_i) \rangle_{0 \leq i \leq k}$ of $\mathcal{P}$ be such that it is failing and $\sigma_0 \vDash \mathcal{I}$. We have to show that a failing run exists for the new program. The proof is by induction on the number of occurrences of s_1 in $\mathbf{q}$. Base case of 0 occurrences is trivial. Let there be $n + 1$ occurrences of s_1 and let the leftmost occurrence be in the transition $(\sigma_{i-1}, \Delta_{i-1}) \xrightarrow{(s_1,t)} (\sigma_i, \Delta_i)$. Then, by definition of simulation, either $(\sigma_{i-1}, \Delta_{i-1}) \xrightarrow{(s_2,t)} (\sigma_i, \Delta_i)$ holds, or there are two states $(\sigma_{i-1}', \Delta_{i-1}'), (\sigma_i', \Delta_i')$ such that $(\sigma_{i-1}', \Delta_{i-1}') \xrightarrow{(s_2,t)} (\sigma_i[\mathsf{err} \mapsto -1], \Delta_i)$, $(\sigma_{i-1}[\mathsf{err} \mapsto 1], \Delta_{i-1}) \xrightarrow{(s_2,t)} (\sigma_i', \Delta_i')$, $\sigma_{i-1}'(\mathsf{err}) = -2$, $\sigma_i'(\mathsf{err}) = 2$. In the former case, we obtain a new failing run with n occurrences of s_1. In the latter case, if q was a forward failing run, then the run from (σ_0, Δ_0) to (σ_i', Δ_i') is a witness to a forward failing run. Similarly, if q was a backward failing run, then the run from $(\sigma_{i-1}', \Delta_{i-1}')$ to (σ_k, Δ_k) is a witness to a backward failing run with n occurrences of s. □

Reduction. In order to make sense of the reduction proof rules given in the following section, we need to formalize the notion of *mover*. Let $\mathbf{l}$ be a sequence of labels and (σ, Δ) be a state. An assert of $\mathbf{l}$ fails at (σ, Δ), written $(\sigma, \Delta) \notmid \mathbf{l}$, if there exists a state (σ', Δ') such that $\sigma'(\mathsf{err}) = 2$ and $(\sigma[\mathsf{err} \mapsto 1], \Delta) \xrightarrow{1} (\sigma', \Delta')$. Similarly, a tressa of $\mathbf{l}$ fails at (σ, Δ), $\mathbf{l} \notmid (\sigma, \Delta)$, if there exists a state (σ', Δ') such that $\sigma'(\mathsf{err}) = -2$ and $(\sigma', \Delta') \xrightarrow{1} (\sigma[\mathsf{err} \mapsto -1], \Delta)$.

Definition 3 (Mover). *Let $s_1, s_2 \in Atoms(\mathcal{P})$. We say that s_1 commutes to the right of s_2 in $\mathcal{I}$ if, for all labels $l_1 = (s_1, t), l_2 = (s_2, u)$ with $t \neq u$ and for states $(\sigma_1, \Delta_1), (\sigma_2, \Delta_2)$ in $\mathcal{I}$, whenever $(\sigma_1, \Delta_1) \xrightarrow{\langle l_1 l_2 \rangle} (\sigma_2, \Delta_2)$, we have*

- **X:** $(\sigma_1, \Delta_1) \xrightarrow{\langle l_2 l_1 \rangle} (\sigma_2, \Delta_2)$, or
- **RI:** $(\sigma_1, \Delta_1) \notin \langle l_1 \rangle$ and $\langle l_1 \rangle \notin (\sigma_2, \Delta_2)$, or
- **Rf:** $(\sigma_1, \Delta_1) \notin \langle l_2 \rangle$ and **Rb:** $\langle l_2 l_1 \rangle \notin (\sigma_1, \Delta_1)$.

Intuitively, s_1 commutes to the right of s_2, if at any state q_1 executing (s_1, t) followed by (s_2, u) leads to q_3, then either (**RI**) the assert and tressa of (s_1, t) fail at q_1 and q_3 respectively, or after reversing the order of execution either (**X**) the same end state is reached, or (**Rf+Rb**) it is possible to obtain both forward and backward failing runs. If we replace **RI** with (**LI**) $(\sigma_1, \Delta_1) \notin \langle l_2 \rangle$ and $\langle l_2 \rangle \notin (\sigma_2, \Delta_2)$, **Rf** with (**Lf**) $(\sigma_1, \Delta_1) \notin \langle l_2 l_1 \rangle$, and **Rb** with (**Lb**) $\langle l_1 \rangle \notin (\sigma_2, \Delta_2)$, s_2 is said to *commute to the left* of s_1. Similar to simulation, if the program does not contain any assertions, then conditions relating to assertion failures are ignored (first part of **RI/LI** and **Rf/Lf**); if there are no tressa claims, tressa failure conditions are ignored (second part of **RI/LI** and **Rb/Lb**).

A statement $s \in Atoms(\mathcal{P})$ is *right mover* (left mover, resp.) with respect to $\mathcal{I}$ if it commutes to the right (left, resp.) of every statement in $Atoms(\mathcal{P})$ for every state in $\mathcal{I}$. For $\mu \in \{\mathbb{R}, \mathbb{L}\}$, $\mathcal{I} \vdash (\mathcal{P}, s) : \mu$ denotes that the atomic statement s has mover type μ in program $\mathcal{P}$.

Lemma 2 (Sequential Reduction). *Let $s_1 ; s_2$ be a statement in $\mathcal{P}$ such that $s_1, s_2 \in Atoms(\mathcal{P})$ and let $\mathcal{I}$ be an invariant of $\mathcal{P}$. Assume further that either $\mathcal{I} \vdash (\mathcal{P}, s_1) : \mathbb{R}$ or $\mathcal{I} \vdash (\mathcal{P}, s_2) : \mathbb{L}$. Then, the program $\mathcal{P}[s_1 ; s_2 \mapsto s_1 \circ s_2]$ is failing for $\mathcal{I}$ if $\mathcal{P}$ is failing for $\mathcal{I}$.*

3.1 Proof Rules

A *proof frame* is a pair $(\mathcal{P}, \mathcal{I})$, where $\mathcal{I}$ is an invariant for program $\mathcal{P}$. A *proof* is a sequence of proof frames $\langle \mathcal{P}_i, \mathcal{I}_i \rangle_{0 \leq i \leq n}$ such that each $(\mathcal{P}_{i+1}, \mathcal{I}_{i+1})$ is obtained from $(\mathcal{P}_i, \mathcal{I}_i)$ by an application of a proof rule. The proof rules of our system are given in Fig. 3.

Modified Rules. With the exception of ANNOT-P, the proof rules are almost the same as those of [1]. The main difference is due to the modification in the concepts of simulation and mover types both of which take into account forward and backward reasoning. The rule ANNOT-H is for annotating simple statements with a new (history) variable. The rule INV is for strengthening of the invariant. The rule SIM is for abstracting an action by replacing it with one that simulates it. The rules RED-L, RED-S, RED-C are for reducing loops, sequential composition and conditional branches of two atomic statements, respectively.

Prophecy Introduction Rule. Let $a =: e$, *reverse assignment*, be a syntactic sugar for $\{\text{assume } a == e' ; \text{ havoc } a ; \text{ assume } a == x ; \text{ havoc } x\}$, where x is a new variable and e' is the same as e except every free occurrence of a is replaced with x.

The main concern when adding a new variable into the program is to annotate statements so that no terminating execution of the original program is left out. That is why the ANNOT-H rule for introducing history variables into the program requires a transition for every valuation of the auxiliary variable: if the original program makes a transition over a certain valuation of variables, so will the new

ANNOT-H
$$\frac{Simple(\mathcal{P}) = \{s_i\}_{i \in J} \quad a \notin Var(P) \quad \forall i.(\tilde{s}_i = (a:=e_i) \circ s_i)}{\mathcal{P}, \mathcal{I} \dashrightarrow \mathcal{P}[gV \mapsto gV \cup \{a\}, \forall i.s_i \mapsto \tilde{s}_i], \mathcal{I}}$$

INV
$$\frac{\mathcal{I}_2 \Rightarrow \mathcal{I}_1 \quad \mathcal{I}_2 \rightleftarrows \mathcal{P}}{\mathcal{P}, \mathcal{I}_1 \dashrightarrow \mathcal{P}, \mathcal{I}_2}$$

SIM
$$\frac{\mathcal{I} \vdash s \preceq \tilde{s}}{\mathcal{P}, \mathcal{I} \dashrightarrow \mathcal{P}[s \mapsto \tilde{s}], \mathcal{I}}$$

RED-L
$$\frac{\mathcal{I} \vdash (\mathcal{P}, s) : \mu \quad \mu \in \{\mathbb{R}, \mathbb{L}\} \quad \mathcal{I} \rightleftarrows \tilde{s} \quad \mathcal{I} \vdash skip \preceq \tilde{s} \quad \mathcal{I} \vdash \tilde{s} \circ s \preceq \tilde{s}}{\mathcal{P}, \mathcal{I} \dashrightarrow \mathcal{P}[while\,(*)\,\{s\} \mapsto \tilde{s}], \mathcal{I}}$$

RED-S
$$\frac{\mathcal{I} \vdash (\mathcal{P}, s) : \mathbb{R} \; or \; \mathcal{I} \vdash (\mathcal{P}, \tilde{s}) : \mathbb{L}}{\mathcal{P}, \mathcal{I} \dashrightarrow \mathcal{P}[s;\tilde{s} \mapsto s \circ \tilde{s}], \mathcal{I}}$$

RED-C
$$\frac{s = if(*)\,\{atomic\{s_1\}\}\,else\{atomic\{s_2\}\} \quad \tilde{s} = atomic\{if(*)\,\{s_1\}\,else\{s_2\}\}}{\mathcal{P}, \mathcal{I} \dashrightarrow \mathcal{P}[s \mapsto \tilde{s}], \mathcal{I}}$$

ANNOT-P
$$\frac{Simple(\mathcal{P}) = \{s_i\}_{i \in J} \quad a \notin Var(P) \quad \forall i.(\tilde{s}_i = (a=:e_i) \circ s_i)}{\mathcal{P}, \mathcal{I} \dashrightarrow \mathcal{P}[gV \mapsto gV \cup \{a\}, \forall i.s_i \mapsto \tilde{s}_i], \mathcal{I}}$$

Fig. 3. Rules of the proof system

program over the same valuation for any value of the history variable. Prophecy variables satisfy a similar requirement. The condition that has to be satisfied for prophecy variables, however, is the dual of that of a history variable. Prophecy variable introduction requires the new transition be defined for all next state values of the prophecy variable. In other words, prophecy variables are non-blocking in the backward direction for any value they can assume much like history variables are non-blocking in the forward direction. This leads to the following lemma.

Lemma 3. *Let $\rho_1 = (\mathcal{P}_1, \mathcal{I}_1)$ be a proof frame. Let ρ_2 be the proof frame obtained from ρ_1 by an application of the* ANNOT-P *rule. Let $\langle q_i \rangle_{0 \le i \le k}$ be a run of $\mathcal{P}_1$. Then, there exists a run $\langle q_i' \rangle_{0 \le i \le n}$ of $\mathcal{P}_2$ such that for all i, q_i and q_i' coincide on every component except the value of the prophecy variable a introduced by the* ANNOT-P *rule.*

Proof (Sketch). By induction on the length of the run, k. Construct the run backwards, starting from the end state q_k and make the observation that for each state, due to the premise of the ANNOT-P rule, there always exists a value of the prophecy variable in the preceding state such that the transition of $\mathcal{P}_1$ is enabled in $\mathcal{P}_2$. □

We close this section by stating the soundness of the proof system claiming that failing runs are preserved. A program $\mathcal{P}$ is safe for $\mathcal{I}$ if $\mathcal{P}$ has no failing run that starts at a state in $\mathcal{I}$.

Theorem 1 (Soundness). *Let $(\mathcal{P}_0, \mathcal{I}_0) \dashrightarrow^* (\mathcal{P}_n, \mathcal{I}_n)$ be a proof. If $\mathcal{P}_n$ is safe for $\mathcal{I}_n$, then $\mathcal{P}_0$ is safe for $\mathcal{I}_n$.*

4   Overview of a Sample Proof

Figure 4 presents the Lookup and Insert methods implementing a bounded set of non-negative integers. Set elements are stored in an array in which duplicates are allowed. An array slot is taken to be empty if it contains -1. Initially, all slots are assumed to be empty. The contents of the set are given by the set of values in non-empty slots. Reads and writes to each array index are atomic.

The Insert method starts from an arbitrary array index in order to reduce conflicts between concurrent executions of Insert on early array indices. It examines array slots in increasing order of indices and wraps around at the end of the array. Insert returns true (succeeds) when it either finds an empty slot to which it atomically writes the new element, or it finds an occupied slot containing the element it was trying to insert. It returns false (fails) if all array slots are occupied by other elements. In this simplified implementation, there is no removal whose presence would make the other methods non-atomic. Lookup(x) searches in increasing order of indices for x. It returns true iff for some array index i, q[i] == x. Since Insert can start from an arbitrary index, Lookup must examine the entire array before deciding whether or not x is in the set.

We would like to prove that the Lookup method is behaviorally equivalent to an atomic block that returns true iff for some array index i, q[i] == x.

```
procedure Insert(y: Data)
returns success: bool;
{
  havoc j;          // arbitrary
  assume 0<=j<n;   // array slot

  cnt := 0; success := false;

  while (cnt<n && !success) {
    if (*) {
      atomic{
        assume q[j]==-1; q[j] := y;
        success := true; } }
    else if (*) {
      atomic{
        assume q[j]==y;
        success := true; } }
    else {
      j := j+1 mod n;
      cnt := cnt+1; }
  }
}
```

(a) The code for the Insert procedure

```
procedure Lookup(x: Data)
  returns found: bool;
{
  found := false;
  i := 0;

  while (i<n && !found) {
    found := (q[i]==x);
    i := i+1;
  }
}
```

(b) The Lookup procedure

Fig. 4. An implementation of a bounded set

Intuition for Atomicity. Observe that all actions of Lookup except the read of q[i] are thread-local, i.e., they are both movers. Then the only potential conflict is between the read of q[i] and the update to q[i] done by the Insert method when q[i] == -1.

Call an iteration of the Lookup loop for some i *failing* if q[i] != x (denoted by $F(i)$) and *succeeding* (denoted by $S(i)$) otherwise. Executions of Lookup that return false are of the following form

$$..., F(0), ..., F(1), ..., F(2), ..., F(n-1), ..., F(n), ...$$

while executions that return true are of the following form

$$..., F(0), ..., F(1), ..., F(2), ..., F(i-1), ..., S(i), ...$$

where ... represents a sequence of actions by other threads. The reduction-based proof is based on the following intuition. Let "commit action" denote the action that all other actions of Lookup will be moved and be made adjacent to. For Lookup(x)'s that return false is $F(0)$ because the set may contain x later in the execution. For Lookup's that return true, the commit action is $S(i)$, since the action that writes the only x to an array slot may immediately precede $S(i)$.

In order to reduce the entire execution of the loop to an atomic action, for Lookup's that return false, we need all $F(k)$ to be left-movers in order to group them next to $F(0)$, while, for Lookup's that return true, all $F(k)$'s must be right movers in order to move immediately to the left of $S(i)$. The two kinds of lookups require different applications of reduction to prove atomicity.

```
procedure Lookup(x: Data) returns found: bool;
{
 if (*)                           else
   { atomic{                        { atomic{
       found := false;                  found := false;
       i := 0; }                        i := 0; }
     while (*) {                      while (*) {
       chkL(i,x);                       chkR(i,x);
     }                                }
     assume !found;                   assume found;
   }                                }
}
```

Fig. 5. The Lookup procedure after code transformation

Proof Highlights. To enable different reduction proofs for succeeding and failing executions of Lookup, we transform Lookup as shown in Fig. 5. This version of the code is arrived at after the following sound code transformation:

Let s be the statement representing the body of Lookup. Replace s with if(*) { s; assume!found;} else{ s; assume found;}.

This transformation is sound because found is a thread-local variable. In the following, we only present the atomicity proof for the failing branch of Lookup, as this is the path that involves the use of tressa. Let chk(i,x) be shorthand for the following atomic statement that is the body of the while loop in Lookup and wrt(j,y) denote the update action of Insert.

$$\text{chk(i,x)} \triangleq \{\text{assume i<n \&\& !found; found := (q[i]==x); i := i+1;}\}$$
$$\text{wrt(j,y)} \triangleq \{\text{assume (q[j]==-1); q[j] := y}\}$$

After the code transformation given in Fig. 5, we let chkL(i,x) denote the copy of chk(i,x) that resides in the failing branch. chkR(i,x) is the copy of chk(i,x) in the succeeding branch. chkL(i,x) and chkR(i,x) are syntactically identical. Observe that chkL(i,x), as it stands, is neither a right nor a left-mover, since it does not commute with wrt(j,y) if j == i and x == y. The key use of the tressa construct will be to annotate the action chkL(i,x) with the information that it is part of the failing branch of Lookup, and, therefore, cannot be immediately preceded by wrt(i,x). An alternative statement of this fact is as follows. If wrt(i,x) were followed by chkL(i,x), then, when the assume !found statement is reached at the end of the failing branch, the execution would block, i.e., only the artificial blocking executions that are by-products of the code split and not real executions of the program can contain wrt(i,x) followed by chkL(i,x). We encode this information in the form of a tressa annotation and abstract chkL(i,x) as atomic{ chkL(i,x); tressa !found;} which yields the code snippet given in Fig. 6. Executions which violate !found right after chkL(i,x) have "chosen the wrong branch", i.e., in order for these executions to terminate, control should have gone down the other non-deterministic branch.

Let us define LHS as the pair of transitions wrt(i,x) executed by thread $t1$ followed by atomic{ chkL(i,x); tressa !found} executed by thread $t2$. Let RHS be the same sequence in reverse order; that is, atomic{chkL(i,x); tressa !found} executed by thread $t2$ followed by wrt(i,x) executed by thread $t1$. Recall the left-mover check in Sec. 3. Initial-final state pairs (q_1, q_2) that LHS can give rise to must be matched by RHS only if !found holds in q_2 (due to **LI**). But, wrt(i,x) followed by chkL(i,x) always gives rise to found being true. Therefore, the mover check vacuously holds.

```
procedure Lookup(x: Data) returns found: bool;
{
  ...
  while (*) {
   atomic{ chkL(i,x); tressa !found; }//left-mover
  }
  assume !found;
  ...
}
```

Fig. 6. The failing iterations annotated with tressa

Intuitively, at this stage of the proof, we make the assumption that if found is true after chkL(i,x) is executed, then this is an artificially blocking execution that can be ignored. We will have to validate this assumption later. Using our loop reduction rule, we can prove that the following action summarizes the while loop in the failing branch of the Lookup.

```
atomic{
 if (*) { skip; }
 else { havoc i,found; tressa !found;
        assume i<=n;
        assume !found <==> (∀j. j<i ==> q[j]!=x)); }
}
```

This loop summary and the assume !found following it are combined into a single atomic block using the reduce-sequential rule. Once this level of atomicity is reached, the proof assumption that we had expressed as a tressa annotation is discharged easily by reasoning backwards within the atomic block.

5   Conclusion

In this paper, we incorporated backward reasoning into static verification. We achieved this by augmenting the static verification tool QED with a new construct, tressa, along with a new proof rule for the introduction of prophecy variables. We re-defined correctness, simulation and mover checks to allow for reasoning in both forward and backward executions. We have demonstrated the usage of this new approach in the atomicity proof of a non-trivial set implementation.

Tressa claims reflect the user's belief that any time the tressa is executed, the remaining execution leads to safe termination only when its claim is satisfied. A tressa claim can thus be used in specifying properties a program should satisfy much like an assertion. We are preparing a companion paper in which the use of tressa claims at the specification level is discussed along with a framework which can be used in debugging programs whose specifications are given via tressa claims.

On the static verification front, our next goal is to statically verify STM (Software Transactional Memory) implementations. Actually, the need for backward reasoning and prophecy variables in a static setting manifested itself while we were doing preliminary work on STM verification.

References

1. Elmas, T., Qadeer, S., Tasiran, S.: A calculus of atomic actions. In: POPL 2009, pp. 2–15. ACM, New York (2009)
2. Lipton, R.J.: Reduction: a method of proving properties of parallel programs. Commun. ACM 18(12), 717–721 (1975)
3. Larus, J.R., Rajwar, R.: Transactional Memory. Morgan & Claypool (2006)

4. Ashcroft, E.A.: Proving assertions about parallel programs. J. Comput. Syst. Sci. 10(1), 110–135 (1975)
5. Owicki, S., Gries, D.: Verifying properties of parallel programs: an axiomatic approach. Commun. ACM 19(5), 279–285 (1976)
6. Wang, L., Stoller, S.D.: Static analysis for programs with non-blocking synchronization. In: PPoPP 2005. ACM Press, New York (2005)
7. O'Hearn, P.W.: Resources, concurrency, and local reasoning. Theor. Comput. Sci. 375(1-3), 271–307 (2007)
8. Flanagan, C., Qadeer, S.: A type and effect system for atomicity. SIGPLAN Not. 38(5), 338–349 (2003)
9. Freund, S.N., Qadeer, S.: Checking concise specifications for multithreaded software. Journal of Object Technology 3 (2004)
10. Freund, S.N., Qadeer, S., Flanagan, C.: Exploiting purity for atomicity. IEEE Trans. Softw. Eng. 31(4), 275–291 (2005)
11. Abadi, M., Lamport, L.: The existence of refinement mappings. Theor. Comput. Sci. 82(2), 253–284 (1991)
12. Hesselink, W.H.: Simulation refinement for concurrency verification. Electr. Notes Theor. Comput. Sci. 214, 3–23 (2008)
13. Kesten, Y., Pnueli, A., Shahar, E., Zuck, L.D.: Network invariants in action. In: Brim, L., Jančar, P., Křetínský, M., Kucera, A. (eds.) CONCUR 2002. LNCS, vol. 2421, pp. 101–115. Springer, Heidelberg (2002)
14. Colvin, R., Groves, L., Luchangco, V., Moir, M.: Formal verification of a lazy concurrent list-based set algorithm. In: Ball, T., Jones, R.B. (eds.) CAV 2006. LNCS, vol. 4144, pp. 475–488. Springer, Heidelberg (2006)
15. Lynch, N.A., Tuttle, M.R.: An introduction to input/output automata. CWI Quarterly 2, 219–246 (1989)
16. Marcus, M., Pnueli, A.: Using ghost variables to prove refinement. In: Nivat, M., Wirsing, M. (eds.) AMAST 1996. LNCS, vol. 1101, pp. 226–240. Springer, Heidelberg (1996)

Automated Verification of a Small Hypervisor

Eyad Alkassar[1,*], Mark A. Hillebrand[2,*], Wolfgang J. Paul[1],
and Elena Petrova[1,*]

[1] Saarland University, Computer Science Dept., Saarbrücken, Germany
{eyad, wjp, petrova}@wjpserver.cs.uni-saarland.de
[2] German Research Center for Artificial Intelligence (DFKI), Saarbrücken, Germany
mah@dfki.de

Abstract. Hypervisors are system software programs that virtualize the architecture they run on. They are typically small, safety-critical, and hard to debug, which makes them a feasible and interesting target for formal verification. Previous functional verifications of system software were all based on interactive theorem proving, requiring substantial human effort complemented by expert prover knowledge. In this paper we present the first functional verification of a small hypervisor using VCC, an automatic verifier for (suitably annotated) C developed at Microsoft. To achieve this goal we introduce necessary system verification techniques, such as accurate modeling of software/hardware interaction and simulation proofs in a first-order logic setting.

1   Introduction

Hypervisors are small system software programs that virtualize the underlying architecture, allowing to run a number of guest machines (also called partitions) on a single physical host. Invented in the 1970s for use in mainframes, hypervisors are becoming more and more important today with shared multi-threading and shared multiprocessing being part of computer mainstream. Because they are hard to debug, and because of their small size yet high criticality, hypervisors make a viable and interesting target for (system) software verification. Hypervisor verification is also challenging: a hypervisor functions correctly if it simulates the execution of its guest systems. Thus, functional correctness of a hypervisor cannot be established by only proving shallow properties of the code.

In this paper we present the formal verification of a simple hypervisor, which we call baby hypervisor, using VCC, an automatic verifier for concurrent C (with annotations) developed at Microsoft [5]. The verification of the baby hypervisor is part of the Verisoft XT project, which also aims at the verification of the hypervisor of Microsoft's Hyper-V[TM]. In comparison, the baby hypervisor and the architecture it virtualizes are very simple (e.g., neither a multi-core architecture nor concurrent code are considered). In the project, the baby hypervisor has played an important role of driving the development of the VCC technology and

* Work funded by the German Federal Ministry of Education and Research (BMBF) in the framework of the Verisoft XT project under grant 01 IS 07 008.

G.T. Leavens, P. O'Hearn, and S.K. Rajamani (Eds.): VSTTE 2010, LNCS 6217, pp. 40–54, 2010.

applying it to system verification. For example, the region-based memory model of previous VCC versions exhibited serious performance problems in an earlier verification attempt of the baby hypervisor, which also led to the development of VCC's current memory model [6]. The baby hypervisor can serve a similar purpose outside the Verisoft XT project, and act as a benchmark or challenge for other verification tools.[1]

Our contribution is twofold: (i) We present the first verification of a hypervisor. It includes the initialization of the guest partitions and a simple shadow page table algorithm for memory virtualization. We verified the simulation of the guest partitions, and, since our modeling starts at host reset time, the assumptions are few and well-defined. (ii) We demonstrate how to apply automated verification to system software. In particular, we show a way to do simulation proofs in a first-order prover setting, how to model the underlying hardware, and reason about its interaction with the (mixed C and assembly) code.

The remainder of this paper is structured as follows. In Sect. 2 we give an overview of related work. In Sect. 3 we introduce VCC. In Sect. 4 we present an overview of our architecture, called *baby VAMP*, which we have formalized in VCC. In Sect. 5 we introduce the framework we use here for the verification of system software with VCC. System behavior is modeled by the execution of a *system program* that consists of an infinite loop of steps of the host architecture; system correctness is an invariant of this loop. In Sect. 6 we present an overview of the baby hypervisor data structures and invariants, and instantiate the simulation framework. The two main proof obligations are (i) the correctness of the hypervisor's top-level function and (ii) the simulation of guest steps by steps on the host in which no host exceptions. In Sects. 7 and 8 we evaluate and conclude.

2   Related Work

There are several projects with substantial results in the system verification area. The seminal work in pervasive systems verification was the CLI stack, which included the (very simple) KIT operating system [4]. More recent work was done in the projects FLINT, L4.verified, and Verisoft. FLINT focuses on the development of an infrastructure for the verification of systems software [8]. In L4.verified, the functional correctness of a high-performance C implementation of a microkernel was proven [9]. In Verisoft [13] large parts of the 'academic system', comprising hardware, system software, and applications, have been verified (e.g., cf. [1, 2] for work on the lower system software layers). In contrast to the present work, all the work above was based on interactive theorem proving, requiring significant human interaction and expertise. Of the above work, only KIT and Verisoft take into account user processes like we do. For microkernels this might be an acceptable compromise, assuming that a provably correct implementation of the kernel API already covers a substantial portion of overall system correctness. For hypervisors, however, the major part of its functionality is the simulation of the base architecture, and its verification should not be dodged.

---

[1] Verified source is available at http://www.verisoftxt.de/PublicationPage.html

There is also related but in-progress work in hypervisor verification. The Robin project aimed at verifying the Nova microhypervisor using interactive theorem proving [12]. Although on the specification side much progress has been made, only small portions of the actual hypervisor code are reported to be verified. In the Verisoft XT project [14], which the baby hypervisor verification was also part of, the verification of the hypervisor of Microsoft's Hyper-V™ using VCC is being attempted (cf. [10] for verification status). No code or specs are shared between these hypervisors; our work drove VCC development early on and thus helped empower VCC for more complex tasks.

3   VCC Overview

The Verifying C Compiler (VCC) is a verifier for concurrent C being developed at Microsoft Research, Redmond, USA, and the European Microsoft Innovation Center (EMIC), Aachen, Germany. Binaries and source are openly available and free for academic use. The VCC methodology aims at a broad class of programs and algorithms. Our overview here is focussed on our verification target (e.g., we do not consider concurrency); more information on VCC is available from [5,11].

Workflow. VCC supports adding specifications (e.g., in the form of function contracts or data invariants) directly into the C source code. During regular build, these annotations are ignored. From the annotated program, VCC generates verification conditions for (partial) correctness, which it then tries to discharge (under the hoods using the Boogie verifier [3] and the automatic theorem prover Z3 [7]). Ideally, all verification conditions can be proven. Otherwise, a counter example is produced or a violation of resource bounds is reported.

Memory Model. The C standard defines memory as a collection of byte sequences. Using this model directly proved to be inefficient. Instead, as a sound abstraction of the standard model, VCC now implements a typed memory model [6]. Pointers are modeled as pairs of types and addresses. We distinguish pointers to primitive types (e.g., integer) from pointers to non-primitive types (e.g., structs); the latter are also called 'object pointers'. Memory content is a mapping from primitive pointers to data. To ensure that differently typed pointers (and fields of different objects) do not overlap, VCC maintains a typedness predicate on pointers together with appropriate invariants, and inserts verification conditions that only typed memory is referenced. Typedness of pointers is inferred along structural type dependencies, e.g., a pointer to a field of a structure is known to be typed if the pointer to the structure is typed, and vice versa. These dependencies are also used to infer non-aliasing of pointers. For example, two typed references $\&p{\rightarrow}f$ and $\&q{\rightarrow}g$ can be disambiguated if $p{\neq}q$ or $f{\neq}g$.

To allow for the framing of function calls, VCC maintains a predicate for writability. At the beginning of a function, all pointers given by the function contract's writes clause are writable (and typed). For function calls, writability of the writes clauses is checked, and after the call memory contents, typedness and writability for non-written pointers are preserved. Pointers in the writes clauses are still writable if the function ensures them to remain typed. Moreover, pointers may also be ensured as 'freshly typed', which will make them writable.

Ownership and Invariants. On top of the memory model, VCC implements and enforces an ownership model. For each object (i.e., non-primitive pointer), VCC maintains an owner field and a closed bit. The owner field of an object indicates which object it is owned by. If an object is closed, all objects it owns must be closed. The *domain* of a closed object is the set of all objects it transitively owns (and their fields). The currently executing thread (denoted as **me**) is a special owner, which plays a role in memory reference checking. Pointers owned by it are called *wrapped* if closed and *mutable* otherwise. Extending the earlier checks, reading of a pointer is allowed if it is mutable or in the domain of a wrapped object. Writing to a pointer is allowed, if it is mutable and marked writable. Thus, while a domain remains unopened, its data cannot change. This allows for extended framing of calls. Ownership information is manipulated via ghost operations (setting the owner, wrapping, and unwrapping). These operations require write permissions on the objects they manipulate. Unwrapping a wrapped object opens it; its fields and owned objects become writable and wrapped. Wrapping a mutable object with wrapped closed objects closes it; its fields and owned objects will lose writability.

Objects can be annotated with invariants, which are meant to hold while the object is closed. Since invariants are only checked when wrapping they cannot talk about arbitrary state. Rather they may only refer to their domain, which is checked by VCC in an invariant admissibility check.

Ghosts. In addition to C types, VCC provides ghost types for use in annotations. The additional primitive types include unbounded integers, records, and maps. Moreover, VCC supports non-primitive ghost structures and ghost unions, which are fully-fledged objects with invariants. Ghost functions and data can be used for abstraction and for overcoming limitations of VCC's first order prover setting. For example, a linked list may be abstracted as a set of pointers to list elements with reachability relations being maintained with maps. The modification of implementation data in such scenarios typically involves doing a suitable ghost update. Such updates are done in *ghost code* inserted by the annotator. For soundness reasons, ghost code needs to be terminating and may not modify implementation variables (preventing information flow from ghost to implementation data). VCC checks this by a mixture of static and dynamic conditions.

Syntax. Object invariants are added to struct declarations using **invariant** clauses. Function contracts are given after the function signature. Writes clauses are given by **writes**. Pre- and postconditions are specified using **requires** and **ensures**; the clause **maintains** means both. In postconditions, **old** can be used to evaluate an expression in the prestate, **result** refers to the function's return value, and **returns**(x) abbreviates **ensures**(**result**≡ x). Listing 1 shows a small program with annotations. In the function *triple*, the bound requirement is needed to pass the overflow check generated for the arithmetic, the **writes**

```
struct Even {                              {
  unsigned v; invariant(v%2≡ 0)              unsigned x = e→v;
};                                           unwrap(e);
unsigned triple(struct Even *e)              e→v = x + x + x;
  requires(e→v < 4711)                       wrap(e);
  maintains(wrapped(e))                      return x;
  writes(e) returns(old(e→v))              }
  ensures(e→v≡ 3*old(e→v))
```

Listing 1. VCC Syntax Example

clause is needed to allow unwrapping the object e, and the proof that the object invariant holds when wrapping e requires that validity of the invariant after unwrapping.

4   Architecture

The *baby VAMP* architecture is a 32-bit RISC architecture with 44 instructions, two privilege levels (user and system mode), single-level address translation (without TLB), and interrupt handling. In this section we describe the specification model of the baby VAMP hardware architecture. In VCC, architecture state and steps are defined using ghost types and functions, respectively. We use the model to specify (i) transitions of the *VAMP simulator* modeling steps of the system (cf. Sect. 5), (ii) effects of assembly code execution, and (iii) transitions of the abstract guest machines.

Configuration. Words and addresses of the machine are encoded as 32-bit integers. The memory m is modeled as a map from addresses to words. A page is an aligned chunk of $PG\_SZ:=1024$ words in memory. Accordingly, an address a is decomposed into a page and a word index, $PX(a):=a \;/\; PG\_SZ$ and $WX(a):=a$ % PG_SZ. For a page index px we define $PA(px):=px*PG\_SZ$.

Listing 2 shows the configuration of the VAMP machine (making use of VCC maps and records). It consists of the word addressable memory and the processor configuration. The latter consists of the normal and delayed program counters *pcp* and *dpc* (there is one delay slot) and the general- and special-purpose register files *gpr* and *spr*. For this paper the following special-purpose registers are

```
typedef unsigned _int32 v_word;         typedef struct vcc(record) v_mach {
typedef v_word v_mem[unsigned];           v_mem m;
typedef struct vcc(record) v_proc {       v_proc p;
  v_word gpr[unsigned],                 } v_mach;
    spr[unsigned], dpc, pcp;
} v_proc;
```

Listing 2. Baby VAMP Configuration

of interest: (i) *PTO* and *PTL* for the page table's origin and maximum index, (ii) *MODE*, equal to *0* and *1* in system / user mode, respectively, and (iii) *EPC*, *EDPC*, *EMODE*, *EDATA* for registers used to save the current program counters, mode, and additional data (as exception cause and data) in case of an interrupt.

Memory Access. In user mode a memory access to a virtual address is subject to address translation. This translation is done via a page table in main memory, which maps virtual page indices to page table entries (PTEs). The start of the currently active page table is designated by the (physical) page index of its first entry and the length by its maximum index, stored in the *PTO* and *PTL* registers. Each page table entry *pte* is a machine word encoding three components: (i) the valid bit $V(pte):=pte$ & *1024* indicating whether the entry can be used for any access, (ii) the protection bit $P(pte):=pte$ & *2048* indicating whether the entry cannot be used for write access, and (iii) the physical page index $PPX(pte):=PX(pte)$ indicating the location of the page in physical memory. To compute the translation of a virtual address a via a page table at a certain origin *pto*, we first compute the address of the corresponding page table entry as $v\_ptea(pto, a):=PA(pto)+ PX(a)$. Second, we look up the entry in the memory, $v\_pte(m, a, pto):=m[v\_ptea(pto,a)]$. Finally, the translated address is obtained by concatenating the PTE's page index and the word index of the input address, $v\_ta(m, a, pto):=PA(PPX(v\_pte(m,a,pto)))+ WX(a)$. Given a memory, an input adress, a translation flag, and a page table origin a memory read result is defined as $v\_mem\_read(m, a, t, pto):=m[(t$? $v\_ta(m,a,pto): a)]$. Likewise, writing v is formalized with the function $v\_mem\_write(v, a, t, pto, m)$, which returns an updated memory.

Memory accesses may fail and cause an interrupt (a bus error or page fault). Untranslated accesses fail in case of a bus error, i.e., if the accessed address lies outside the physical memory whose size is given by the maximum physical page index *max_ppx*, a machine parameter. Translated accesses fail if (i) the virtual address is outside virtual memory (virtual page index outside the page table), (ii) the page-table entry address is outside physical memory, (iii) the page-table entry is invalid, (iv) the page-table entry is protected and a write is attempted, or (v) the translated address is outside physical memory. Given the memory, the maximum physical page index, the address to access, the translation flag, the page table origin and a flag indicating write or read access, the predicate $v\_pf(m, max\_ppx, a, t, pto, ptl, w)$ indicates the presence of such a failure.

Interrupt Handling. Interrupts may trigger due to internal events like page faults, illegal / unprivileged instructions, and traps, or due to external events like reset and device interrupts. For the baby hypervisor verification, the only external interrupt considered is reset. Interrupts may be masked by the programmer, i.e., disabled, by setting corresponding bits in the special-purpose status register *SR*. We distinguish between maskable, i.e., interrupts which can be disabled, and non-maskable interrupts (in our case only reset).

If an interrupt occurs, the interrupt service routine (ISR) is invoked by: (i) setting exception cause and data registers and saving program counters, mode, and status registers to the SPR, (ii) setting the program counters to the start of the ISR, which handles the interrupt, and (iii) masking all maskable interrupts by setting the status register to zero.

Semantics. The architecture's main function is the step function with the following signature: **v_mach** v_step(**v_mach** mach, **v_word** max_ppx, **bool** reset). It takes as input the current machine state, the maximum physical memory space, and a reset signal. It returns an updated machine state which is either computed by fetching and executing a single instruction of the machine, or by jumping to the interrupt service routine. Given a machine configuration, instruction fetch is defined as a simple memory read v_mem_read(mach.m, mach.p.dpc, mach.p.spr[MODE], mach.p.spr[PTO])). An interrupt is triggered by the reset signal, by a page fault during instruction fetch, or during instruction execution.

5   Simulation Framework

In this section we show how to bring VCC and system verification together, allowing to reason on overall system correctness in an efficient and pervasive manner. To do this, we model the architecture state and steps in VCC such that later program verification is not made hard. We then show how to express top-level system correctness as a *system program*.

Representing the Architecture. Since C memory is sufficiently low-level, we use a prefix of it, starting from address zero, to represent the architecture's memory. We hold the processor state in a separate structure **proc_t** *h located outside this region; it matches its abstract counterpart **v_proc** with the exception of arrays being used instead of maps. We define abs_p(h) to abstract the processor state and abs_m(max_ppx, m):=λ(a; a < PA(max_ppx+1)? m[a] : 0) to abstract memory. Using these definitions, the function abs0(h) abstracts from a processor configuration and a zero-based memory, returning a state of type **v_mach**.

We perform machine steps by statements of the form il = sim_vamp(h,reset). The function *sim_vamp* takes as inputs the processor state, a Boolean flag indicating reset, and, implicitly, the zero-based memory. It operates directly on the processor state and the VCC memory, simulating a single instruction. For simplicity, it also returns the interrupt level associated with the instruction (or *IL_NONE* if the instruction did not cause an exception and no reset occurred).

The contracts of *sim_vamp* have to be chosen carefully. Contradictory postconditions would make VCC unsound. We ensures consistency of the sim_vamp contracts by verifying them (in VCC) against a concrete implementation, which we refer to as the *baby VAMP simulator*. Moreover, the contracts have to comply to the (trusted) architecture specification described in the previous section. The obvious way to achieve this is by describing the effects of sim_vamp using the abstraction abs0 and the transition function v_step in a postcondition **ensures**(abs0(h)≡ **old**(v_step(abs0(h),max_ppx,reset))). However, this straightforward contract is impractical, since the caller of sim_vamp would have to ensure that the complete memory is uniformly typed and writable. We realize a less invasive approach: only the specific memory cells that the architecture accesses in a certain step need to be typed and mutable (and in case of the store operand also writable).

Basic Simulation Pattern. A convenient way to show system correctness is to prove a simulation theorem between the concrete system and some abstraction of it. The simplest description of a system (which we call *system program*) is given by an infinite loop executing steps of the architecture modeled by *sim_vamp*. The simulation property is stated as a loop invariant. This invariant relates the initial (i.e., before entering the loop) and the current states of the system under the abstraction, and claims that the current abstract state is reachable from the initial abstract state taking steps of the abstract transition system.

In general, reachability cannot be stated in first-order logic. We avoid this problem by introducing a counter increased in each step. Let **mathint** denote the type of unbounded integers. Given an abstract step relation S, the predicate $R(s,t,n) \iff (s \equiv t \wedge n \equiv 0) \vee (n > 0 \wedge \exists(\textbf{mathint } u; R(s,u,n-1) \wedge S(u,t)))$ is an exact first-order definition of n-step reachability.

With the abstraction denoted as $A(\textbf{proc\_t } *h)$ and additional implementation invariants as I, a basic simulation pattern in VCC has the following form (where **old()** here evaluates an expression in the state before entering the loop):

```
sim_vamp(h, true);
while (1)
    invariant(I ∧ ∃(mathint n; R(old(A(h)), A(h), n)))
    sim_vamp(h, false);
```

Extended Simulation Pattern. Next we want to combine code verification with the execution of the architecture. Note, that in the system program above we can first unroll the **while**-loop, group chunks of *sim_vamp* computations together, and finally describe their effects by contracts. Such a chunk may be given, e.g., by the execution of assembly instructions, where the semantics of each instruction can be expressed in terms of *sim_vamp*. Similarly a chunk may consist of compiled C code. Since we use the same VCC memory model for the architecture and the C code verification, and by assuming compiler correctness, we can describe these chunks by their corresponding C implementation.

We show how to unroll and divide the **while**-loop into four parts as they might occur in a typical (sequential) OS kernel verification. (i) The architecture executes under *sim_vamp* until some interrupt occurs. (ii) The kernel is entered and the interrupted state (here: the processor registers) must be saved, which must be implemented in assembly rather than in pure C. The semantics of assembly instructions can be fully expressed by *sim_vamp* and the effects of the complete code by the contracts of a function *kernel_entry(h)*. (iii) The kernel's main function *kernel_main(il)* implemented in C then handles the interrupt. (iv) Exiting the kernel and switching to the user again requires an assembly implementation, the effects of which we specify by the contracts of the function *kernel_exit(h)*. Accordingly, we define a more elaborate simulation pattern, which combines reasoning on C code, assembly code, and user steps into a single, pervasive correctness proof:

```
il = sim_vamp(h, true);
while (1)
    invariant(I ∧ ∃(mathint n; R(old(A(h)), A(h), n)))
{ kernel_entry(h); kernel_main(il); kernel_exit(h);
    do il = sim_vamp(h, false); while (il≡ IL_NONE); }
```

6   Hypervisor Implementation and Correctness

We present the implementation and verification of a simple hypervisor, which we call *baby hypervisor*. The baby hypervisor virtualizes the architecture defined in Sect. 4, and its correctness is expressed and verified using the previously presented simulation framework.

The recipe for virtualizing the different guest architecture is simple. We always make the guests run in user mode on the host, regardless of the mode they think they are in. Hence, we obtain full control over guests, as they run translated and unprivileged. Under hardware address translation, we virtualize guest memory by setting up so-called host and shadow page tables for the guest running in system and user mode, respectively. The host page tables will map injectively into host memory with different regions allocated for each guest. The shadow page table of a guest is set up as the 'concatenation' of the guest's own page table and its host page table. To make sure that the guest cannot break this invariant, we map all host or shadow page table entries to the guest page table as read-only. Thus, attempts of a guest to edit its page table and also to perform a privileged operation (e.g., change the page-table origin) will cause an exception on the host and be intercepted by the hypervisor. The hypervisor will then emulate the exception operation in software.

We express the whole system verification scenario following the pattern of our simulation framework introduced in Sect. 5. The state of the system we intend to simulate consists of a vector of architecture states (cf. Sect. 4), where each state represents the state of a guest partition. The transition function is almost identical to the architecture's transition function; deviations are that guest traps in system mode are used to issue hypercalls (we only implement a simple 'yield' call for cooperative partition scheduling), and (for implementation reasons) the guest's page table length needs to be bounded by a maximum virtual page index parameter. Based on the hypervisor's data structure we then define an abstraction from the implementation state into the simulated, i.e., the guest's, state. The instantiation of the system program features the different code parts of the hypervisor (the hypervisor main function implemented in C, and assembly portions for hypervisor entry and exit), and architecture steps to model guest execution on the host. For simulation, we state the reachability of (abstracted) guest configurations from their initial state as an invariant of the main loop.

```
typedef struct guest_t {              typedef struct hv_t {
  proc_t pcb;                           v_word ng;
  v_word max_ppx, max_vpx,              guest_t *g, *cg;
    *gm, gmo, *hpt, hpto, *spt, spto;  } hv_t;
} guest_t;
```

Listing 3. Hypervisor Data Structures

Parameters and Memory Map. The hypervisor is configured at boot time by four parameters encoded in four bytes at the beginning of its data segment at address *DS_START*: (i) the data segment size *DS_SIZE*, (ii) the number of guests *NG*, (iii) the maximum physical page index for each guest *MAX_PPX*, and (iv) the maximum virtual page index for each guest *MAX_VPX*. At boot time, the data segment is a byte array *DS:=**as_array**((**uint8_t**∗)DS_START,DS_SIZE)* (where **as_array***(a,n)* denotes an array object with base *a* and size *n*). Given the last three parameters, we can compute the size to allocate and align all global data structures of the hypervisor. This size must not be larger than *DS_SIZE*, a condition that we abbreviate as *VALID_DS*.

Data Structures. Listing 3 shows the two main data structures of the hypervisor implementation without invariants. The structure **guest_t** holds all data for a single partition: (i) the maximum physical and virtual page index for the guest (that remain constant after initialization), (ii) the processor registers when suspended (modeled by the struct type **proc_t** already used in Sect. 5), (iii) pointers to the guest's memory as well as the host and shadow page tables, and (iv) for each of these, the index of the first (host) page they are stored in. The top-level data structure **hv_t** holds the number of guests, a pointer to an array of their data structures, and the current guest pointing into that array. When the boot procedure completes, a wrapped **hv_t** data structure is returned at the beginning of the data segment; we abbreviate *HV:=((**hv_t**∗)DS_START)*.

Invariants. All data structures have been annotated with invariants on subtypes, typedness / non-aliasing, ownership, and, in general, data. Importantly, by the non-aliasing and ownership invariants, all of the guests' data structures are separated. The most complex invariants are those for the host and shadow page tables entries, declared in the **guest_t** structure. Let *in_pt* indicate if a page index falls into a page table given by *pto* and *ptl*, i.e., *in_pt(x, pto, ptl):=pto* $\leq x \wedge (x \leq pto + (ptl / 1024))$ where *1024* is the number of page-table entries per page. A host PTE with index x must be valid, point to the guest page x as stored on the host, and be protected if covered by the guest's page table:

bool inv_hpt_entry(**guest_t** *g, **v_word** x)
   returns(V(g→hpt[x]) $\wedge$ PPX(g→hpt[x])≡ g→gmo + x $\wedge$
    (P(g→hpt[x]) $\Longleftrightarrow$ in_pt(x, g→pcb.spr[PTO], g→pcb.spr[PTL])));

A shadow PTE with index x is valid iff the translation yields no guest bus error (i.e. if the address is not in range) and the guest PTE is valid. Validity of the shadow PTE then implies that it points to the host page designated by guest and host translation and it is protected if the guest page is protected or part of the guest page table. We define

bool inv_spt_entry(**guest_t** *g, **v_word** x)
  returns((V(g→spt[x]) ⟺
    ¬v_bus_error(v_ptea(o, PA(x)),g→max_ppx) ∧ PPX(e) ≤ g→max_ppx ∧ V(e)) ∧
    (V(g→spt[x]) ⟹ (PPX(g→spt[x]) ≡ PPX(g→hpt[PPX(e)]) ∧
    (P(e) ∨ in_pt(PPX(e),o,l)) ⟹ P(g→spt[x]))))));

where $o:=g{\to}pcb.spr[PTO]$, $l:=g{\to}pcb.spr[PTL]$, and $e:=g{\to}gm[v\_ptea(o,\ x)]$.

Abstraction. Given a guest's implementation data structure, we can construct an abstract machine state in terms of the architecture definition from Sect. 4. This involves constructing the guest's memory and processor state. The latter is done in two contexts. When the hypervisor executes, all registers are held in the guest's *pcb* structure. In this case, the abstraction just operates on a guest pointer g (the expression *(R){...}* defines a record constant):

v_mach abs_g(**guest_t** *g)
  returns((**v_mach**) { .p = abs_p(&g→pcb), .m = abs_m(g→max_ppx,g→gm) });

When a guest executes on the host, the partition control block only stores the guest SPR (accesses to those are emulated) while the GPR and program counters are stored in the actual host's processor state. With the host processor state denoted as *h* we define guest abstraction in this case as follows (the expression *r* / {.a = b} denotes record update):

v_mach abs_gh(**guest_t** *g, **proc_t** *h)
  returns((**v_mach**) { .p = abs_p(h) / { .spr = abs_p(&g→pcb).spr },
      .m = abs_m(g→max_ppx, g→gm) });

Let us define how the host's SPR are set up while the guest runs on it. When guests execute, the SPR is set up to use address translation and the shadow or host page table depending on the guest mode; in guest system mode the host page table origin and the maximum physical page index are used, in guest user mode the shadow page table origin and the guest's page table length index are used. Given a guest structure g and a host processor state h we define

bool spr_inv(**guest_t** *g, **proc_t** *h)
  returns(H.spr[MODE] ∧ (G.spr[MODE]
    ? H.spr[PTO]≡ g→spto ∧ H.spr[PTL]≡ G.spr[PTL]
    : H.spr[PTO]≡ g→hpto ∧ H.spr[PTL]≡ g→max_ppx));

where $H:=abs\_p(h)$ and $G:=abs\_p(g)$. Given this setup, we can (in VCC) prove the equivalence of memory operations: (i) the absence of host page faults implies the absence of guest page faults and (ii) if there's no host page fault the result of reads (a data word) and writes (an updated memory) are equal.

Simulation Loop. Listing 4 shows the instantiatation of the system program for the baby hypervisor, where the relation *R* is *n*-step reachability of guest transitions. As a boot requirement (i.e., a *sim* precondition) a writable, large-enough

```
void sim(proc_t *h)
  requires(VALID_DS ∧ wrapped(h)) writes(h, extent(DS))
{
  spec(v_word ng = NG, max_ppx = MAX_PPX;)
  v_il il;
  sim_vamp(h, true);
  hv_dispatch(h→spr[ECA],h→spr[EDATA]);
  spec(v_mach G0[unsigned] = λ(unsigned i; i < ng; abs_g(HV→g+i));)
  do
    invariant(∀(unsigned i; i < ng; ∃(mathint n;
      R(G0[i],abs_g(HV→g+i),max_ppx,n))))
    invariant(wrapped(HV) ∧ wrapped(h))
  {
    restore_guest(h,&HV→cg→pcb);
    do
      invariant(∀(unsigned i; i < ng; ∃(mathint n; R(G0[i],
        HV→g+i≡ HV→cg ? abs_gh(HV→cg, h) : abs_g(HV→g+i), max_ppx, n))))
      il = sim_vamp(h, false);
    while (il≡ IL_NONE);
    save_guest(&HV→cg→pcb,h);
    hv_dispatch(h→spr[ECA], h→spr[EDATA]);
  } while (1);
}
```

Listing 4. Hypervisor Simulation Loop

data segment and a wrapped and writable host processor state are assumed (note that we have not yet formalized remaining memory layout, such as the stack and code segment). Ghost code and declarations are given using the VCC keyword *spec* (e.g., the map of initial abstract guest machine configurations). The code that runs on the host architecture is represented by assembly portions *save_guest* and *restore_guest* (used on kernel entry and exit), *hv_dispatch*, and (for generic host execution) by *sim_vamp* (cf. Sect. 5). The hypervisor's main function *hv_dispatch* takes the architecture's exception cause and data as parameters *eca* and *edata*. The main code paths of the hypervisor are initialization (function *handle_reset*) and handling exceptions caused by guests (functions *handle_illegal* and *handle_pf*); calling *hv_dispatch* with eca≡ *IL_NONE* is not allowed. We sketch the individual components in a little more detail below.

Assembly Parts. A single assembly routine is located at the start of the interrupt service routine (i.e., address 0). It consists of three parts: (i) save the registers of the current guest (unless on reset), (ii) set up the stack and call the main C function of the hypervisor, *hv_dispatch*, (iii) restore the registers of the (possibly new) current guest. In the simulation loop (which shows dynamic instances of this code in the execution) we have represented this code in slightly abstracted form; calls to the dispatcher (including setting up the stack and the parameters) are represented as a regular call to *hv_dispatch*, we only specify the effects of save and restore via function contracts *save_guest* and *restore_guest*, and we simply omit the save part after reset.[2] The specifications of save and restore describe the copying of register between a guest's partition control block and the host.

Boot. Calling *hv_dispatch* with *eca*≡ *IL_RESET* will lead to the execution of the reset procedure of the hypervisor. Just as *sim*, the function in this case requires a writable and valid data segment. Using a boot-time allocator, the reset code of the hypervisor allocates and initializes its data structures in the data segment, i.e., the hypervisor structure, the individual guest structures, and for each guest its memory, shadow page table, and host page table. For verifying this code we make use of VCC's memory reinterpretation feature, which allows us to split and convert the data segment (initially a byte array) into the necessary (page-aligned) typed objects. As a postcondition, *hv_dispatch* guarantees to return *HV* wrapped and with properly initialized guests.

Host Exceptions. On host interrupts *hv_dispatch* gets called after saving the guest state with a non-reset exception cause *eca*. Unless the guest issues a hypercall (which it does by executing a trap in system mode), the dispatcher has to emulate an interrupt, a privileged operation, or a page table writes of a guest. Interrupt injection is mostly done in *hv_dispatch* directly, while the latter two cases are implemented by the functions *handle_illegal* and *handle_pf*, respectively.

The non-reset contracts for *hv_dispatch* requires the hypervisor structure *HV* to be wrapped and writable and that *eca* contains an actual interrupt level that occurred on the host while executing the current guest $HV{\rightarrow}cg$. The function ensures to return a wrapped hypervisor structure. For non-continue type interrupts (in our case every interrupt but a trap), it also guarantees to emulate a guest step. Trap interrupts are special for two reasons: (i) Traps that the guest executes in system mode are used to issue hypercalls. There is only a single hypercall in the baby hypervisor, which is a *yield* call to switch execution round-robin fashion to the next guest partition. From a guest's point of view, that call is just a nop (i.e., it only increments program counters). (ii) Traps reach the hypervisor with the guest's program counters already pointing to the next instruction. When emulating traps the hypervisor must not increment them again. We currently express these peculiarities by a special post condition describing the guest processor updates. In the context of the simulation loop, the combined effect of hardware and hypervisor updates give the complete semantics of the guest step.

7   Evaluation

Our work consists of four components (VAMP spec and simulator, hypervisor implementation, and system program) comprising 2.5k C code tokens and 7.7k annotation tokens, which comprise data invariants, function contracts (including loop invariants), ghost code, and (proof) assertions. Roughly a quarter of the

---

[2] Justifying the abstractions is the subject of future work. Note that almost identical assembly code has been verified previously [1].

Table 1. Annotation Effort (Tokens) and Runtimes (Average, Standard Deviation)

	Code	Contract		Ghost Code		Proof		∅	σ
hv_dispatch	158	198	(1.3)	90	(0.6)	441	(2.8)	930s	574s
handle_reset	60	150	(2.5)	30	(0.5)	42	(0.7)	545s	295s
handle_pf	102	96	(0.9)	40	(0.4)	208	(2.0)	473s	414s
reset_guest	125	131	(1.0)	46	(0.4)	53	(0.4)	213s	38s
handle_movi2ptl	93	238	(2.6)	6	(0.1)	66	(0.7)	98s	31s
handle_movi2pto	69	162	(2.3)	6	(0.1)	57	(0.8)	74s	20s
handle_illegal	90	47	(0.5)	48	(0.5)	149	(1.7)	53s	8s
update_spt	62	175	(2.8)	0	(0.0)	140	(2.3)	14s	6s
System program	54	587	(10.9)	205	(4.6)	378	(7.0)	1241s	794s

annotation tokens belong to the architecture specification and another quarter to the system program. Overall proof time is ca. 1 hour on one core of a 2.66 GHz Intel Core Duo machine, depending on random seeds for Z3's heuristics. The hypervisor C code consists of 9 loops in 45 functions. In Table 1 we list token counts and runtimes (for 20 runs) of its 8 most complex functions and the system program. Particularly, we give ratios of contract, ghost code, and proof tokens versus C tokens in brackets. The latter ratio may be considered an upper bound, and will likely decrease with better automation. Measuring person effort is hard, because VCC has undergone major development since we started, and therefore annotations had to be often revised. The hypervisor was never tested, and a number of bugs could be found and fixed during the verification. Notably, some of these became apparent when doing the proof of the system program, at the HW/SW boundary (e.g., emulating guest traps, cf. Sect. 6).

8   Future Work and Conclusion

We have presented a technique and framework for pervasively verifying system correctness based on automated methods. Our approach precisely models the underlying system architecture and represents it in a first-order logic based program prover (in our case VCC), which is then used to prove the mixed-language system software correct. We used this framework to show for the first time (i) the functional correctness of a small hypervisor, expressed as the architecture-conforming simulation of guest machines by the host system, and (ii) the feasibility of applying automated methods in the context of functional (systems) verification. We are confident that much of the presented methods can be used as a basis for further extensions, and that our verification may serve as a valuable benchmark for the automated reasoning and software verification community. Meanwhile, the feedback (in form of bug reports and optimization suggestions) provided by the baby hypervisor verification as first complex and completed proof target substantially contributed to the development of VCC.

There are several directions of future work, some of them ongoing. The assembly portions of the hypervisor have been specified but not yet verified against their implementation which almost only consists of straightforward code to copy register contents. Our framework allows for a seamless integration of assembly verification into VCC (using the VAMP simulator). Still, a detailed soundness proof of the presented approach (including compiler calling convention and correctness), is ongoing work. Moreover, the presented framework should be extended to more complex software and hardware designs. On the hardware side, this should cover the modeling of multi-core systems, buffers (e.g., TLBs), and devices. On the software side, the step to the verification of multi-threaded or preemptive kernels is crucial. Parallelism in the code and in the architecture can be dealt with by using VCC's concurrency features, as e.g., two-state invariants. We plan to use two-state invariants for a more general way to express simulation, which should also scale to a concurrent setting. Adaptation to this new form will presumably require only little additional proof effort.

Acknowledgments. We wish to thank Ernie Cohen and Michał Moskal for many helpful comments and discussions of our work.

References

1. Alkassar, E., Hillebrand, M.A., Leinenbach, D.C., Schirmer, N.W., Starostin, A., Tsyban, A.: Balancing the load: Leveraging a semantics stack for systems verification. JAR 42(2-4), 389–454 (2009)
2. Alkassar, E., Paul, W., Starostin, A., Tsyban, A.: Pervasive verification of an OS microkernel: Inline assembly, memory consumption, concurrent devices. In: Leavens, G.T., O'Hearn, P., Rajamani, S. (eds.) VSTTE 2010. LNCS, vol. 6217, pp. 71–85. Springer, Heidelberg (2010)
3. Barnett, M., Chang, B.-Y.E., DeLine, R., Jacobs, B., Leino, K.R.M.: Boogie: A modular reusable verifier for object-oriented programs. In: de Boer, F.S., Bonsangue, M.M., Graf, S., de Roever, W.-P. (eds.) FMCO 2005. LNCS, vol. 4111, pp. 364–387. Springer, Heidelberg (2006)
4. Bevier, W.R.: Kit and the short stack. JAR 5(4), 519–530 (1989)
5. Cohen, E., Dahlweid, M., Hillebrand, M., Leinenbach, D., Moskal, M., Santen, T., Schulte, W., Tobies, S.: VCC: A practical system for verifying concurrent C. In: Urban, C. (ed.) TPHOLs 2009. LNCS, vol. 5674, pp. 1–22. Springer, Heidelberg (2009)
6. Cohen, E., Moskal, M., Schulte, W., Tobies, S.: A precise yet efficient memory model for C. In: SSV 2009. ENTCS, vol. 254, pp. 85–103. Elsevier, Amsterdam (2009)
7. de Moura, L., Bjørner, N.: Z3: An efficient SMT solver. In: Ramakrishnan, C.R., Rehof, J. (eds.) TACAS 2008. LNCS, vol. 4963, pp. 337–340. Springer, Heidelberg (2008)
8. Feng, X., Shao, Z., Guo, Y., Dong, Y.: Certifying low-level programs with hardware interrupts and preemptive threads. JAR 42(2-4), 301–347 (2009)
9. Klein, G., Elphinstone, K., Heiser, G., et al.: seL4: Formal verification of an OS kernel. In: SOSP 2009, pp. 207–220. ACM, New York (2009)
10. Leinenbach, D., Santen, T.: Verifying the Microsoft Hyper-V Hypervisor with VCC. In: Cavalcanti, A., Dams, D.R. (eds.) FM 2009. LNCS, vol. 5850, pp. 806–809. Springer, Heidelberg (2009)
11. Microsoft Corp. VCC: A C Verifier, http://vcc.codeplex.com/
12. Tews, H., Völp, M., Weber, T.: Formal memory models for the verification of low-level operating-system code. JAR 42(2-4), 189–227 (2009)
13. The Verisoft Project (2003), http://www.verisoft.de/
14. The Verisoft XT Project (2007), http://www.verisoftxt.de/

A Rely-Guarantee Proof System for x86-TSO

Tom Ridge

University of Leicester

Abstract. Current multiprocessors provide weak or relaxed memory models. Existing program logics assume sequential consistency, and are therefore typically unsound for weak memory. We introduce a novel Rely-Guarantee style proof system for reasoning about x86 assembly programs running against the weak x86-TSO memory model. Interesting features of the logic include processor assertions which can refer to the local state of other processors (including their program counters), and a syntactic operation of closing an assertion under write buffer interference. We use the expressivity of the proof system to construct a new correctness proof for an x86-TSO version of Simpson's four slot algorithm. Mechanization in the Hol theorem prover provides a flexible tool to support semi-automated verification.

1 Introduction

Multiprocessors are now widespread, but real multiprocessors provide subtle relaxed (or weak) memory models. Typically sequential consistency (SC) can be recovered by appropriate programming disciplines eg the use of locks to guard access to shared memory. However, there are several areas where the use of locks is either not possible, or would impose unacceptably high performance costs. For example, operating system lock implementations cannot assume that locks are already provided, and non-blocking synchronization techniques avoid the use of locks to provide good performance and strong progress guarantees. However, these programs are directly exposed to the weak memory models of the underlying processors, and consequently there is often considerable doubt about whether they are correct [Lin99]. Unfortunately existing program logics are typically no longer sound in this setting.

Our main contribution in Sect. 5 is a proof system for processors executing x86 assembly code with the x86-TSO memory model, proved sound with respect to the operational semantics. In Sect. 6 we show that the system is pragmatically useful by using it to give a novel proof of Simpson's four slot algorithm [Sim90]. The Hol mechanization[1] is a formal version of this paper, including complete definitions, formal proof rules, formal soundness proofs, the example application to Simpson's algorithm, and a mechanized proof environment to tackle further examples. We now discuss some interesting features of our program logic.

A rigorous semantics for the relaxed x86-TSO memory model has been defined in higher-order logic and mechanized in the Hol theorem prover [OSS09], see

---

[1] Available online at http://www.cs.le.ac.uk/people/tr61/vstte2010

G.T. Leavens, P. O'Hearn, and S.K. Rajamani (Eds.): VSTTE 2010, LNCS 6217, pp. 55–70, 2010.
© Springer-Verlag Berlin Heidelberg 2010

Sect. 3. We extend this model with an operational semantics for x86 assembly code in Sect. 4. For x86-TSO, every processor is connected to main memory by a FIFO write buffer modelled as a list of (address, value) pairs. Each write buffer process repeatedly removes a write from the head of the queue, and commits the write to main memory. A processor indirects via its write buffer: a read returns the value of the last buffered write to the address, if any, otherwise the value of the address in main memory, as usual. *We treat write buffers as active processes.* This is not straightforward: in traditional models, processes cannot write to or read from each other's local state, whereas here a processor affects the local state of its write buffer whenever it tries to write to a memory address. For x86-TSO, a processor's write buffer state is writable by that processor, but inaccessible to other processors. The need for *private state, that is shared between two related processes*, is built into our proof system. Write buffers also affect the semantics of assertions. Traditionally, the validity of a process assertion should not be affected by the behaviour of other processes. We require that the *validity is unaffected by the behaviour of the write buffer processes.* Writing syntactic assertions that satisfy this constraint is difficult, so we introduce a *syntactic operation of "closing an assertion under write buffer interference".* This is a key step towards making x86-TSO verification tractable.

The main challenge of low-level x86 assembly code is the *non-atomic nature of individual instructions.* For example, the mov$_{iload}$ eax, ebx (indirect load) instruction loads the register eax with the value of the memory address pointed to by ebx. This accounts for three separate memory/register read/writes. Interference from other processors can occur between each of these steps. The problem here is that individual instructions are *not* atomic. We do not give a general solution, but try hard to make the proof rules as simple as possible.

In traditional proof systems the notion of state is restricted: program counters (or equivalent) are not part of the state, and process assertions cannot refer to the local state of other processes. *We lift both these restrictions*, thereby dramatically increasing the expressivity of the system. The new elegant proof of Simpson's algorithm we present uses *processor assertions that refer to the private state of other processors.* Moreover, it seems very natural to talk about processes executing different regions of their code, and this essentially involves *assertions about processes' program counters.* A specific motivation for x86-TSO is that a processor assertion will often refer to the state of the processor's write buffer. Unfortunately this increases the complexity of the proof rules. For example, the familiar assertion $\{P\}$ nop $\{P\}$ is no longer valid eg if P is "the next instruction is nop", and nop is followed by a non-nop instruction. In order to recover the familiar $\{P\}$ nop $\{P\}$ rule, we require that the assertion P is invariant under changes to the processor's current instruction. Fortunately these side conditions are trivial in practice.

Notation. Formal definitions have been lightly edited before inclusion here. We use the following notation: function update $(f \oplus (x, y))$; list concatenation $(xs \mathbin{+\!\!+} ys)$; head and tail of a list (HD xs and TL xs); records with fields having values ($\{$ fld $= v; \ \ldots \ \}$); record update of a field with a value

(r with { fld $= v$ }); domain of a function (DOM f); image of a function or relation on a set (IMAGE f S); restriction of the domain of a function or relation to a set ($f|_S$); function application (f pid or f_{pid}).

2   Preview of the Proof System

In this section we give the syntax and semantics of the main proof system judgement informally. The familiar Hoare triple $\vdash \{P\}$ c $\{Q\}$ is valid iff starting from a state satisfying P, execution of the x86 assembly instruction c ends in a state satisfying Q [Flo67, Hoa69]. To this we add the standard Rely-Guarantee relations (R, G) to give the judgement $(R, G) \vdash \{P\}$ c $\{Q\}$: We now consider the execution of c interleaved with steps of other processes, which we can *assume* are approximated by the set of transitions R (Rely assumption). Dually we must *prove* that G approximates c steps (Guarantee commitment) [Jon81]. The judgement is valid iff starting from P, executing c steps interleaved with R steps, execution ends in Q and furthermore every c step is contained in G^2. Finally we must address what happens when execution jumps to some other address. We include in the judgement a component J such that J.invs is a partial map from code points, to invariants that must hold when execution reaches that point [CH72]. In the case that c terminates by jumping to a code point lbl, the final state must satisfy J.invs lbl rather than Q. To this we add the processor pid that is executing c and the code point ma of the current instruction (both of which can typically be ignored) to get pid, (R, G), J, $ma \vdash \{P\}$ c $\{Q\}$. If the judgement is valid, we write pid, (R, G), J, $ma \models \{P\}$ c $\{Q\}$. Some example judgements are:

- pid, $(\{\}, \{(s, s') \mid \mathsf{T}\})$, J, $ma \vdash \{\mathsf{T}\}$ nop $\{\mathsf{ma} = ma + 1;\ \mathsf{ci} = [ma + 1]\}$, where the precondition $\{\mathsf{T}\}$ is unconstrained, and the post-condition states that the current code point is $ma + 1$ and the current instruction is whatever instruction was stored in memory at address $ma + 1$.
- pid, $(\{\}, \{(s, s') \mid \mathsf{T}\})$, J, $ma \vdash \{J.\mathsf{invs}\ lbl\}$ jump lbl $\{\bot\}$, where the invariant that must hold after the jump is already established in the pre-condition.

An example proof rule concerns the instruction $\mathsf{mov_{ri}}(r, n)$, which sets local register r to the value n:

$$\frac{\begin{array}{c} \mathsf{wf}\ (pid,\ (R, G),\ J,\ ma \vdash \{P\}\ \mathsf{mov_{ri}}(r,\ n)\ \{Q\}) \\ \mathsf{nop\_conditions}\ pid\ P\ Q\ G \\ f = \mathsf{update\_f}\ pid\ (\lambda\ ll.\ ll\ \mathsf{with}\ \{\ \mathsf{l} = ll.\mathsf{l} \oplus (r, n);\ \mathsf{ci} = \mathsf{nop}\ \}) \\ \mathsf{IMAGE}\ f\ P \subseteq Q \qquad f\ |_P \subseteq G \end{array}}{pid,\ (R, G),\ J,\ ma \models \{P\}\ \mathsf{mov_{ri}}(r,\ n)\ \{Q\}}\ \text{MOV}_{\text{RI}}$$

The first condition checks that the judgement is well-formed, which includes the usual Rely-Guarantee requirement that P and Q are closed under R^3. A formal

---

[2] A key point for x86-TSO (but not in the semantics presented in this section) is that R includes *at least* all those steps that can be taken by write buffers. Thus, to prove a judgement valid using our proof system, it is necessary to take into account the behaviour of all write buffers.

[3] A set P is closed under a relation R iff for all s in P, for all s', if (s, s') in R then s' is also in P.

definition of judgement well-formedness will be given shortly. In addition there is a technical side-condition related to nop transitions, which can be safely ignored for now. The operational semantics for $mov_{ri}(r, n)$ simply updates the local state $ll.l$ of processor pid at register r with the value n whilst also updating the current instruction ci to nop. This is captured by the update function f. The judgement is valid iff starting from a state $s \in P$, the update function results in a state $f\ s \in Q$ (ie IMAGE $f\ P \subseteq Q$), and in addition the update is allowed by the guarantee G (ie $f\ |_P \subseteq G$, where the function f is considered as a set of pairs).

3   The x86-TSO Memory Model

We briefly review the x86-TSO memory model [OSS09], which usefully abstracts from the details of x86 assembly instructions. The model consists of processors

Read from memory

$$\frac{\text{not\_blocked } s\ p \qquad s.M\ a = \text{SOME } v \qquad \text{no\_pending } (s.B\ p)\ a}{s\ \xrightarrow{\text{Evt } p\ (\text{Access } R\ (\text{Location\_mem } a)\ v)}\ s}$$

Read from write buffer

$$\frac{\text{not\_blocked } s\ p \qquad s.B\ p = b1 + [(a, v)] + b2 \qquad \text{no\_pending } b1\ a}{s\ \xrightarrow{\text{Evt } p\ (\text{Access } R\ (\text{Location\_mem } a)\ v)}\ s}$$

Read from register

$$\frac{s.R\ p\ r = \text{SOME } v}{s\ \xrightarrow{\text{Evt } p\ (\text{Access } R\ (\text{Location\_reg } p\ r)\ v)}\ s}$$

Write to write buffer

$$s\ \xrightarrow{\text{Evt } p\ (\text{Access } W\ (\text{Location\_mem } a)\ v)}\ s \text{ with } \{\ B = s.B \oplus (p, [(a, v)] + (s.B\ p))\ \}$$

Write from write buffer to memory

$$\frac{\text{not\_blocked } s\ p \qquad s.B\ p = b + [(a, v)]}{s\ \xrightarrow{\text{Tau}}\ s \text{ with } \{\ M = s.M \oplus (a, \text{SOME } v);\ B = s.B \oplus (p, b)\ \}}$$

Write to register

$$s\ \xrightarrow{\text{Evt } p\ (\text{Access } W\ (\text{Location\_reg } p\ r)\ v)}\ s \text{ with } \{\ R = s.R \oplus (p,\ (s.R\ p) \oplus (r,\ \text{SOME } v))\ \}$$

Barrier

$$\frac{s.B\ p = []}{s\ \xrightarrow{\text{Evt } p\ (\text{Barrier Mfence})}\ s}$$

Lock

$$\frac{s.L = \text{NONE} \qquad s.B\ p = []}{s\ \xrightarrow{\text{lock } p}\ s \text{ with } \{\ L = \text{SOME } p\ \}}$$

Unlock

$$\frac{s.L = \text{SOME } p \qquad s.B\ p = []}{s\ \xrightarrow{\text{unlock } p}\ s \text{ with } \{\ L = \text{NONE}\ \}}$$

Fig. 1. The x86-TSO machine behaviour [OSS09]

connected via write buffers to a single shared main memory. The model also includes details of the per-processor local registers. *Individual* x86 instructions can be locked (and so execute atomically) which is captured by a lock value L, indicating which processor if any currently holds the lock. The states of the x86-TSO machine are records with the following fields:

```
machine_state = {
    R  :  proc → reg → value option;      // per processor registers
    M  :  address → value option;         // main memory
    B  :  proc → (address × value) list;  // per processor write buffers
    L  :  proc option                     // which processor holds the lock, if any
}
```

The behaviour of the system is described by the labelled transition relation $s \xrightarrow{lbl} s'$ in Fig. 1. The datatype of labels is label = Tau | Evt of proc × action | lock of proc | unlock of proc where an action is either a memory barrier or a read or write to a register or memory address. The predicate not_blocked $s\ p$ holds if the lock is owned by processor p, or if the lock is not held by any processor. The predicate no_pending $xs\ a$ checks that there are no writes to address a in write buffer xs.

4   x86 Assembly Code

We rephrase the model of the previous section and extend it with a model of x86 assembly code. The syntax of assembly instructions is expressed as a datatype:

```
instruction =                              | mov_iload of reg_name × reg_name
    | nop                                  | jump of flag_condition × code_point
    | mov_ri of reg_name × value           | lock of instruction
    | mov_rr of reg_name × reg_name        | Barrier Mfence
    | mov_rm of reg_name × data_address    | ...
```

The state of the system, type S, is a record with a field g giving the contents of the shared memory, a field f giving the local state for each processor, and a field lck giving the processor that holds the lock, if any. The local state LL for each processor consists of some code, the address of the current instruction ma, the state of the current instruction ci, the values of the processor-local registers l, and the pending writes in the write buffer w.

```
S = {                                      LL = {
    g : data_address →_fin value;              code : code_point →_fin instruction;
    f : proc →_fin LL;                         ma : code_point;
    lck : proc option                          ci : instruction;
}                                              l : reg_name →_fin value;
                                               w : (data_address × value) list
                                           }
```

The proc_view function gives a processor's view of memory, taking into account pending writes in the write buffer:

```
proc_view pid s = list.FOLDR (λ (a, v). λ g. g ⊕ (a, v)) s.g (s.f pid).w
```

The semantics is then expressed as a (small-step) state transition relation TransP pid (s, s'). This uses several auxiliary relations. The first, PreTransP, gives the basic semantics of commands.

```
PreTransP pid s =
  case (s.f pid).ci of
  nop → failwith "PreTransP : nop"
  || movri(r, n) → update_f pid (λ ll. ll with { l = ll.l ⊕ (r, n); ci = nop }) s
  || movrm(r, a) → update_f pid (λ ll. ll with { ci = movri(r, proc_view pid s a) }) s
...
```

Note that most instructions (including locked instructions) are eventually rewritten to nop. The evaluation of a nop instruction involves getting the next instruction at address ma + 1 and releasing the lock if it is taken.

```
XnopTrans pid (s, s') =
  let ll = s.f pid in
  case ll.ci of
  nop → (
      let ma' = ll.ma + 1 in
      if ma' ∉ DOM ll.code then ⊥ else
      let s1 = update_f pid (λ ll. ll with { ma = ma'; ci = (ll.code ma') }) s in
      let s2 = unset_lock s1 in
      s' = s2)
  || _ → ⊥
```

The lock and jump transitions are handled similarly. TransP is then

```
TransP pid (s, s') =
  pid ∈ DOM s.f ∧ not_blocked pid s ∧ let ll = s.f pid in
  case ll.ci of
  nop → (XnopTrans pid (s, s'))
  || lock c → (XlockTrans pid (s, s'))
  || jump(c, n) → (XjumpTrans pid (s, s'))
  || _ → (s' = PreTransP pid s)
```

The write buffer for processor pid simply takes the first pending write of value v to address a and updates the global memory g.

```
TransWb pid (s, s')  =
  let ll = s.f pid in
  let (a, v) = HD ll.w in
  let s1 = s with { g = s.g ⊕ (a, v) } in
  let s2 = update_f pid (λ ll. ll with { w = TL ll.w }) s1 in
  pid ∈ DOM s.f ∧ ll.w ≠ [] ∧ (s' = s2)
```

The transitions of the system are simply the union of the individual processor and write buffer transitions, TransS = $\bigcup_{pid}$\{TransP pid ∪ TransWb pid\}.

For example, a simple instruction such as $\text{mov}_{ri}(r, n)$ executes in two steps, the first PreTransP transition updates the local state, and changes the current instruction to nop. The second XnopTrans transition gets the next instruction from memory, then updates the current instruction and current address. In the concurrent setting, these steps are interleaved with steps of write buffers and other processors. More complicated instructions take more than two steps to execute, and each step may involve accessing an address in memory or a local register. This lack of atomicity impacts considerably on the proof system.

5   Rely-Guarantee Proof System

In this section we give our main contribution, a Rely-Guarantee proof system for x86 assembly code with the x86-TSO memory model. In Sect. 2 we gave the syntax and semantics of our judgement, and discussed the MOV_{RI} rule. In Fig. 2 we give selected rules covering further x86 instructions and logical aspects such as weakening.

Judgement well-formedness and soundness. The non-logical rules use a judgement well-formedness condition wf, and typically also include a nop_conditions side condition. The main aim of these conditions is to reduce the complexity of rules, which results from the liberal notion of state and the non-atomic nature of individual instructions, by making assumptions about P, Q, R, G. We motivate these conditions by discussing in more detail the soundness proof for rule MOV_{RI} from Sect. 2. The execution of $\text{mov}_{\text{ri}}(r, n)$ is interleaved with R-steps as follows:

$$s_0 \xrightarrow{R^*} s_1 \xrightarrow{\text{PreTransP}} s_2 \xrightarrow{R^*} s_3 \xrightarrow{\text{XnopTrans}} s_4 \xrightarrow{R^*} s_5$$

We are given that $s_0 \in P$, and we need to show $s_5 \in Q$. Our well-formedness assumption gives that P and Q are closed under R (this is a standard assumption), so it suffices to assume $s_1 \in P$, and show $s_4 \in Q$. Formally, wf is defined as follows:

---
wf j = case j of pid (R, G) J $ma \vdash P$ c $Q \rightarrow$
  wf_R pid R $\wedge$ wf_G pid G $\wedge$ (closed P R) $\wedge$ (closed Q R)

The judgements wf_R, wf_G are technical conditions that assert eg that the rely for a processor preserves for values of that processor's local registers. The nop_conditions in the premises of the rule require Q to be closed under XnopTrans pid transitions:

---
nop_conditions pid P Q G =
  closed Q (XnopTrans pid)
  $\wedge$ { (s, s') | $(s, s') \in$ XnopTrans pid $\wedge$ $s' \in Q$ } $\subseteq G$

---

so it suffices to show $s_2 \in Q$ (using again the fact that Q is closed under R). In practice, assertions for processor pid do not mention pid's program counter, and the side condition is trivial. Let $f = $ update_f pid $(\lambda$ $ll.$ ll with { $l = ll.l \oplus (r, n)$; ci = nop }). From the definition of PreTransP, we have that $s_2 = f$ s_1 ie $s_2 \in$ IMAGE f P. So the rule is sound only if IMAGE f $P \subseteq Q$, one of the premises of the rule. A similar argument can be used to prove that the Guarantee commitment is satisfied only if $f|_P \subseteq G$.

Composition. Our judgement concerns a single processor pid executing in some environment R which has so far been largely unconstrained. For x86-TSO, R should include the transitions of other processors and all write buffers. The move from the global view of the system with many processors and write buffers, to the local view of a single processor in environment R is handled

$$\frac{pid,\ (R,G),\ J,\ ma \models \{P'\}\ c\ \{Q'\} \qquad P \subseteq P' \qquad Q' \subseteq Q}{pid,\ (R,G),\ J,\ ma \models \{P\}\ c\ \{Q\}}\ \text{WEAKEN}$$

$$\frac{pid,\ (R',G'),\ J,\ ma \models \{P\}\ c\ \{Q\} \qquad R \subseteq R' \qquad G' \subseteq G}{pid,\ (R,G),\ J,\ ma \models \{P\}\ c\ \{Q\}}\ \text{WEAKENRG}$$

$$\frac{pid,\ (R,G),\ J',\ ma \models \{P\}\ c\ \{Q\} \qquad J' \subseteq J}{pid,\ (R,G),\ J,\ ma \models \{P\}\ c\ \{Q\}}\ \text{WEAKENJ}$$

$$\frac{pid,\ (R,G),\ J,\ ma \models \{P\}\ c\ \{Q\} \qquad pid,\ (R,G),\ J,\ ma \models \{P'\}\ c\ \{Q'\}}{pid,\ (R,G),\ J,\ ma \models \{P \wedge P'\}\ c\ \{Q \wedge Q'\}}\ \text{CONJ}$$

$$\frac{\text{wf}\ (pid,\ (R,G),\ J,\ ma \vdash \{P\}\ \text{nop}\ \{P\}) \qquad nop\_conditions\ pid\ P\ P\ G}{pid,\ (R,G),\ J,\ ma \models \{P\}\ \text{nop}\ \{P\}}\ \text{NOP}$$

$$\frac{\begin{array}{c} \text{wf}\ (pid,\ (R,G),\ J,\ ma \vdash \{P\}\ \text{mov}_{\text{rr}}(r1,\ r2)\ \{Q\}) \qquad s \in P \\ v = (s.\text{f}\ pid).\text{l}\ r2 \qquad f = \text{update\_f}\ pid\ (\lambda\ ll.\ ll\ \text{with}\ \{\ \text{ci} = \text{mov}_{\text{ri}}(r1,v)\ \}) \\ (s,f\ s) \in G \qquad pid,\ (R,G),\ J,\ ma \models \{f\ s\}\ \text{mov}_{\text{ri}}(r1,v)\ \{Q\} \end{array}}{pid,\ (R,G),\ J,\ ma \models \{P\}\ \text{mov}_{\text{rr}}(r1,\ r2)\ \{Q\}}\ \text{MOV}_{\text{RR}}$$

$$\frac{\begin{array}{c} \text{wf}\ (pid,\ (R,G),\ J,\ ma \vdash \{P\}\ \text{mov}_{\text{rm}}(r,\ a)\ \{Q\}) \qquad s \in P \\ v = \text{proc\_view}\ pid\ s\ a \qquad f = \text{update\_f}\ pid\ (\lambda\ ll.\ ll\ \text{with}\ \{\ \text{ci} = \text{mov}_{\text{ri}}(r,v)\ \}) \\ (s,f\ s) \in G \qquad pid,\ (R,G),\ J,\ ma \models \{f\ s\}\ \text{mov}_{\text{ri}}(r,v)\ \{Q\} \end{array}}{pid,\ (R,G),\ J,\ ma \models \{P\}\ \text{mov}_{\text{rm}}(r,a)\ \{Q\}}\ \text{MOV}_{\text{RM}}$$

$$\frac{\begin{array}{c} \text{wf}\ (pid,\ (R,G),\ J,\ ma \vdash \{P\}\ \text{mov}_{\text{iload}}(r1,\ r2)\ \{Q\}) \qquad s \in P \\ a = (s.\text{f}\ pid).\text{l}\ r2 \qquad f = \text{update\_f}\ pid\ (\lambda\ ll.\ ll\ \text{with}\ \{\ \text{ci} = \text{mov}_{\text{rm}}(r1,a)\ \}) \\ (s,f\ s) \in G \qquad pid,\ (R,G),\ J,\ ma \models \{f\ s\}\ \text{mov}_{\text{rm}}(r1,a)\ \{Q\} \end{array}}{pid,\ (R,G),\ J,\ ma \models \{P\}\ \text{mov}_{\text{iload}}(r1,\ r2)\ \{Q\}}\ \text{MOV}_{\text{ILOAD}}$$

$$\frac{\begin{array}{c} \text{wf}\ (pid,\ (R,G),\ J,\ ma \vdash \{P\}\ \text{jump}(cnd,\ ma')\ \{Q\}) \\ nop\_conditions\ pid\ P\ Q\ G \\ \text{closed}\ (J.\text{invs}\ ma')\ R \qquad \text{IMAGE XjumpTrans}_{pid}\ (P \cap cnd) \subseteq J.\text{invs}\ ma' \\ \text{IMAGE XjumpTrans}_{pid}\ (P \cap \neg cnd) \subseteq Q \qquad \text{XjumpTrans}_{pid}|_P \subseteq G \end{array}}{pid,\ (R,G),\ J,\ ma \models \{P\}\ \text{jump}(cnd,\ ma')\ \{Q\}}\ \text{JUMP}$$

$$\frac{\begin{array}{c} \text{wf}\ (pid,\ (R,G),\ J,\ ma \vdash \{P\}\ \text{lock}(c)\ \{Q\}) \\ pid,\ (\{\},\ G),\ J,\ ma \models \{P\}\ c\ \{Q\} \qquad \text{XlockTrans}_{pid}|_P \subseteq G \end{array}}{pid,\ (R,G),\ J,\ ma \models \{P\}\ \text{lock}(c)\ \{Q\}}\ \text{LOCK}$$

$$\frac{\begin{array}{c} \text{wf}\ \hat{J} \wedge \exists\ \hat{R}\ \exists\ \hat{G} \\ (\forall\ pid.\ \bigcup_{pid' \neq pid}(\hat{G}\ pid') \subseteq (\hat{R}\ pid)) \\ \wedge\ (\forall\ pid.\ \bigcup_{pid'}(\text{TransWb}\ pid') \subseteq (\hat{R}\ pid)) \\ \wedge\ (\forall\ ma.\ \text{let}\ J = \hat{J}\ pid\ \text{in} \\ \text{let}\ (R,\ G) = (\hat{R}\ pid,\ \hat{G}\ pid)\ \text{in} \\ pid,\ (R,G),\ J,\ ma \models \{J.\text{invs}\ ma\}\ J.\text{code}\ ma\ \{J.\text{invs}\ (ma+1)\}) \end{array}}{\models_{\text{j}} \hat{J}}\ \text{COMP}$$

Fig. 2. Selected proof rules

by the COMP rule. $\hat{J}$ is a function that for each pid gives a $J = \hat{J}\ pid$. Well-formedness of $\hat{J}$ means that each J should provide a pre and post condition for each code point (not just jump targets). Similarly $\hat{R}$, $\hat{G}$ give rise to R and G. The first Rely-Guarantee requirement is that $\hat{R}\ pid$, the rely for pid, should contain the guarantees of the other processors pid'. The second requirement is that the rely also contain all write buffer transitions. The final conjunct requires that for every instruction $c = J.\text{code}\ ma$, there is a valid judgement $pid,\ (R, G),\ J,\ ma \models \{J.\text{invs}\ ma\}\ c\ \{J.\text{invs}\ (ma + 1)\}$. The meaning of the conclusion $\models_j \hat{J}$ is that, providing the system starts in a state s where the instruction executed by pid and identified by ma is such that $s \in (\hat{J}\ pid).\text{invs}\ ma$, then all further invariants given by $(\hat{J}\ pid).\text{invs}\ ma'$ hold whenever execution of pid reaches ma'. Thus $\models_j \hat{J}$ represents the conjunction of invariants, each of which are indexed by pid and ma. The invariants themselves can be arbitrary formulas in higher-order logic, over the whole system state (including program counters).

The logic in practice. The COMP rule requires that the Rely relations include at least the transitions of the write buffers. A consequence is that the proof rules for instructions require assertions to be closed under write buffer transitions. For example, suppose we write a value v to an address a. We might incorrectly annotate the write as $\{w = []\}a := v\{w = [(a, v)]\}$, where w informally refers to the write buffer of the process. However, the assertion $\{w = [(a, v)]\}$ is not closed, because at any point after the instruction executes, the write buffer could flush the write and become empty. A correct assertion, that is closed under write buffer interference, is $\{w = [(a, v)] \lor w = []\}$. Rather than expanding various possible states as disjuncts, a more succinct approach is to allow assertions to be explicitly closed with respect to write buffer interference. If P is an assertion $\{\dots\}$, we write the closure under R as $\{\dots\}^R$. For example, if R represents interference from the write buffer, then $\{w = [(a, v)]\}^R = \{w = [(a, v)] \lor w = []\}$. In practice, rather than deal with the whole write buffer, we often want to refer to pending writes to a particular address. We introduce the syntax $\{a \doteq xs\}$ to mean that the contents of the write buffer, filtered to address a (and then projected onto the written values), is xs. For example, if $a \neq b$, then a write buffer $[(b, 0); (a, 1); (b, 2); (a, 3)]$ satisfies the assertion $\{a \doteq [1, 3]\}$.

A key point is that our assertions are higher-order logic predicates over the entire system state S, and can therefore be almost arbitrarily complicated. Moreover, the fact that our system is embedded in higher-order logic means that we can readily introduce new syntax for common assertions that arise in practice.

6 Simpson's Four Slot Algorithm

In this section we show how to apply the proof system to verify Simpson's four slot algorithm. We looked at several other examples (Peterson's mutual exclusion algorithm and the Linux spin-lock implementation), but Simpson's algorithm is considerably more interesting, and exercises several novel features

STATE

data$[0..1, 0..1]$
slot$[0..1]$ // *read-only by the reader,* slot$[\_] \in \{0, 1\}$
latest $= 0$ // *read-only by the reader,* latest $\in \{0, 1\}$
reading $= 0$ // *read-only by the writer,* reading $\in \{0, 1\}$
pair$_W$, index$_W$ // *writer local state,*   pair$_W \in \{0, 1\}$, index$_W \in \{0, 1\}$
pair$_R$, index$_R$ // *reader local state,*   pair$_R \in \{0, 1\}$, index$_R \in \{0, 1\}$

WRITER CODE

pair$_W = \neg$reading

index$_W = \neg$slot$[$pair$_W]$

$\ldots$ // *critical section, write to* data$[$pair$_W,$ index$_W]$

slot$[$pair$_W] =$ index$_W$

latest $=$ pair$_W$

READER CODE

pair$_R =$ latest

reading $=$ pair$_R$

index$_R =$ slot$[$pair$_R]$

$\ldots$ // *critical section, read from* data$[$pair$_R,$ index$_R]$

Fig. 3. Simpson's four slot algorithm in pseudo-code

of our proof system, such as processor assertions that refer to the private state of other processors (essential for the direct proof we give here). Our approach mirrors informal algorithm development for weak memory models: First, we consider the SC case for high-level pseudo-code. Then we incorporate the x86-TSO memory model, and modify the algorithm by including memory barriers. A key point is that the proof of correctness in the SC case dictates the positioning of the memory barriers in the weak case. Finally we refine the pseudo-code to low-level assembly code. Another key point is that we retain the high-level assertions in the low-level code, however the reasoning is substantially more complicated due to the non-atomic execution of individual instructions.

Simpson's four slot algorithm is designed to ensure mutual exclusion between a single reader and a single writer of a multi-word datum. Simpson's algorithm also satisfies several other desirable properties, but here we focus solely on mutual exclusion. Simpson's algorithm is non-blocking: the reader can still read even when the writer is delayed in the critical section, and vice-versa. This is achieved essentially by maintaining four copies of the underlying data in an array data$[0..1, 0..1]$ and ensuring that the reader and writer access different slots when running concurrently.

The code in Fig. 3 describes the entry and exit protocol run by the reader and the writer before and after the data array is accessed (the exit protocol for the reader is trivial). This entry and exit code is invoked whenever the writer wants to write to data, or the reader wants to read from data. Thus, the code

WRITER CODE

$\mathsf{pair}_W = \neg\mathsf{reading}$

$\{\,\mathsf{pc}_R \in \boxdot \longrightarrow (\mathsf{pair}_W = \mathsf{reading}) \longrightarrow (\mathsf{index}_R = \mathsf{slot}[\mathsf{reading}])\,\}$

$\mathsf{index}_W = \neg\mathsf{slot}[\mathsf{pair}_W]$

$\{\,\mathsf{pc}_R \in \boxdot \longrightarrow (\mathsf{pair}_W = \mathsf{reading}) \longrightarrow (\mathsf{index}_R = \mathsf{slot}[\mathsf{reading}]),\ \mathsf{index}_W = \neg\mathsf{slot}[\mathsf{pair}_W]\}$

$\ldots$ // *critical section, write to* $\mathsf{data}[\mathsf{pair}_W, \mathsf{index}_W]$

$\mathsf{slot}[\mathsf{pair}_W] = \mathsf{index}_W$

$\mathsf{latest} = \mathsf{pair}_W$

READER CODE

$\mathsf{pair}_R = \mathsf{latest}$

$\mathsf{reading} = \mathsf{pair}_R$

$\{\,\mathsf{pc}_R \in \cdot\,\square,\ \mathsf{pair}_R = \mathsf{reading}\,\}$

$\mathsf{index}_R = \mathsf{slot}[\mathsf{pair}_R]$

$\{\,\mathsf{pc}_R \in \boxdot,\ \mathsf{pair}_R = \mathsf{reading}\,\}$

$\ldots$ // *critical section, read from* $\mathsf{data}[\mathsf{pair}_R, \mathsf{index}_R]$

Fig. 4. Annotated pseudo-code for SC

above could be executed many times. Between executions, arbitrary other code may be executed, but crucially it should not access data.

Simpson's algorithm is correct in the sense that, if the reader and writer are both in their critical sections, then they access different entries in the data array. More formally, we introduce the notation $\mathsf{pc}_R \in \boxdot$ ($\mathsf{pc}_R \in \cdot\,\square$) to mean that the reader is (is not) in the critical section. We then have the following:

$\{\,\mathsf{pc}_W \in \boxdot \longrightarrow \mathsf{pc}_R \in \boxdot \longrightarrow (\mathsf{pair}_W, \mathsf{index}_W) \neq (\mathsf{pair}_R, \mathsf{index}_R)\}$

$=\qquad$ // *by propositional reasoning*

$\{\,\mathsf{pc}_W \in \boxdot \longrightarrow \mathsf{pc}_R \in \boxdot \longrightarrow (\mathsf{pair}_W = \mathsf{pair}_R) \longrightarrow (\mathsf{index}_R \neq \mathsf{index}_W)\}$

$=\qquad$ // *since* $\mathsf{pc}_R \in \boxdot \longrightarrow (\mathsf{pair}_R = \mathsf{reading})$

$\{\,\mathsf{pc}_W \in \boxdot \longrightarrow \mathsf{pc}_R \in \boxdot \longrightarrow (\mathsf{pair}_W = \mathsf{reading}) \longrightarrow (\mathsf{index}_R \neq \mathsf{index}_W)\}$

$=\qquad$ // *since* $\mathsf{pc}_W \in \boxdot \longrightarrow (\mathsf{index}_W = \neg\mathsf{slot}[\mathsf{pair}_W])$

$\{\,\mathsf{pc}_W \in \boxdot \longrightarrow \mathsf{pc}_R \in \boxdot \longrightarrow (\mathsf{pair}_W = \mathsf{reading}) \longrightarrow (\mathsf{index}_R = \mathsf{slot}[\mathsf{reading}])\}$

ie the algorithm is correct provided the *main correctness assertion* $\mathsf{pc}_R \in \boxdot \longrightarrow (\mathsf{pair}_W = \mathsf{reading}) \longrightarrow (\mathsf{index}_R = \mathsf{slot}[\mathsf{reading}])$ holds in the writer's critical section. Of course, we must also ensure that the auxiliary facts we used in the equality proof above are valid, but this is easy to see from the code. Note that this writer assertion refers to the program counter and private register state of the reader. The annotated code is in Fig. 4.

The writer assertions in Fig. 4 are trivially true for the writer if there is no reader. In the concurrent setting, following Rely-Guarantee [Jon81], we must check that these assertions are true regardless of steps taken by the reader: we check that the properties are closed under interference from the reader. First we express the interference from the reader as a relation between states. The notation $S \rightsquigarrow S'$ represents the relation $S \times S'$. Consider the Fig. 4

annotated code for the reader. Since these statements concern reader thread-local state pc_R and $pair_R$, or global state reading that is read-only by the writer, these assertions are closed under writer interference. Examining this annotated code reveals the interference from the reader consists of: Updates to reading outside the critical section: $(pc_R \in \cdot\square, \text{reading} = i) \rightsquigarrow (pc_R \in \cdot\square, \text{reading} = j)$, $i \in \{0,1\}$, $j \in \{0,1\}$; Entrance to the critical region: $(pc_R \in \cdot\square, pair_R = \text{reading}) \rightsquigarrow (pc_R \in \boxdot, pair_R = \text{reading}, \text{index}_R = slot[pair_R])$; Exit from the critical region: $(pc_R \in \boxdot) \rightsquigarrow (pc_R \in \cdot\square)$. The only non-trivial interference involves the reader entering the critical section, but it is immediate that this preserves the main correctness assertion. A key point is that the reader interference is dependent on which region of code the reader is executing ($pc_R \in \cdot\square$, $pc_R \in \boxdot$). This is the main motivation for our liberal notion of state, which can be incorporated into traditional proof systems unrelated to weak memory. In general, we expect more complicated algorithms will involve many more "regions". The key idea here is to index the rely and guarantee relations by the region in which the code is executing.

Simpson's algorithm for x86-TSO. A common approach to adapting algorithms to weak memory models is to insert memory synchronization operations eg memory barriers. One option is to insert barriers between every instruction, which is sufficient to regain SC behaviour for x86-TSO. However, synchronization operations are typically very expensive, so for performance reasons it is important to minimize their use. In this section we show how the SC proof dictates where to place memory barriers in the weak case.

We first examine the interference from the reader, specifically interference when entering the critical section. The first reader assertion in Fig. 4 states that the value of the reader's thread-local register $pair_R$ is equal to the main memory value at address reading. Unfortunately, since writes to memory may be buffered, this assertion no longer holds. The fix is to insert a memory barrier after the write to reading.

Now consider the first writer assertion in Fig. 4. Whilst the assertion is closed under interference from the reader, the writer's own write buffer may asynchronously flush a write to memory which invalidates the assertion. For example, there may be a write to $slot[pair_W]$ from a previous execution of the writer's exit protocol which is still in the write buffer. The problem is that the assertion is not closed under write buffer transitions, as required by the proof system. The simplest fix is to ensure that there are no pending writes in the write buffer to addresses which are involved in the assertion. The assertion mentions two addresses, reading and $slot[pair_W]$. The write buffer will never contain writes to reading since it is read-only by the writer. Thus, an invariant for the writer is the assertion $\{\text{reading} \doteq []\}$. To rule out the possibility of a write to slot from a previous execution of the writer exit protocol, we can insert a memory barrier at the end of the writer code, see Fig. 5. The alternative, placing the barrier immediately after the write to $slot[pair_W]$ means that the write to latest may be delayed, potentially reducing performance, though not correctness.

‌$\boxed{\text{WRITER CODE}}$

$\{\,\mathsf{reading} \doteq [\,], \;\mathsf{slot}[\_] \doteq [\,] \,\}$

   $\mathsf{pair}_W = \neg\mathsf{reading}$

$\{\,\mathsf{reading} \doteq [\,], \;\mathsf{slot}[\_] \doteq [\,], \;\mathsf{pc}_R \in \boxdot \longrightarrow (\mathsf{pair}_W = \mathsf{reading}) \longrightarrow (\mathsf{index}_R = \mathsf{slot}[\mathsf{reading}])\}$

   $\mathsf{index}_W = \neg\mathsf{slot}[\mathsf{pair}_W]$

$\{\,\mathsf{reading} \doteq [\,], \;\mathsf{slot}[\_] \doteq [\,], \;\mathsf{pc}_R \in \boxdot \longrightarrow (\mathsf{pair}_W = \mathsf{reading}) \longrightarrow (\mathsf{index}_R = \mathsf{slot}[\mathsf{reading}])\}$

   $\ldots //$ *critical section, write to* $\mathsf{data}[\mathsf{pair}_W, \mathsf{index}_W]$

   $\mathsf{slot}[\mathsf{pair}_W] = \mathsf{index}_W$

   $\mathsf{latest} = \mathsf{pair}_W$

   $\mathsf{barrier}\ \mathsf{mfence}$

$\{\,\mathsf{reading} \doteq [\,], \;\mathsf{slot}[\_] \doteq [\,] \,\}$

Fig. 5. Annotated pseudo-code for x86-TSO

Simpson's algorithm in x86 assembly code with x86-TSO. We now refine the high-level pseudo-code of the preceding section to low-level x86 assembly code. This makes the whole development more realistic, but the length of the code increases dramatically, and although high-level assertions are preserved at the low-level, there are now many intermediate assertions which obscure the main correctness argument.

The writer pseudo-code starts with $\mathsf{pair}_W = \neg\mathsf{reading}$, which translates to the three x86 assembly instructions in Fig. 6. The initial and final assertions are exactly those of the pseudo-code version, and the expected intermediate assertions do indeed hold, but for far from obvious reasons. Interested readers may consult the formal development for further details. To clarify the exposition, we suppress the trivial assertions $\mathsf{reading} \doteq [\,], \;\mathsf{slot}[\_] \doteq [\,]$ in these intermediate assertions. The remaining pseudo-code instructions are tackled in a similar way.

7   Related Work

We have included references to the main sources in the body of the text. The x86-TSO memory model [OSS09] was introduced in two provably-equivalent styles, axiomatic and operational, but here it suffices to consider only the operational model (called the "abstract machine memory model" in [OSS09]). In order to make our development self-contained, we have reproduced this memory model, and in addition incorporated a model of x86 instructions. It would be reasonably straightforward to establish a formal connection between our model and x86-TSO. Our x86 instruction model is based on that of Myreen [MSG08] which has been extensively validated in the sequential case; we believe the model is accurate for the concurrent case considered here. Whilst the model is not intended to be exhaustive, it should be straightforward to extend it. One of the challenges of this work was dealing with non-atomic x86 assembly instructions. Similar issues are the subject of ongoing research [Col08].

WRITER CODE

$\{\, \mathsf{reading} \doteq [], \; \mathsf{slot}[\_] \doteq [] \,\}$

  $\mathsf{mov_{rm}(eax, \; reading)}$

$\{\, \mathsf{pc}_R \in \boxdot \longrightarrow (1 \; - \; \mathsf{eax} = \mathsf{reading}) \longrightarrow (\mathsf{index}_R = \mathsf{slot} \; (\mathsf{reading})) \,\}$

  $\mathsf{mov_{ri}(pair_W, \; 1)}$

$\{\, \mathsf{pc}_R \in \boxdot \longrightarrow (1 \; - \; \mathsf{eax} = \mathsf{reading}) \longrightarrow (\mathsf{index}_R = \mathsf{slot} \; (\mathsf{reading})), \; \mathsf{pair}_W = 1 \,\}$

  $\mathsf{sub_{rr}(pair_W, \; eax)}$

$\{\, \mathsf{reading} \doteq [], \; \mathsf{slot}[\_] \doteq [], \; \mathsf{pc}_R \in \boxdot \longrightarrow (\mathsf{pair}_W = \mathsf{reading}) \longrightarrow (\mathsf{index}_R = \mathsf{slot}[\mathsf{reading}]) \,\}$

Fig. 6. Annotated x86 assembly code for x86-TSO

Our proof for Simpson's algorithm in the SC case is new, as far as we are aware. Many other proofs for SC exist in the literature eg [Hen03, Rus02]. As discussed in previous sections, our proof is unsuited to traditional program logics because of the need to refer to the private state of other processors. There are several other approaches to ensuring correctness of programs running on weak memory models. Data-race free (DRF) programs can be reasoned about using SC techniques. A strengthening of DRF techniques to x86-TSO is [Owe10]. An interesting approach that shares some similarities with DRF techniques is [CS09]. Model checking is another technique that has been fruitfully applied in this area [PD95], and one can always resort to direct operational proofs [Rid07].

8   Conclusion

We presented a proof system for concurrent low-level assembly code and the x86-TSO memory model. Some features of the proof system, such as the liberal notion of state, are independent of the memory model and may find use elsewhere. Some features are specific to x86-TSO, such as the need to use assertions closed under write buffer interference (and the practical importance of having a syntactic "closure under write buffer interference" operation) and how to incorporate a smooth treatment of write buffers as degenerate processes.

Mechanization revealed several unexpected areas for future work. For example, intermediate assertions at the assembly code level involved substantially more complicated proofs than at higher-levels, although intuitively the proof effort should be similar. One possible explanation is that our proof system can distinguish intermediate states in the execution of a single instruction, however in practice assertions do not make such distinctions. Therefore one may expect that the proof system can be simplified by making further assumptions about the nature of assertions. Clearly there is a trade-off here between the complexity of the judgement semantics and the complexity of the proof rules: in this paper we have chosen to keep the judgement semantics as simple as possible, but other choices are certainly possible. Our argument for the correctness of the high-level pseudo-code running against x86-TSO should be made formal, by taking an appropriate model of a high-level language (eg Xavier Leroy's Clight [BL09]) and exposing the low-level memory model. This would involve tracking the memory model through the different stages of the compilation process. A much easier alternative would be to design an operational semantics of a high-level language that incorporates x86-TSO from scratch, and carry out the proofs of correctness against this model.

We believe that our proof system makes the presentation of proofs much more palatable. However, the reasoning is still very low-level and operational, and creating a proof takes significant effort. Having talked with low-level programmers, it appears that most think very operationally about these programs, and that few high-level abstractions or concepts have emerged. One can incorporate other orthogonal abstractions such as separation logic but it is not clear that this would make these programs essentially easier to reason about. This work has uncovered several key requirements, but a key challenge remains: to establish higher-level notions for reasoning about programs executing with relaxed memory models. The author acknowledges funding from EPSRC grants EP/F036345 and EP/F019394.

References

[BL09]   Blazy, S., Leroy, X.: Mechanized semantics for the Clight subset of the C language. CoRR, abs/0901.3619 (2009)

[CH72]   Clint, M., Hoare, C.A.R.: Program proving: Jumps and functions. Acta Informatica 1, 214–224 (1972)

[Col08]   Coleman, J.W.: Expression decomposition in a Rely/Guarantee context. In: Shankar, N., Woodcock, J. (eds.) VSTTE 2008. LNCS, vol. 5295, pp. 146–160. Springer, Heidelberg (2008)

[CS09]   Cohen, E., Schirmer, N.: A better reduction theorem for store buffers. Technical report (2009)

[Flo67]   Floyd, R.W.: Assigning meanings to programs. In: Proc. American Mathematical Society Symposia in Applied Mathematics, vol. 19 (1967)

[Hen03]   Henderson, N.: Proving the correctness of Simpson's 4-slot ACM using an assertional Rely-Guarantee proof method. In: Araki, K., Gnesi, S., Mandrioli, D. (eds.) FME 2003. LNCS, vol. 2805, pp. 244–263. Springer, Heidelberg (2003)

[Hoa69]   Hoare: An axiomatic basis for computer programming. CACM: Communications of the ACM 12 (1969)

[Jon81]   Jones, C.B.: Development Methods for Computer Programmes Including a Notion of Interference. PhD thesis, Prgr. Res. Grp. 25, Oxford Univ., Comp. Lab., UK (June 1981)

[Lin99]   Linux Kernel mailing list, thread "spin_unlock optimization(i386)", 119 messages (November 20 - December 7, 1999), http://www.gossamer-threads.com/lists/engine?post=105365;list=linux (Accessed 2009/11/18)

[MSG08]   Myreen, M.O., Slind, K., Gordon, M.J.C.: Machine-code verification for multiple architectures: An application of decompilation into logic. In: Proc. FMCAD (2008)

[OSS09]   Owens, S., Sarkar, S., Sewell, P.: A better x86 memory model: x86-TSO. In: Urban, C. (ed.) TPHOLs 2009. LNCS, vol. 5674, pp. 391–407. Springer, Heidelberg (2009)

[Owe10]   Owens, S.: Reasoning about the implementation of concurrency abstractions on x86-TSO. In: D'Hondt, T. (ed.) ECOOP 2010. LNCS, vol. 6183, pp. 478–503. Springer, Heidelberg (2010)

[PD95]   Park, Dill: An executable specification, analyzer and verifier for RMO (relaxed memory order). In: SPAA: Annual ACM Symposium on Parallel Algorithms and Architectures (1995)

[Rid07]   Ridge, T.: Operational reasoning for concurrent Caml programs and weak memory models. In: Schneider, K., Brandt, J. (eds.) TPHOLs 2007. LNCS, vol. 4732, pp. 278–293. Springer, Heidelberg (2007)

[Rus02]   Rushby, J.: Model checking Simpson's four-slot fully asynchronous communication mechanism (2002)

[Sim90]   Simpson, H.R.: Four-slot fully asynchronous communication mechanism. IEE Proceedings, Computers and Digital Techniques 137(1), 17–30 (1990)

Pervasive Verification of an OS Microkernel
Inline Assembly, Memory Consumption, Concurrent Devices

Eyad Alkassar[*,***], Wolfgang J. Paul,
Artem Starostin[**,***], and Alexandra Tsyban[***]

Computer Science Department - Saarland University
{eyad,wjp,starostin,azul}@wjpserver.cs.uni-saarland.de

Abstract. We report on the first formal *pervasive* verification of an operating system microkernel featuring the correctness of inline assembly, large non-trivial C portions, and concurrent devices in a single seamless formal proof. We integrated all relevant verification results we had achieved so far [21,20,2,5,4] into a single top-level theorem of microkernel correctness. This theorem states the simulation of user processes with own, separate virtual memories — via the microkernel — by the underlying hardware with devices. All models, theorems, and proofs are formalized in the interactive proof system Isabelle/HOL.

1 Introduction

Pervasive Verification: Why Bother? A program proven correct in a high-level programming language may not execute as expected on a particular computer. Such correctness proof ignores irregular patterns of control flow which take place due to multitasking and interrupts on the computer. High-level data types and operations used to implement the program and formulate its correctness criteria differ from flip-flops and signals that occur in the hardware. The gap between what has been proven about the program in the high-level language semantics and what is actually executed on the underlying hardware may be a source of errors. The solution to the problem is to verify the execution environment of the program: the operating system to ensure correct assignment of hardware resources to the program and non-interference with other programs, the compiler and assembler to guarantee correct translation from high-level data types and operations to the machine instruction level, the actual hardware implementation to make certain that it meets the instruction set architecture. This is known as *pervasive* verification [18].

Pervasive verification of complete computer systems stacks from the gate-level hardware implementation up to the application level is the aim of the

---

[*] Work was supported by the German Research Foundation (DFG) within the program 'Performance Guarantees for Computer Systems'.

[**] Work was supported by the International Max Planck Research School for Computer Science (IMPRS-CS).

[***] Work was supported by the German Federal Ministry of Education and Research (BMBF) within the Verisoft project under grant 01 IS C38.

G.T. Leavens, P. O'Hearn, and S.K. Rajamani (Eds.): VSTTE 2010, LNCS 6217, pp. 71–85, 2010.

German Verisoft project[1]. The context of the current work is 'academic system', a subproject of Verisoft, which covers, among others, a processor with devices, a microkernel, and an operating system.

In order to ensure that interfaces of all components of the program's execution environment fit together a common formal framework — like Isabelle/HOL [23] in our project — has to be used. By choosing the implementation model of each layer to be the specification of the next lower layer it is possible to combine the components into a verified stack. With the program on top of the stack one achieves the *highest* degree of assurance in program correctness.

The Challenges in Pervasive Verification of an OS Microkernel. It is fair to put an operating system microkernel at the heart of a hardware-software stack. By design, a microkernel inevitably features (i) inline assembly portions — to access resources beyond the visibility of C variables, e.g., hardware registers, (ii) large sequential C parts — to implement resource management policies, e.g., user process scheduling, and (iii) interleaving communications of the processor with devices — to support, e.g., demand paging. Hence, the task of formal pervasive verification of a microkernel requires a feasible technology for efficient reasoning — in a single proof context — about the aforementioned features. In our experience, the complexity of the problem turns out to be not in verification of individual components comprised by a system, but rather in formal integration of different correctness results achieved separately. For instance, integration of functional correctness properties of sequential C code into an interleaved hardware computation requires additional reasoning about the memory consumption.

Contributions. This paper gives a bird's eye view on the first pervasive correctness proof of an operating system microkernel including such challenging components as demand paging, devices communications, and process-context switch. We report on the top-level correctness theorem and its completed (modulo symmetric cases) formal proof. This proof has motivated development of formal theories to reason, among others, about inline assembly, memory consumption, and concurrent devices.

Related Work. As Klein's article [16] provides an excellent and comprehensive overview of the history and current state of the art in operating systems verification we limit this paragraph to highlight the peculiarities of our work. We extend the seminal work on the CLI stack [6] by integrating devices into our model and targeting a more realistic system architecture regarding both hard and software. The project L4.verified [11] focuses on the verification of an efficient microkernel, rather than on formal pervasiveness, as no compiler correctness or an accurate device interaction is considered. The project produced a 200k-line formal correctness proof of the seL4 microkernel implementation. In the FLINT project, an assembly code verification framework is developed and a preemptive thread implementation together with synchronization primitives on a x86 architecture were formally proven correct [13]. A program logic for assembly

---

[1] www.verisoft.de

code as well as techniques for combining domain-specific and foundational logics are presented [12], but no integration of results into high-level programming languages is undertaken. The relevant references to our own previous work covering single pieces of the overall correctness puzzle are as follows: [21] reports on process-context switch verification, [20] describes the correctness of microkernel primitives, [2] elaborates on interleaved driver verification, and [5] shows verification of a page-fault handler. The semantic stack used to verify the microkernel is covered in large detail in [4]. The current paper reports for the first time on integrating all mentioned previous results into a single formal top-level correctness theorem of a microkernel.

Outline. In Sect. 2 we introduce CVM, our programming model for microkernels. Sect. 3 states its top-level correctness theorem. Sect. 4 introduces a semantics stack used for the theorem's proof outlined in Sect. 5. We conclude in Sect. 6.

2   CVM Programming Model

We discuss operating system microkernels built following the model of communicating virtual machines (CVM) [14], a programming model for concurrent user processes interacting with a microkernel and devices. The purpose of this model is to provide to the programmer of a microkernel a layer implementing separate virtual user processes.

CVM is implemented in C with inline assembly as a framework [15,22] featuring isolated processes, virtual memory, demand paging [5,19], and low-level inter-process and devices communications [2,1]. Most of these features are implemented in the form of so called microkernel primitives [20]. Primitives are functions with inline assembly parts realizing basic operations which constitute the kernel's functionality. The framework can be linked on the source code level with an abstract kernel, an interface to users, in order to obtain a concrete kernel, a program that can be translated and run on a target machine, the VAMP processor [7] with devices in our case. As CVM is only parametrized with an abstract kernel, its computations do not depend on particular shapes of abstract kernels. Two different abstract kernels were used in Verisoft: a general purpose microkernel VAMOS [9] and an OSEKtime-like microkernel OLOS [10].

Specification. The state space of the CVM comprises components for (i) user processes, (ii) the abstract kernel, (iii) devices, (iv) shared interrupt mask, and (v) the current process identifier. User processes are modeled as a vector of separate VAMP assembly machines (cf. Sect. 4) with own, large virtual memories. The abstract kernel is a pure C program with no inline assembly portions. Its computations are modeled by the small-step semantics of C0 (cf. Sect. 4), a C-dialect used in Verisoft [17]. Besides ordinary C0 functions the abstract kernel can call a number of special functions, called CVM primitives [20]. These functions have no implementation within the abstract kernel, and are therefore called externally. CVM primitives can alter states of user processes and devices and implement basic means needed for a microkernel programmer: copy data

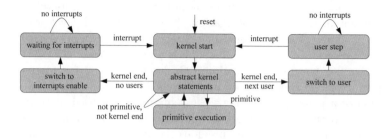

Fig. 1. States and transitions of CVM model

between processes, manage size of virtual memory given to processes, send data to devices, etc. Devices are modeled as deterministic transition systems communicating with an external environment and the processor via a specified memory interface. The external environment is used to model non-determinism and communication.

The transition function of the CVM model (cf. Fig. 1) distinguishes, therefore, three top-level cases of an execution corresponding to the mentioned CVM components: an *user step*, a *kernel step*, and a *devices step*.

A user step distinguishes three cases: (i) an uninterrupted step, (ii) an interrupted step with an abort of user execution, and (iii) a step with interrupt which nevertheless allows us to perform a step of the user machine before interrupt handling. In the first case the step boils down to an update of the user process configuration according to the VAMP assembly semantics. In case an interrupt occurs during the user step, the user has to be suspended and the kernel's interrupt handling routine has to be invoked. The actions taken in the third case are simply a composition of the first and the second case.

Kernel steps come in three flavors: (i) the kernel stays in the idle 'wait' state, (ii) the kernel finishes its execution by switching to the idle state or to a user process, and (iii) the kernel performs a step of the abstract kernel component. The last step distinguishes between an ordinary C0 small-step semantics step of the abstract kernel and a primitive execution. For the case of a primitive invocation the CVM transition function defines which effect the primitive has on the user processes and/or the kernel.

A devices step boils down to an external step of the specified device. The effect of a device step is to update the devices component of the CVM model.

Target Hardware Platform. The main purpose of a microkernel is to provide multiple users access to shared computational resources like physical memory and devices. Therefore, a particular target hardware model has to be considered while reasoning about microkernel correctness. We use the VAMP [7] with devices hardware platform to run the compiled microkernel.

The VAMP instruction set architecture is a sequential specification of the VAMP gate-level hardware. The model is defined by a transition function over the states which comprise bit-vector representations of components for the program counters, general and special purpose registers, and memory. The model features two execution modes, system and user, and address translation in user mode. VAMP ISA computations could be broken by interrupt signals, either internal, or external. In this case the execution is switched to the system mode, and the program counters are set to the start address of the compiled kernel.

Below, we briefly highlight how this hardware platform allows us to implement some fundamental features of a microkernel. Physical memory sharing is realized in CVM by memory virtualization: the kernel ensures that each user process has a notion of its own large address space. User processes access memory by virtual addresses which are translated to physical ones by a memory management unit [8] on the hardware side, or by the kernel on the software. We allow address spaces of user processes to exceed real memory of the physical hardware. This feature is supported by means of demand paging [5]: we partition available physical memory into small consecutive portions of data, called pages, which are stored either in fast but strongly limited in size *physical memory*, or in large but slower auxiliary memory, called *swap memory*. We store the swap memory on a hard disk [2]. The address translation algorithm of VAMP can determine where a certain page lies. In case the desired pages resides in the physical memory the kernel can provide an immediate access. Otherwise, the page is on the hard disk. The processor signals it by raising a data or instruction page-fault interrupt. The kernel's page-fault handler reacts to this interrupt by transferring the page from the hard disk to the main memory.

Communication of user processes with devices is supported by memory-mapped devices of the VAMP with devices. Devices are modeled as deterministic transition systems communicating with an external environment and the processor. The processor accesses a device by reading or writing special addresses. The devices, in turn, can signal interrupts to the processor. Interaction with the external environment is modeled by non-deterministic input/output. Several devices and a processor model could be coupled into a combined system which interleaves devices and processor steps. We refer to this system as VAMP ISA with devices. Computations of this system are guided by an external oracle, called an execution sequence, which defines for each point of time which of the computational sources, either the processor or some device, makes a step.

Implementation. CVM provides a microkernel architecture consisting of two layers. The general idea behind this layering is to separate a kernel into two parts: the abstract kernel that can be purely implemented in a high-level programming language, and the framework that inevitably contains inline assembly code because it provides operations which access hardware registers, devices, etc. The CVM framework is implemented with approximately 1500 lines of code from which 20% constitute inline assembly code. The implementation contains the following routines.

Process-context switch procedures init_() and cvm_start() are used for saving and restoring of contexts of user processes, respectively. The function init_() distinguishes a reset and non-reset cases. The former occurs after the power was switched on on the VAMP processor — the kernel memory structure is created.

In a non-reset case the procedure saves by means of inline assembly code the content of hardware registers into a special kernel data structure and invokes the elementary dispatcher of the CVM framework. The cvm_start() procedure is basically an inverse of the context save in a non-reset case. Context-switch procedures are almost fully implemented in inline assembly.

The page-fault handler of CVM pfh_touch_addr() features all operations on handling page faults, software address translation, and guaranteeing for a certain page to reside in the main memory for a specified period. The necessarily needed assembly code for talking to the hard disk is isolated in elementary hard-disk drivers write_to_disk() and read_from_disk().

The function dispatcher() is an elementary dispatcher of the CVM framework. It handles possible page faults by invoking pfh_touch_addr() and calls dispatcher_kernel(), the dispatcher of the abstract kernel. This dispatcher returns to the CVM framework an identifier of the next-scheduled process or a special value in case there is no active processes. In the former case the elementary dispatcher starts the scheduled process by means of cvm_start(). In the latter case cvm_wait() is called which implements the kernel idle state.

The remaining part of the CVM framework contains 14 primitives for different operations for user processes.

3   Verification Objective

The CVM verification objective is to justify correctness of (pseudo-)parallel executions of user processes and the kernel on the underlying hardware (cf. Fig. 2). This is expressed as a simulation theorem between the VAMP ISA with devices and virtual machines interleaving with the kernel. States of the CVM and VAMP ISA with devices models are coupled by a simulation relation which is a conjunction of the claims like (i) the kernel relation which defines how an abstract kernel is related to the concrete one and — through the C0 compiler correctness

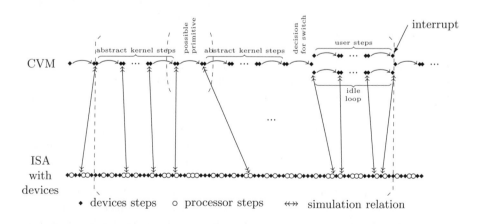

Fig. 2. Different cases of the CVM correctness theorem

statement [17] — how the latter is mapped to the VAMP ISA machine, (ii) the devices relation which claims that devices in CVM and hardware configurations are equal except for the swap hard disk which is invisible in the CVM model, (iii) the relation for user processes which states that the user process configurations are encoded in the configuration of the hardware with devices model. Thus, the top-level correctness theorem of the CVM can be stated as follows.

Theorem 1 (CVM correctness). *Given an execution of the VAMP ISA with devices model we can construct an execution of the CVM model such that the simulation relation between both holds after each CVM step.*

To prove that the CVM abstraction relation holds throughout CVM executions a number of invariants over the CVM implementation as well as the underlying hardware model have to hold. The reader can find complete definitions of the simulation relation and invariants in [22].

4   Semantics Stack

Ultimately, the right level to express overall correctness of system software, as the CVM kernel, is VAMP ISA with devices; only there all relevant components, as for example the mode register, become visible. Still, conducting all the code verification (or even the implementation) at this level seems to be infeasible. Rather, we introduced a pervasive semantics stack (depicted in Fig. 3), reaching from the high-level programming language C0, down to VAMP ISA with devices. On the one hand this semantics stack should provide for each single verification target with the most adequate reasoning environment. On the other hand the stack must be sound, i.e. allowing to integrate results of different levels into a single proof and finally propagate correctness to the low-level hardware model.

The overwhelming part of the microkernel is written in the language C0. C0 was designed as a subset of C which is expressive enough to allow implementations of all encountered system code in the Verisoft project, while remaining handy enough for verification. Therefore, we restricted ourselves to a type-safe fragment of C, without pointer arithmetic. However in the context of system-code verification we also have to deal with portions of inline assembly code that break the abstraction of structured C0 programs: low-level hardware intrinsics as processor registers, explicit memory model and devices become visible.

The semantics stack of the Verisoft project comprises three flavors of C0 reasoning [4]: Hoare logic, small-step semantics and an intermediate big-step semantics. The Hoare logic provides sufficient means to reason about pre- and postconditions of sequential, type-safe, and assembly-free C0 programs. In contrast to small-step semantics, the Hoare logic features split heap, compound variables, and implicit typing. The heap model we use excludes explicit address arithmetic but it is capable to efficiently represent heap structures like lists.

Compiler correctness allows to transfer properties proven in the C0 small step semantics to the so called VAMP Assembly with devices model [17]. While attempting to show correctness of assembly portions we have concluded that

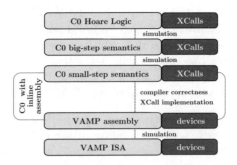

Fig. 3. Semantics stack

reasoning about the code in the VAMP ISA semantics is unnecessarily hard for a number of reasons like bit-vector representation of operands and presence of unwanted interrupts. As a response to this issue we introduced a convenient abstraction, the VAMP assembly model [22].

Having in mind that devices are executed in parallel with the processor, and that computations of the processor may be interrupted, only a C0 small-step semantics is adequate for verifying drivers and interleaved applications. Still, conducting all the code verification at the level of small step semantics or even below is not intended. Otherwise, one would abdicate the whole power of Hoare logic and the corresponding verification condition generator. The solution is to abstract low-level components by an extended state and to encapsulate the effects of inline assembly code by so called XCalls, which are atomic specifications manipulating both the extended state and the original C0 machine. First, by enriching the semantics stack with XCalls, we lift assembly code and driver semantics into Hoare logic. Then, by proving implementation correctness of XCalls we transfer results proven in Hoare logic down to VAMP assembly with devices [1].

All verification levels are glued together by respective simulation theorems [3,4]. This gives us freedom to choose the most efficient level of verification for each individual parts of the kernel and subsequently — via the simulation theorems — combine the results at the lowest level, the VAMP ISA.

Next we will describe in more detail three important extensions to the basic semantics stack which enable us to reason on system software correctness.

Concurrent Devices and Reordering. Device drivers are often an integral part of operating system kernels. For instance, since CVM features demand paging it needs correctly implemented hard-disk drivers. Hence, any approach to pervasive verification of operating system kernels should deal with driver correctness. Nonetheless, when proving functional driver correctness it does not suffice to reason only about code running on a processor. Devices themselves and their interaction with the processor also have to be formalized.

Obviously, when proving correctness of a concrete driver, an interleaved semantics of all devices is extremely cumbersome. Integration of results into traditional Hoare logic proofs also becomes hardly manageable. Preferably, we would like to maintain a sequential programming model or at least, only bother with interleaved steps of those devices controlled by the driver we attempt to verify. A basic observation of our overall model is that device and processor steps that do not interfere with each other can be swapped. For a processor and a device step, this is the case if the processor does not access the device and the device does not cause an interrupt. Similarly, we can swap steps of devices not communicating with each other. Utilizing this observation we reorder execution sequences into parts where the processor accesses no device or only one device. All interleaved and non-interfering device steps are moved to the end of the considered part and hence a (partially) sequential programming model is obtained.

Note that compiled, pure C0 programs never access devices, because data and code segments must not overlap with device addresses. Hence, all interleaved device steps can be delayed until some inline assembler statement is encountered. More generally, the execution of drivers controlling different (non-interfering) devices can also be separated, enabling modular verification of device drivers [1].

Inline Assembly and XCalls. The simulation theorems described in Sect. 4 allow us to transfer program properties from the Hoare logic down to the assembly level. Recall that CVM contains large chunks of C code involving heap data structures and, at the same time, rare calls to functions with inline assembly. It is highly desirable to verify these parts in the Hoare logics, however inline assembly portions break the abstraction of structured C0 programs: low-level entities (like the state of a device) may become visible even in the specification of code that is only a client to the inline assembly parts. To avoid doing all the verification in the lower semantic levels we extend the Hoare logic to represent the low-level actions on an abstract extension of the state space by the concept of XCalls.

XCalls capture the semantical effects of function calls by atomic specifications. Particularly, when specifying functions with inline assembly portions, as for example drivers, the use of XCalls is appealing. First, we extend the C0 configuration by additional *meta variables*, representing those parts of the processor which are accessed by the assembly code. More general, these ghost variables — in the following called *extended state* — may abstract from arbitrary low-level entities which lie outside the scope of C0, e.g. memory, registers or even device states. An XCall describes the effect of a function call on the C0 configuration and on the extended state by one atomic state update. Compiler correctness remains applicable only in case implementation correctness proofs are provided for each of the XCalls.

The main charm of XCalls is that they enable us to argue on effects of inline assembly portions without caring about assembly semantics. Thus, by enriching the semantics stack with XCalls, we can lift assembly code and driver semantics up to the Hoare logic level. Then, by proving implementation correctness of XCalls we transfer results proven in Hoare logic down to VAMP assembly with devices. Note, that for drivers XCalls abstract interleaved executions to sequential atomic specifications. This is justified by the reordering theory [5,1].

Memory Consumption. Any code verification effort claiming the label *pervasive* has to deal with the concrete memory consumption of the given program and with memory restrictions of the target machine. The compiler correctness theorem, for example, is only applicable if in each step sufficient heap and stack memory is available in the assembly machine. Often such assumptions are silently ignored because they are not visible in the semantics of the given high-level language. As in the C0 small-step semantics, those models assume some infinite memory. Memory restrictions do not emerge until results are propagated down to lower levels, as in the case of the driver correctness.

Conditions on memory consumption should be formalized and verified in a modular way, i.e., in form of function contracts which do not depend on the invocation context. Moreover, they should be discharged for the high-level programming language, rather than at the level of the target machine.

For the kernel verification we have applied and verified the soundness of two different approaches to deal with memory restrictions:

- Static (syntactical) program code analysis. An upper bound of the stack consumption of functions with no recursive calls and no pointers to functions can be computed by a static analysis of the program. In short, this approach determines the deepest path (in terms of stack consumption) in the invocation tree of the given code. The soundness of this approach is established by verifying that executing the analyzed function (in any context) will never consume more stack memory than the computed upper bound.
- Extending the programming logic. In this approach we extend the Hoare logic by a ghost variable, which keeps track of the so far consumed heap memory. Moreover we have to adapt the inference rules for memory allocation to check and update the meta-variable. The soundness proof of this approach is part of the soundness proof of the transfer theorems from Hoare logic to C0 small step semantics. A similar approach could also be used to compute the stack memory consumption of a program. Note, that this methodology exploits our knowledge about the C0 compiler, in particular the sizes of its types.

5   Verifying CVM

The proof of the CVM correctness theorem (Theorem 1) is split according to various types of steps that can be made within the model (cf. Fig. 1). The statement of this theorem is formulated for all possible interleavings of the VAMP hardware with devices. Many steps of the hardware might be mapped to a single step of the CVM model (or even be invisible in it). The execution sequence of the CVM model must be constructed from the hardware one taking care about points where the processors detects interrupts. The theorem is proven by induction on the number of processor steps in the CVM execution sequence. The construction of this sequence is the starting point in proofs of all cases of the CVM correctness theorem. We partition all possible cases from Fig. 1 into two groups on verification of which we elaborate below: the kernel step and the

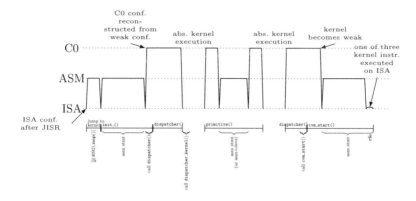

Fig. 4. Verification of a kernel step

user step. For each of them we examine the relevant code parts and show their functional correctness. From that the top-level simulation relation is inferred.

Kernel Step. The kernel step corresponds to such parts of the CVM implementation as (i) kernel initialization (after reset), (ii) process-context switch: switch to user and kernel initialization after user interrupt, (iii) primitives execution, (iv) waiting for interrupts, and (v) abstract kernel step.

Since this part of the CVM implementation features — beside the C code — many inline assembly portions, its verification proceed in the C0 small-step semantics and VAMP assembly semantics. Moreover, reasoning about instructions which switch process execution modes involves even the VAMP ISA semantics because the VAMP assembly model by design lacks support of modes. For each part of the code we would like to do the formal verification on the highest possible level of abstraction. Fig. 4–5 reflect this approach and depict correspondence between the CVM implementation parts and the semantics of verification.

The kernel step (cf. Fig. 4) starts right after the processor detects an interrupt and the JISR (jump to interrupt service routine) signal is activated. The latter sets the program counters to the start address of the *zero page* which, essentially, is used as a draft to store intermediate results of assembly computations. The first two instructions of the zero page, however, implement a jump to the kernel and are verified in the VAMP assembly semantics. The target of this jump is the function init_() which is responsible for the process-context save as well as kernel initialization and is implemented in inline assembly. The last statement of init_() is a C-call to the CVM's elementary dispatcher. We verify this call and the body of the dispatcher in C0 small-step semantics. In order to proceed with that we have to reconstruct the C0 configuration from the state of VAMP assembly. For that we maintain an invariant which states that the parts of C0 configuration — called the *weak* C0 configuration— are permanently encoded in the VAMP assembly memory. This technique is described in detail in [21]. Next, the CVM's dispatcher invokes the abstract kernel whereas the latter might

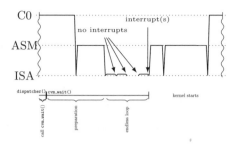

Fig. 5. Verification of the 'wait' case (idle loop)

invoke some CVM primitive. Primitives are verified [20] on C and assembly levels as they access user memory regions and devices. Further verification of the kernel step is split depending on whether there is at least one user process which has to be resumed. In case there is one, the verification of the remaining part is symmetrical: correctness proof of a C call to the process-context restore cvm_start() is followed by reasoning in assembly semantics about its body. The last instruction of the kernel step chain is the 'rfe' (return from exception) which switches the processor mode to user, and, therefore, has effects defined only in the VAMP ISA semantics. In case there is no user processes to be resumed the kernel goes to an idle loop by calling cvm_wait() (cf. Fig. 5). Here we are pending interrupts and, therefore, reason on the VAMP ISA level.

User step. User processes are modeled as virtual assembly machines with an illusion of their own, large, and isolated memory. Memory virtualization is transparent to user processes: within the CVM model page faults that might occur during a user step are handled silently by the low-level kernel functionality such that user can continue its run. During a single user step up to two page faults might occur: instruction page fault (*ipf*) and data page fault (*dpf*). The former might happen on instruction fetch whereas the latter could take place if we execute a memory operation. Our page-fault handler is designed in a way that it guarantees that no more than two page faults occur while processing a single instruction. The following five situations are possible regarding page faults: (i) there are no page faults, (ii) there is only an instruction page fault, (iii) there is only a data page fault, (iv) there is an instruction page fault followed by a data page fault, and (v) there is a data page fault followed by an instruction page fault. Fig. 6 depicts verification scheme for these cases. Essentially, the proof of the user step correctness boils down to a multiple application of the page-fault handler correctness theorem [5,19].

Page-Fault Handler. The page-fault handler is one of the most involved code portions of the CVM implementation. It maintains doubly-linked lists on the heap to implement the user virtual memory management policy and at the same time calls assembly subroutines implementing the hard disk driver. We verify the

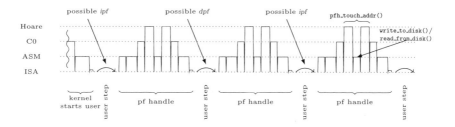

Fig. 6. Verification of a user step

page-fault handler in the Hoare logic and then transfer its functional correctness properties down to the level of VAMP ISA with devices semantics. The semantics of the assembly implemented hard disk drivers is encapsulated in XCalls. While justifying the correctness of XCalls implementation we have to deal with such peculiarities as devices steps reordering and estimating the memory consumption (cf. Sect. 4).

Besides loading the missing pages to the physical memory the page-fault handler servers as a single entry point for the software emulation of address translation in the kernel. In order to show the correctness of the latter the page-fault handler maintains a solid number of validity invariants over the page table and page management lists. One example of such invariants is that the page table entries always point outside the kernel region. This invariant turns out to be crucial for tackling the following problem.

Dealing with Self-Modifying Code. Suppose, we want to run the microkernel on a processor supporting self-modifying code: we can write at the address we have already fetched from. In system mode this peculiarity is resolved by the hardware. In user mode, however, the problem is affected by the address translation since now during the fetch we read not only at the fetch address but also the page tables. In this scenario we have to guarantee that user processes do not write page tables. By exploiting the aforementioned page-fault handler validity invariant we conclude that the translated address always lie in the user range.

6   Conclusion

We reported on the first formal and pervasive verification of a microkernel. Claiming pervasiveness means that all results can be (soundly) translated into and expressed at the low-level hardware model. We were forced to reason about many aspects and conditions of the system which are usually under the veil of 'technically but simple'. They don't show up until pervasive and formal verification is conducted. These conditions may be crucial for system correctness, as we illustrated for memory consumption. We are confident that the verification methods introduced to deal with inline assembly code, device drivers, and memory restrictions, within the framework of a high-level programming logic as Hoare logic, can be applied to other, more complex system verification targets.

All models, theorems and proofs leading to the top-level correctness statement of the CVM have been verified in Isabelle/HOL — modulo symmetric cases (as the read case of the hard-disk driver and some of the primitives were only specified but not verified). The CVM implementation is made up of 1200 lines of C0 and 300 lines of inline assembly code. Altogether we carried out the CVM verification in almost 100k proof steps in 5k Lemmas.

Integrating the huge amount of specifications, models and proofs emerged as a highly non-trivial and time-consuming engineering task. This covers, among other things, a social process, in which the work of many researchers, located at different places, has to be combined to one uniform and formal Isabelle/HOL theory. More than 250 Isabelle theories developed by more than 10 researchers were either directly or indirectly imported to state and verify the top-level correctness of the microkernel.

Larger efforts should be undertaken to simplify and better organize the formal verification in a computer aided proof system as Isabelle/HOL. On the one hand side it would be desirable to have more proof analysis tools as e.g., proof clones detection. We think, that in projects with such a large theory corpus, 'proof-by-search' technology (as automatically finding already proven similar lemmas) may be highly promising. On the other hand, the use of automatic tools in Verisoft often failed due to a huge overhead caused by the integration of external tools. Linking results obtained by e.g. automatic first-order theorem provers or SAT solvers is often much harder than proving the requested goal by hand.

References

1. Alkassar, E.: OS Verification Extended - On the Formal Verification of Device Drivers and the Correctness of Client/Server Software. PhD thesis, Saarland University, Computer Science Dept. (2009)
2. Alkassar, E., Hillebrand, M.: Formal functional verification of device drivers. In: Shankar, N., Woodcock, J. (eds.) VSTTE 2008. LNCS, vol. 5295, pp. 225–239. Springer, Heidelberg (2008)
3. Alkassar, E., Hillebrand, M., Leinenbach, D., Schirmer, N., Starostin, A.: The verisoft approach to systems verification. In: Shankar, N., Woodcock, J. (eds.) VSTTE 2008. LNCS, vol. 5295, pp. 209–224. Springer, Heidelberg (2008)
4. Alkassar, E., Hillebrand, M., Leinenbach, D., Schirmer, N., Starostin, A., Tsyban, A.: Balancing the load: Leveraging semantics stack for systems verification. J. Autom. Reasoning 42(2-4), 389–454 (2009)
5. Alkassar, E., Schirmer, N., Starostin, A.: Formal pervasive verification of a paging mechanism. In: Ramakrishnan, C.R., Rehof, J. (eds.) TACAS 2008. LNCS, vol. 4963, pp. 109–123. Springer, Heidelberg (2008)
6. Bevier, W.R., Hunt, W.A., Moore, J.S., Young, W.D.: Special issue on system verification. J. Autom. Reasoning 5(4), 409–530 (1989)
7. Beyer, S., Jacobi, C., Kröning, D., Leinenbach, D., Paul, W.: Putting it all together - formal verification of the vamp. STTT Journal, Special Issue on Recent Advances in Hardware Verification (2005)

8. Dalinger, I., Hillebrand, M., Paul, W.: On the verification of memory management mechanisms. In: Borrione, D., Paul, W. (eds.) CHARME 2005. LNCS, vol. 3725, pp. 301–316. Springer, Heidelberg (2005)

9. Daum, M., Dörrenbächer, J., Wolff, B.: Proving fairness and implementation correctness of a microkernel scheduler. J. Autom. Reasoning 42(2-4), 349–388 (2009)

10. Daum, M., Schirmer, N., Schmidt, M.: Implementation correctness of a real-time operating system. In: SEFM 2009, pp. 23–32. IEEE, Los Alamitos (2009)

11. Klein, G., et al.: seL4: Formal verification of an OS kernel. In: SOSP 2009, Big Sky, MT, USA, October 2009, pp. 207–220. ACM, New York (2009)

12. Feng, X., Shao, Z., Guo, Y., Dong, Y.: Combining domain-specific and foundational logics to verify complete software systems. In: Shankar, N., Woodcock, J. (eds.) VSTTE 2008. LNCS, vol. 5295, pp. 54–69. Springer, Heidelberg (2008)

13. Feng, X., Shao, Z., Guo, Y., Dong, Y.: Certifying low-level programs with hardware interrupts and preemptive threads. J. Autom. Reasoning 42(2-4), 301–347 (2009)

14. Gargano, M., Hillebrand, M., Leinenbach, D., Paul, W.: On the correctness of operating system kernels. In: Hurd, J., Melham, T. (eds.) TPHOLs 2005. LNCS, vol. 3603, pp. 1–16. Springer, Heidelberg (2005)

15. In der Rieden, T., Tsyban, A.: Cvm - a verified framework for microkernel programmers. In: Huuck, R., Klein, G., Schlich, B. (eds.) SSV 2008. ENTCS, vol. 217, pp. 151–168. Elsevier Science B.V., Amsterdam (2008)

16. Klein, G.: Operating system verification — an overview. Sādhanā 34(1), 27–69 (2009)

17. Leinenbach, D.: Compiler Verification in the Context of Pervasive System Verification. PhD thesis, Saarland University, Computer Science Dept. (2008)

18. Moore, J.S.: A grand challenge proposal for formal methods: A verified stack. In: Aichernig, B.K., Maibaum, T.S.E. (eds.) Formal Methods at the Crossroads. From Panacea to Foundational Support. LNCS, vol. 2757, pp. 161–172. Springer, Heidelberg (2003)

19. Starostin, A.: Formal Verification of Demand Paging. PhD thesis, Saarland University, Computer Science Dept. (2010)

20. Starostin, A., Tsyban, A.: Correct microkernel primitives. In: Huuck, R., Klein, G., Schlich, B. (eds.) SSV 2008. ENTCS, vol. 217, pp. 169–185. Elsevier Science B. V., Amsterdam (2008)

21. Starostin, A., Tsyban, A.: Verified process-context switch for C-programmed kernels. In: Shankar, N., Woodcock, J. (eds.) VSTTE 2008. LNCS, vol. 5295, pp. 240–254. Springer, Heidelberg (2008)

22. Tsyban, A.: Formal Verification of a Framework for Microkernel Programmers. PhD thesis, Saarland University, Computer Science Dept. (2009)

23. Wenzel, M., Paulson, L.C., Nipkow, T.: The isabelle framework. In: Mohamed, O.A., Muñoz, C., Tahar, S. (eds.) TPHOLs 2008. LNCS, vol. 5170, pp. 33–38. Springer, Heidelberg (2008)

The L4.verified Project — Next Steps

Gerwin Klein

NICTA*, Australia
School of Computer Science and Engineering, UNSW, Sydney, Australia
gerwin.klein@nicta.com.au

Abstract. Last year, the NICTA L4.verified project produced a formal machine-checked Isabelle/HOL proof that the C code of the seL4 OS microkernel correctly implements its abstract implementation. This paper gives a brief overview of the proof together with its main implications and assumptions, and paints a vision on how this verified kernel can be used for gaining assurance of overall system security on the code level for systems of a million lines of code or more.

1 L4.verified

Last year, we reported on the full formal verification of the seL4 microkernel from a high-level model down to very low-level C code [7].

To build a truly trustworthy system, one needs to start at the operating system (OS) and the most critical part of the OS is its kernel. The kernel is defined as the software that executes in the privileged mode of the hardware, meaning that there can be no protection from faults occurring in the kernel, and every single bug can potentially cause arbitrary damage. The kernel is a mandatory part of a system's *trusted computing base* (TCB)—the part of the system that can bypass security [11]. Minimising this TCB is the core concept behind *microkernels*, an idea that goes back 40 years.

A microkernel, as opposed to the more traditional monolithic design of contemporary mainstream OS kernels, is reduced to just the bare minimum of code wrapping hardware mechanisms and needing to run in privileged mode. All OS services are then implemented as normal programs, running entirely in (unprivileged) user mode, and therefore can potentially be excluded from the TCB. Previous implementations of microkernels resulted in communication overheads that made them unattractive compared to monolithic kernels. Modern design and implementation techniques have managed to reduce this overhead to very competitive limits.

A microkernel makes the trustworthiness problem more tractable. A well-designed high-performance microkernel, such as the various representatives of the L4 microkernel family, consists of the order of 10,000 lines of code. We have

---

* NICTA is funded by the Australian Government as represented by the Department of Broadband, Communications and the Digital Economy and the Australian Research Council through the ICT Centre of Excellence program.

G.T. Leavens, P. O'Hearn, and S.K. Rajamani (Eds.): VSTTE 2010, LNCS 6217, pp. 86–96, 2010.

demonstrated that with modern techniques and careful design, an OS microkernel is entirely within the realm of full formal verification.

The approach we used was interactive, machine-assisted and machine-checked proof. Specifically, we used the theorem prover Isabelle/HOL [10]. Formally, our correctness statement is classic refinement: all possible behaviours of the C implementation are already contained in the behaviours of the abstract specification. The C code of the seL4 kernel is directly and automatically translated into Isabelle/HOL. The correctness theorem connects our abstract Isabelle/HOL specification of kernel behaviour with the C code. The main assumptions of the proof are correctness of the C compiler and linker, assembly code, hardware, and boot code. The verification target was the ARM11 uniprocessor version of seL4. There also exists an x86 port of seL4 with optional multi-processor and IOMMU support.

The key benefit of a functional correctness proof is that proofs about the C implementation of the kernel can now be reduced to proofs about the specification if the property under investigation is preserved by refinement. Additionally, our proof has a number of implications, some of them direct security properties that other OS kernels will find hard to claim. If the assumptions of the verification hold, we have mathematical proof that, among other properties, the seL4 kernel is free of buffer overflows, NULL pointer dereferences, memory leaks, and undefined execution. There are other properties that are not implied, for instance general security without further definition of what security is or information flow guaranties that would provide strict secrecy of protected data. A more in-depth description of high-level implications and limitations has appeared elsewhere [6,5].

2   A Secure System with Large Untrusted Components

There are at least two dimensions in which work on the seL4 microkernel could progress from this state: The first is gaining even more assurance, either by working on the assumptions of the proof, e.g. by using a verified compiler [9] or verifying the assembly code in the kernel, or by proving more properties about the kernel such as a general access control model [3,2]. The second dimension is using the kernel and its proof to build large high-assurance systems. Below I explore this second dimension and try to convey a vision of how large, realistic high-assurance systems can feasibly be built with code-level formal proof.

The key idea is the original microkernel idea that is also widely explored in the MILS (multiple independent levels of security and safety) space [1]: using system architectures that ensure security by construction, relying on basic kernel mechanisms to separate trusted from untrusted code. Security in these systems is not an additional feature or requirement, but fundamentally determines the core architecture of how the system is laid out, designed, and implemented. This application space was one of the targets in the design of the seL4 kernel.

The basic process for building a system in this vision could be summarised as follows (not necessarily in this order):

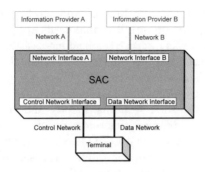

Fig. 1. Secure Access Controller (SAC)

1. Architect the system on a high level such that the trusted computing base is as small as possible for the security property of interest.
2. Map the architecture to a low-level design that preserves the security property and that is directly implementable on the underlying kernel.
3. Formalise the system, preferably on the architecture level.
4. Analyse, preferably formally prove, that it enforces the security property. This analysis formally identifies the trusted computing base.
5. Implement the system, with focus for high assurance on the trusted components.
6. Prove that the behaviour of the trusted components assumed in the security analysis is the behaviour that was implemented.

The key property of the underlying kernel that can make the security analysis feasible is the ability to reduce the overall security of the system to the security mechanisms of the kernel and the behaviour of the trusted components only. Untrusted components will be assumed to do anything in their power to subvert the system. They are constrained only by the kernel and they can be as big and complex as they need to be. Components that need further constraints on their behaviour in the security analysis need to be trusted to follow these constraints. They form the trusted components of the system. Ideally these components are small, simple, and few.

In the following subsections I demonstrate how such an analysis works on an example system, report on some initial progress we had in modelling, designing, formally analysing, and implementing the system, and summarise the steps that are left to gain high assurance of overall system security.

The case study system is a secure access controller (SAC), depicted in Figure 1. It is a small box with the sole purpose of connecting one front-end terminal to either of two back-end networks one at a time. The back-end networks A and B are assumed to be of different classification levels (e.g. top secret and secret) and potentially hostile and collaborating. The property the SAC should enforce is that no information may flow through it between A and B. Information is allowed to flow from A to B through the trusted front-end terminal. The latter may not be a realistic assumption for a real system; the idea is merely to explore

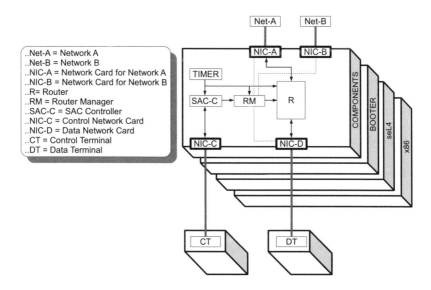

Fig. 2. SAC Architecture

system architectures for the SAC, not to build a multi-level secure product with a secure front-end terminal.

2.1 Architecture

Figure 2 shows the high-level architecture of the system. The boxes stand for software components, the arrows for memory or communication channel access. The main components of the SAC are the SAC Controller (SAC-C), the Router (R), and the Router Manager (RM). The Router Manager is the only trusted user-level component in the system. The system is implemented on top of seL4 and started up by a user-level booter component. The SAC Controller is an embedded Linux instance with a web-server interface to the front-end control network where a user may request to be connected to network A or B. After authenticating and interpreting such requests, the SAC Controller passes them on as simple messages to the Router Manager. The Router Manager receives such switching messages. If, for example, the SAC is currently connected to A, there will be a Router instance running with access to only the front-end data network card and the network card for A. Router instances are again embedded Linuxes with a suitable implementation of TCP/IP, routing etc. If the user requests a switch to network B, the Router Manager will tear down the current A-connected Linux instance, flush all network cards, create a new Router Linux and give it access to network B and the front end only.

The claim is that this architecture enforces the information flow property. Each Router instance is only ever connected to one back-end network and all storage it may have had access to is wiped when switching. The Linux instances are large, untrusted components in the order of a million lines of code each. The trusted Router Manager is small, about 2,000 lines of C.

For this architecture to work, there is an important non-functional requirement on the Linux instances: we must be able to tear down and boot Linux in acceptable time (less than 1-2 seconds). The requirement is not security-critical, so it does not need to be part of the analysis, but it determines if the system is practical. Our implementation achieves this.

So far, we have found an architecture of the system that we think enforces the security property. The next sections explore design/implementation and analysis.

2.2   Design and Implementation

The main task of the low-level design is to take the high-level architecture and map it to seL4 kernel concepts. The seL4 kernel supports a number of objects for threads, virtual memory, communication endpoints, etc. Sets of these map to components in the architecture. Access to these objects is controlled by capabilities: pointers with associated access rights. For a thread to invoke any operation on an object, it must first present a valid capability with sufficient rights to that object.

Figure 3 shows a simplified diagram of the SAC low-level design as it is implemented on seL4. The boxes in the picture stand for seL4 kernel objects, the arrows for seL4 capabilities. The main message of this diagram is that it is significantly more complex than the architecture-level picture we started out with. For the system to run on an x86 system with IOMMU (which is necessary to achieve untrusted device access), a large number of details have to be taken care of. Access to hardware resources has to be carefully divided, large software components will be implemented by sets of seL4 kernel objects with further internal access control structure, communications channels and shared access need to be mapped to seL4 capabilities, and so forth.

The traditional way to implement a picture such as the one in Figure 3 is by writing C code that contains the right sequence of seL4 kernel calls to create the required objects, to configure them with the right initial parameters, and to connect them with the right seL4 capabilities with the correct access rights. The resulting code is tedious to write, full of specific constants, and not easy to get right. Yet, this code is crucial: it provides the known-good initial capability state of the system that the security analysis is later reduced to.

To simplify and aid this task, we have developed the small formal domain-specific language capDL [8] (capability distribution language) that can be used to concisely describe capability and kernel object distributions such as Figure 3. A binary representation of this description is the input for a user-level library in the initial root task of the system and can be used to fully automatically set up the initial set of objects and capabilities. Since capDL has a formal semantics in Isabelle/HOL, the same description can be used as the basis of the security analysis. It can also be used to debug, inspect and visualise the capability state of a running system.

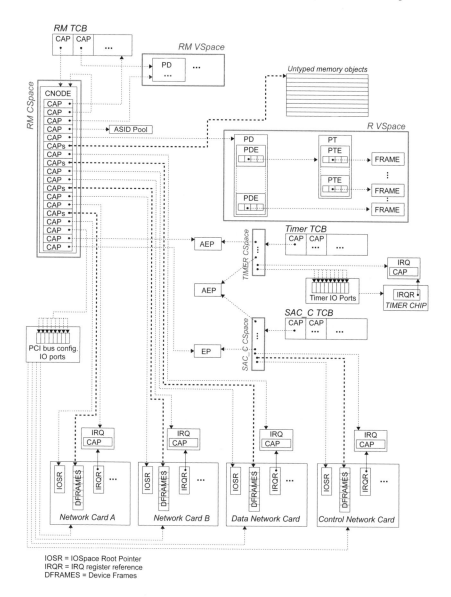

Fig. 3. Low-Level Design

For further assurance, we plan to formally verify the user-level library that translates the static capDL description into a sequence of seL4 system calls. Its main correctness theorem will be that after the sequence of calls has executed, the global capability distribution is the one described in the original description. This will result in a system with a known, fully controlled capability distribution, formally verified at the C code level.

For system architectures that do not rely on known behaviour of trusted components, such as a classic, static separation kernel setup or guest OS virtualisation with complete separation, this will already provide a very strong security argument.

The tool above will automatically instantiate the low-level structure and access-control design into implementation-level C code. What is missing is providing the behaviour of each of the components in the system. Currently, components are implemented in C, and capDL is rich enough to provide a mapping between threads and the respective code segments that implement their behaviour. If the behaviour of any of these components needs to be trusted, this code needs to be verified — either formally, or otherwise to the required level of assurance. There is no reason component behaviour has to be described in C — higher-level languages such as Java or Haskell are being ported to seL4 and may well be better suited for providing assurance.

3   Security Analysis

Next to the conceptual security architecture of the SAC, we have at this stage of the exposition a low-level design mapping the architecture to the underlying platform (seL4), and an implementation in C. The implementation is running and the system seems to perform as expected. This section explores how we can gain confidence that the SAC enforces its security property.

The capDL specification corresponding to Figure 3 is too detailed for this analysis. It contains information that is irrelevant for a security analysis, but is necessary to construct a running system. For instance, for security we need to know which components share virtual memory, but we do not necessarily need to know under which virtual address these shared areas are available to each component. Instead, we would like to conduct the analysis on a more abstract level, closer to the architecture picture that we initially used to describe the SAC.

In previous work, we have investigated different high-level access control models of seL4 that abstract from the specifics of the kernel and reduce the system state to a graph where kernel objects are the nodes and capabilities are the edges, labelled with access rights [3,2]. We can draw a simple formal relationship between capDL specifications and such models, abstracting from seL4 capabilities into general access rights. We can further abstract by grouping multiple kernel objects together and computing the capability edges between these sets of objects as the union of the access rights between the elements of the sets. With suitable grouping of objects, this process results in Figure 4 for the SAC. The figure shows the initial system state after boot, the objects in parentheses (R) and (R-mem) are areas of memory which will later be turned into the main Router thread and its memory frames using the *create* operation, an abstraction of the seL4 system call that will create the underlying objects.

This picture now describes an abstract version of the design. We have currently not formally proved the connection between this model and the capDL

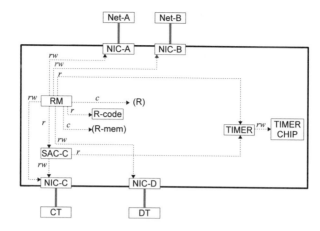

Fig. 4. SAC Abstraction

specification, neither have we formally proved that the grouping of components is a correct abstraction, but it is reasonably clear that both are possible in principle.

The picture is simple enough to analyse. If we proceed with a simple information flow analysis based solely on the capabilities in Figure 4, we would have to conclude that the system is not secure: the component RM possess read/write capabilities to both network A and B and therefore, without further restriction, information may flow between A and B. Of course, RM is the trusted component in the architecture — specifically we trust that it will not transport information between A and B —, and the security analysis should take its behaviour into account.

Details on our experience with this analysis will appear elsewhere, below I only give a short summary.

For a formal analysis, we first need to formally express the behaviour of RM in some way. In this case, we have chosen a small machine-like language with conditionals, jumps, and seL4 kernel calls as primitive operations. Any other formal language would be possible, as long as it has a formal semantics that can be interleaved with the rest of the system. For all other components, we specify that at each system step, they may nondeterministically attempt any operation — it is the job of the kernel configured to the capability distribution in Figure 4 to prevent unwanted accesses.

To express the final information flow property, we choose a label-based security approach in this example and give each component an additional bit of state: it is set if the component potentially has had access to data from NIC A. It is easy to determine which effect each system operation has on this state bit. The property is then simple: in no execution of the system can this bit ever be set for NIC B. This state-based property is slightly weaker than a non-interference based approach [4], because it ignores indirect flows.

Given the behaviour of the trusted component, the initial capability distribution, and the behaviour of the kernel, we can formally define the possible behaviours of the overall system and formally verify that the above property is true. This verification took a 3-4 weeks in Isabelle/HOL and less than a week to conduct in SPIN, although we had to further abstract and simplify the model to make it work in SPIN.

4   What Is Missing?

With the analysis described so far, we do not yet have a high-assurance system. This section explores what would be needed to achieve one.

The main missing piece is to show that the behaviour we have described in a toy machine language for the security analysis is actually implemented by the 2,000 lines of C code of the Router Manager component. Most of these 2,000 lines are not security critical. They deal with setting up Linux instances, providing them with enough information and memory, keeping track of memory used etc. Getting them wrong will make the system unusable, because Linux will fail to boot, but it will not make it break the security property. The main critical parts are the possible sequence of seL4 kernel calls that the Router Manager generates to provide the Linux Router instance with the necessary capabilities to access network cards and memory. Classic refinement as we have used it to prove correctness of seL4 could be used to show correctness of the Router Manager.

Even with this done, there are a number of issues left that I have glossed over in the description so far. Some of these are:

- The SAC uses the unverified x86/IOMMU version of seL4, not the verified ARM version. Our kernel correctness proof would need to be ported first.
- We need to formally show that the security property is preserved by the existing refinement.
- We need to formally connect capDL and access control models. This includes extending the refinement chain of seL4 upwards to the levels of capDL and access control model.
- We need to formally prove that the grouping of components is a correct, security preserving abstraction.
- We need to formally prove that the user-level root task sets up the initial capability distribution correctly and according to the capDL specification of the system.
- We need to formally prove that the information flow abstraction used in the analysis is a faithful representation of what happens in the system. This is essentially an information flow analysis of the kernel: if we formalise in the analysis that a Read operation only transports data from A to B, we need to show that the kernel respects this and that there are no other channels in the system by which additional information may travel. The results of our correctness proof can potentially be used for this, but it goes beyond the properties we have proved so far.

5   Conclusion

In this paper I have not aimed to present finished results, but instead to convey a vision of how one can use a formally verified kernel like seL4 to achieve code-level security proofs of large-scale systems. I have presented some initial, completed steps in this vision, and have shown that even if there is clearly still quite some way to go, there appears to be a feasible path to such theorems.

In an ideal world outcome, the complex proofs such as the information flow analysis based on a precise machine model, could be done once and for all for a given platform, and remaining proofs for specific systems and architectures could be largely or even fully automated: trusted components could be implemented in high-level languages with verified runtimes and compilers, abstractions for security analysis could be derived automatically with minimal user input and automatic correctness proofs, and the security analysis itself could be conducted fully automatically by model checking, potentially exporting proofs. This would mean such systems could be implemented with fairly low cost and extremely high assurance.

Even in a less ideal outcome, high levels of assurance could already be gained. Not all steps have to be justified by formal proof. Once trusted components and protection boundaries are clearly identified, the behaviour of a small trusted component could be assured by code review or testing, or abstractions for the security analysis could be done manually without proof. There is already value in merely following the process and only doing a high-level analysis. In our case study, we found security bugs mainly in the manual, but rigorous abstraction process from low-level design to high-level security model. What the proof provides is assurance that the analysis is complete, at the level of abstraction the theorem provides.

Acknowledgements. The formal security model of the SAC was mostly created by June Andronick. The proof mentioned above was conducted almost entirely by David Greenaway with minor contributions from June Andronick, Xin Gao, and myself. The following people have contributed to the verification and/or design and implementation of seL4 (in alphabetical order): June Andronick, Timothy Bourke, Andrew Boyton, David Cock, Jeremy Dawson, Philip Derrin Dhammika Elkaduwe, Kevin Elphinstone, Kai Engelhardt, Gernot Heiser, Gerwin Klein, Rafal Kolanski, Jia Meng, Catherine Menon, Michael Norrish, Thomas Sewell, David Tsai, Harvey Tuch, and Simon Winwood.

References

1. Boettcher, C., DeLong, R., Rushby, J., Sifre, W.: The MILS component integration approach to secure information sharing. In: 27th IEEE/AIAA Digital Avionics Systems Conference (DASC), St. Paul, MN (October 2008)
2. Boyton, A.: A verified shared capability model. In: Klein, G., Huuck, R., Schlich, B. (eds.) 4th SSV, Aachen, Germany, October 2009. ENTCS, vol. 254, pp. 25–44. Elsevier, Amsterdam (2009)

3. Elkaduwe, D., Klein, G., Elphinstone, K.: Verified protection model of the seL4 microkernel. Technical Report NRL-1474, NICTA (October 2007), http://ertos.nicta.com.au/publications/papers/Elkaduwe_GE_07.pdf

4. Goguen, J., Meseguer, J.: Security policies and security models. In: IEEE Symp. Security & Privacy, Oakland, California, USA, April 1982, pp. 11–20. IEEE Computer Society, Los Alamitos (1982)

5. Klein, G.: Correct OS kernel? proof? done! USENIX ;login: 34(6), 28–34 (2009)

6. Klein, G., Andronick, J., Elphinstone, K., Heiser, G., Cock, D., Derrin, P., Elkaduwe, D., Engelhardt, K., Kolanski, R., Norrish, M., Sewell, T., Tuch, H., Winwood, S.: seL4: Formal verification of an OS kernel. CACM 53(6), 107–115 (2010)

7. Klein, G., Elphinstone, K., Heiser, G., Andronick, J., Cock, D., Derrin, P., Elkaduwe, D., Engelhardt, K., Kolanski, R., Norrish, M., Sewell, T., Tuch, H., Winwood, S.: seL4: Formal verification of an OS kernel. In: 22nd SOSP, Big Sky, MT, USA, October 2009, pp. 207–220. ACM, New York (2009)

8. Kuz, I., Klein, G., Lewis, C., Walker, A.: capDL: A language for describing capability-based systems. In: 1st APSys, New Delhi, India (August 2010) (to appear)

9. Leroy, X.: Formal certification of a compiler back-end, or: Programming a compiler with a proof assistant. In: Morrisett, J.G., Jones, S.L.P. (eds.) 33rd POPL, pp. 42–54. ACM, New York (2006)

10. Nipkow, T., Paulson, L.C., Wenzel, M.T. (eds.): Isabelle/HOL— A Proof Assistant for Higher-Order Logic. LNCS, vol. 2283. Springer, Heidelberg (2002)

11. Saltzer, J.H., Schroeder, M.D.: The protection of information in computer systems. Proc. IEEE 63, 1278–1308 (1975)

An Approach of Requirements Tracing in Formal Refinement

Michael Jastram[1], Stefan Hallerstede[1],
Michael Leuschel[1], and Aryldo G. Russo Jr[2]

[1] Heinrich-Heine Universität Düsseldorf
{jastram, halstefa, leuschel}@cs.uni-duesseldorf.de
[2] Research Institute of State of São Paulo (IPT)
agrj@aes.com.br

Abstract. Formal modeling of computing systems yields models that are intended to be correct with respect to the requirements that have been formalized. The complexity of typical computing systems can be addressed by formal refinement introducing all the necessary details piecemeal. We report on preliminary results that we have obtained for tracing informal natural-language requirements into formal models across refinement levels. The approach uses the WRSPM reference model for requirements modeling, and Event-B for formal modeling and formal refinement. The combined use of WRSPM and Event-B is facilitated by the rudimentary refinement notion of WRSPM, which provides the foundation for tracing requirements to formal refinements.

We assume that requirements are evolving, meaning that we have to cope with frequent changes of the requirements model and the formal model. Our approach is capable of dealing with frequent changes, making use of corresponding techniques already built into the Event-B method.

Keywords: Requirements Traceability, WRSPM, Formal Modeling, Refinement, Event-B.

1 Introduction

We describe an approach for building a formal model from natural language requirements. Our aim is to increase the confidence that the formal model represents the desired system, by explaining how the requirements are "realized" in the formal model. The relationship "realizes" between requirements and formal models is kept informal. Justifications are maintained with each requirement and element of a formal model that are linked by "realizes", tracing requirements into the model, providing the sought explanation. Hence, the technical problem we have to solve is how to trace requirements into a formal model.

Requirements traceability provides a justification for a formal model with respect to the requirements. It is a difficult problem [6,10,15]. Furthermore, it is a cross-disciplinary problem connecting requirements engineering and formal

G.T. Leavens, P. O'Hearn, and S.K. Rajamani (Eds.): VSTTE 2010, LNCS 6217, pp. 97–111, 2010.

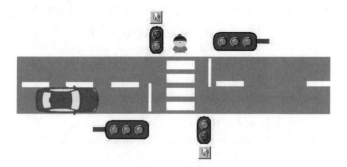

Fig. 1. A traffic light for pedestrians

methods. The benefits of the use of formal methods during requirements engineering has long been recognized. For instance, [5] quantifies the impact of formal methods in requirements engineering based on industrial case studies.

We assume that the requirements and the formal model need to be changed frequently and assume that the requirements are incorporated incrementally into the model. In the process, the requirements may have to be rewritten, corrected, clarified or split. The formal model may have to be modified correspondingly as the requirements become better understood [12].

In this paper, we present an approach for establishing robust traceability between informal requirements and formal models. We focus on natural language requirements and the Event-B formal method [3], but the ideas presented should be applicable more generally. We identified the WRSPM reference model [11] as the foundation for this work.

We consciously limit the scope of our approach. We assume that we start with a set of "reasonable" user requirements, but do not provide a method for eliciting them because good elicitation methods exist [14,9].

1.1 Running Example

In Section 3, we use a traffic light controller, as depicted in Figure 1, to demonstrate our approach. The traffic light for the cars stays green until a pedestrian requests crossing the street by pressing a button. The requirements also describe the sequence of lights and other details. In our preliminary study, we applied our approach to two other examples, a lift controller and a system that controls the access of people to locations in a building. Moreover, the approach is being used in an industrial case of a train door control system, employing the B-Method [1] rather than Event-B.

We show excerpts of the formal model and requirements in boxes, as follows:

Short description
`Excerpt of formal model`

REQ-1	A textual requirement with the identifier REQ-1

1.2   State-Based Modeling and Refinement

We demonstrate our ideas using Event-B [3], a formalism and method for discrete systems modeling. Event-B is a state-based modeling method. The choice of Event-B over similar methods [7,16] is mostly motivated by the built-in formal refinement support and the availability of a tool [4] for experimentation with our approach.

Event-B models are characterized by *proof obligations*. Proof obligations serve to verify properties of the model. To a large degree, such properties originate in requirements that the model is intended to realize. Eventually, we expect that by verifying the formal model we have also established that the requirements to which they correspond are satisfied.

We only provide a brief summary of Event-B in terms of proof obligations. A complete description can be found in [3]. Variables v define the state of a machine. They are constrained by invariants $I(v)$. Possible state changes are described by means of events. Each event is composed of a *guard* $G(t, v)$ and an *action* $\boldsymbol{S}(t, v, v')$, where t are *parameters* of the event. Actions are usually written in the form $v := E(v)$ corresponding to the predicate $v' = E(v)$. The guard states the necessary condition under which an event may occur, and the action describes how the state variables evolve when the event occurs. In Event-B two main properties are proved about formal models: consistency, that is, the invariant $I(v)$ is maintained

$$I(v) \wedge G(t, v) \wedge \boldsymbol{S}(t, v, v') \Rightarrow I(v') \ ,$$

and refinement. Refinement links abstract events to concrete events aiming at the preservation of properties of the abstract event when it is replaced by the concrete event. A concrete event with guard $H(u, w)$ and action $\boldsymbol{T}(u, w, w')$ refines an abstract event with guard $G(t, v)$ and action $\boldsymbol{S}(t, v, v')$ if, whenever the gluing invariant $J(v, w)$ is true:

(i) the guard of of the concrete event is stronger than the guard of abstract event, and

(ii) for every possible execution of concrete event there is a corresponding execution of abstract event which simulates the concrete event such that the gluing invariant remains true after execution of both events.

Formally,

$$I(v) \wedge J(v, w) \wedge H(u, w) \wedge \boldsymbol{T}(u, w, w') \Rightarrow \exists t, v' \cdot G(t, v) \wedge \boldsymbol{S}(t, v, v') \wedge J(v', w') \ .$$

The Event-B method derives proof obligations from these two properties that are easier to handle and can be efficiently generated by a tool [4].

1.3   WRSPM

Our approach is based on WRSPM by Gunter et. al. [11]. WRSPM is a reference model for applying formal methods to the development of user requirements and their reduction to a behavioral system specification.

WRSPM distinguishes between artifacts and phenomena (see Figure 2). Phenomena describe the state space (and state transitions) of the domain and system, while artifacts represent constraints on the state space and the state transitions. The artifacts are broadly classified into groups that pertain mostly to the system versus those that pertain mostly to the environment. These are:

Domain Knowledge (W for World) describes how the world is expected to
behave.
Proper Requirements (R) describe how we would like the world to behave.
Specifications (S) bridge the world and the system.
Program (P) provides an implementation of S.
Programming Platform (M for Machine) provides an execution environ-
ment for P.

In this paper, we use "proper requirements" for the formal artifacts R according the WRSPM terminology. We use just "requirements" when we talk about natural language from the stakeholders. Even though they are called requirements in practice, they may also contain information about the domain, implementation details, general notes, and all kinds of related information. We call those requirements REQ.

Artifacts are descriptions that can be written in various languages. In this paper, we use Event-B. (We discuss some alternatives in Section 4.1.)

We distinguish phenomena by whether they are controlled by the system (belonging to set s) or the environment (belonging to set e). They are disjoint ($s \cap e = \varnothing$), while taken together, they represent all phenomena in the system ($s \cup e =$ "all phenomena"). Furthermore, we distinguish them by visibility. Environmental phenomena may be visible to the system (belonging to e_v) or hidden from it (belonging to e_h). Correspondingly, system phenomena belonging to s_v are visible to the environment, while those belonging to s_h are hidden from it. Those phenomena are disjoint as well ($e_h \cup e_v = e$, $e_h \cap e_v = \varnothing$, $s_h \cup s_v = s$,

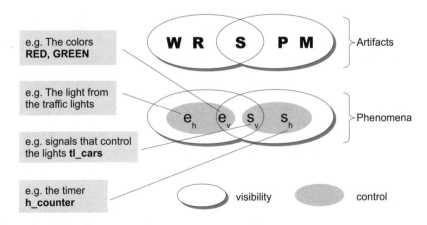

Fig. 2. WRSPM Artifacts and Phenomena, including Examples

$s_h \cap s_v = \varnothing$). Figure 2 illustrates the relationship between artifacts and phenomena, including a few examples for phenomena from the running example.

The distinction between environment and system is an important one; omitting it can lead to misunderstandings during the development. It is sometimes regarded as a matter of taste or convenience where the boundary between environment and system lies, but it has a profound effect on the problem analysis. It clarifies responsibilities and interfaces between the system and the world and between subsystems. If we require ourselves to explicitly make that distinction, we can avoid many problems at an early stage.

In larger projects, where the system is composed of other sub-systems, this concept can be used to determine if all the requirements are covered somewhere in the overall system: Some system phenomena of one sub-system may become the environment phenomena of the other sub-system.

W and R may only be expressed using phenomena that are visible in the environment, which is $e \cup s_v$. Likewise, P and M may only be expressed using phenomena that are visible to the system, which is $s \cup e_v$. S has to be expressed using phenomena that are visible to both the system and the environment, which is $e_v \cup s_v$.

Once a system is modeled following WRSPM, a number of properties can be verified with regard to the model, the first one being *adequacy with respect to S*:

$$\forall e \ s \cdot W \wedge S \implies R \qquad (1)$$

Given both hidden and visible environmental (e) and system (s) phenomena, the system specification (S), under the assumption of the "surrounding" world (W), is strong enough to establish the proper requirements (R). The specification is implemented as the program P in the programming environment M, which allows us to rewrite (1) as

$$\forall e \ s \cdot W \wedge M \wedge P \implies R \qquad (2)$$

2   Combining WRSPM and Event-B for Requirements Tracing

Our goal is to establish requirements traceability from natural language requirements to an Event-B formal model, using WRSPM to provide structure to both the requirements and the model. In the following, we first show how an Event-B model can be structured according to WRSPM, and then how this structure extends to the natural language requirements to support traceability.

2.1   Relationship between WRSPM and Event-B

As we demonstrate our method with Event-B, we need a relation between WRSPM and Event-B, shown in Table 1. An attempt to create a relation between Problem Frames and Event-B [18] provided similar results, thereby confirming our results. Event-B has a number of features that are useful for traceability:

Table 1. Representation of WRSPM elements in Event-B

WRSPM	Event-B
e and s	Phenomena are typically modeled as **constants**, **sets** or **variables**. They are associated with type information (**invariants** for variables, **axioms** for constants and sets). They are associated with **one or two events** that can modify it: Two events are required if both system and environment can modify the phenomenon, otherwise one is sufficient.
e_h	Phenomena hidden from the system are typically not modeled in the formal model. Exceptions are possible (for instance for fault analysis).
W	Domain properties are typically modeled as **invariants** and **axioms**. The line between type information and domain property may be blurry. Domain properties are typically expressed in terms of e. If they require s_v it should be carefully examined whether the artifact is really a domain property and not a proper requirement.
R and S	In Event-B, it is sometimes difficult to separate proper Requirements from Specification. Both are typically expressed in terms of e and s_v. Both are often traced to **invariants** and **axioms**. We also found **dedicated refinements** useful to represent them (see Section 3.4). We can extend tracing further by using **additional formalisms** (see Section 4.1).
P	The final program P is typically implemented with its own execution environment (M). The final refinement is often already an incomplete implementation of P. A conversion into P is often straight forward.

First, many artifacts can be expressed as invariants. Once a proper requirement is expressed as an invariant, we can use proof obligations to guarantee that the invariant will not be violated. Proper requirements that cannot be easily expressed as invariants can be structured using refinement (see Section 3.4), or modeled in a different formalism (see Section 4.1).

Second, Event-B supports refinement as described above. WRSPM comes with a simplified view of refinement very similar to the one described in the introduction of [13]:

$$\forall e\ s \cdot W \wedge M \wedge P \implies S \tag{3}$$

If (1) holds, then (3) holds as well, P being a refinement of S. In practice, an Event-B model consists of several refinements, forming a chain of machines. Refinements can be used to incorporate more proper requirements R, to make modeling decisions S or to provide implementation detail P. Event-B allows to mix these three purposes in one refinement, but we suggest to give every refinement just one single purpose (described in Section 3.4).

Third, if all Event-B proof obligations are discharged, then we know that the model is consistent in the sense described above.

Last, Event-B has no intrinsic mechanism to distinguish W, R, P and S. This means that we have to be careful to track the meaning of Event-B elements in the context of WRSPM. We suggest to use refinements for structuring and naming conventions.

To demonstrate that the WRSPM model does the right thing, we want to show that

$$\forall e \; s \cdot W \wedge R \wedge S \wedge P \text{ realize } REQ \qquad (4)$$

We use "realize" instead of an implication, because REQ is informal. We cannot prove that (4) holds, we can merely justify it. The aim of our approach is to make this justification systematic and scalable (see Section 2.3).

The requirements REQ are rarely ready to be modelled according to our approach in their initial form, as provided by the stakeholders. Figure 4 depicts the iterative process for building the WRSPM-artifacts from the requirements.

2.2   Traceability to Natural Language Requirements

A key contribution of this paper is the traceability between natural language requirements and the Event-B model which is structured according to WRSPM. It allows us to cope with changes in the model and changes in the requirements. Our approach distinguishes the following three types of traces:

Evolution Traces: As the model evolves over time, there is traceability from one iteration to the next (as indicated by the horizontal arrows in Figure 3). This is particularly useful for the stakeholders to verify that changes to the requirements reflect their intentions. This can be done by exploring the requirement's evolution over time, allowing the stakeholder to compare the original requirement to the modeler's revision.

Explicit Traces: Each non-formal requirement is explicitly linked to at least one formal statement. These traces are annotated with a justification that explains why the formal statement corresponds to the non-formal requirement.

Implicit Traces: There is implicit traceability within the Event-B model. Those traces can be discovered via the model relationships (e.g. refinement relationships, references to model elements or proof obligations). For instance, a guard that ensures that an invariant holds is implicitly linked to that invariant via a proof obligation. Furthermore, it is possible to use the identifiers

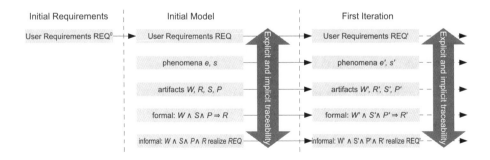

Fig. 3. Traceability between Iterations and within Iterations

of phenomena in the non-formal requirements, in addition to their use in the formal model. This would allow for implicit traceability to *REQ* as well, if we use the identifiers consistently in the natural language requirements.

Tracing an element of the formal model to an original requirement may require following a chain of traces.

2.3   Dealing with Change in Requirements and Model

The established traceability allows us to *validate* systematically that every requirement has been modeled as intended. We validate a requirement by using the justifications of the traces to reason about the requirement and the corresponding model elements.

The Event-B model may contain elements that are not directly associated with a requirement through a trace. These are elements that are necessary for making the model consistent. For instance, events may have guards that are necessary to prevent invariants from being violated. Such elements are implicitly traced, and can ultimately be traced all the way back to a requirement through a chain of traces. Allowing to annotate those implicit traces could be useful at times to explain the shape of a model.

There are also Event-B elements that are part of the design or implementation. Such elements are not always traced, as the information contained in them may not be part of *REQ*. They should be annotated in order to make the model understandable.

3   Application of the Approach

Now that we introduced our approach, we will demonstrate the concepts with the running example from Section 1.1. We follow the process depicted in Figure 4 by selecting a requirement to start with.

REQ-2	The traffic light for the cars has the colors red, yellow and green

3.1   Modeling Phenomena

We identify the following five phenomena in the text of REQ-2. We provide the Event-B identifier in parentheses[1]:

s_v: **traffic light for the cars (tl_cars).** We model the traffic light as the variable tl_cars, controlled by the system and visible to the environment.

e_v: **colors (COLORS).** We model colors as a set. This is a phenomenon of the environment that is visible to the system and provides typing of tl_cars.

---

[1] As a convention, we write environmental phenomena in uppercase and system phenomena in lowercase.

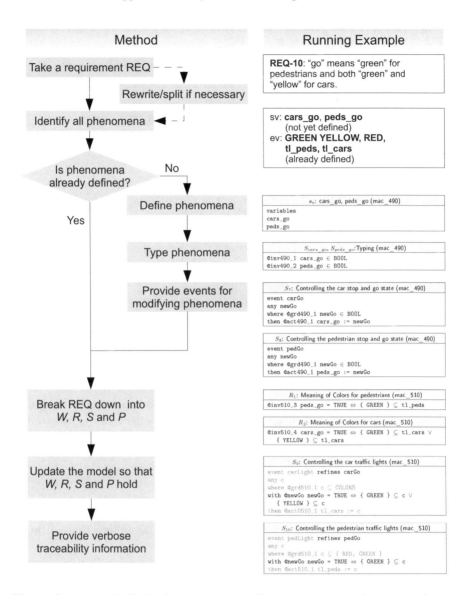

Fig. 4. Processing individual requirements. The running example is described in Section 3.3.

e_v: **red, yellow, green** (RED, YELLOW, GREEN). We model the actual color values as constants of type COLOR.

With this information we can rephrase REQ-2 and model the phenomena in Event-B. First we decompose REQ-2 into two requirements REQ-2-1 and REQ-2-2. These are connected by evolution traces to REQ-2:

REQ-2-1	`tl_cars` consists of `COLORS`

REQ-2-2	`COLORS` is the set of `RED`, `YELLOW` and `GREEN`

After declaring the phenomena in Event-B, we can create explicit declaration traces to the corresponding requirements REQ-2-1 and REQ-2-2.

The phenomena are defined through typing invariants (for instance, the typing of `tl_cars` is $tl\_cars \subseteq COLORS$). These traces are implicit, as they can be extracted from the formal Event-B model.

The requirement REQ-2-1 is realized as an invariant (the same as the typing invariant) and REQ-2-2 as an axiom (the partitioning of colors). These are explicit traces that we have to establish by hand.

Last, we have to provide an event to modify the state of the traffic light. There is an implicit trace ("changed by") between this event and the variable `tl_cars`. This is expressed in Event-B as follows:

```
Controlling the car traffic lights
event carLight
any c where c ⊆ COLORS
then tl_cars := c
```

Note that there is nothing yet constraining which of the three lights are on or off. At this stage, the system could still evolve into a disco light, because REQ-2 describes the domain, rather than how it is supposed to behave (the model elements are part of W). In subsequent refinements, the behavior is constrained more and more, as new requirements and design are incorporated into the model. We will demonstrate this in Section 3.4.

3.2 Modeling Requirements as Invariants

If possible, we model requirements as invariants. Once modeled this way, Event-B ensures that the invariant will never be violated (assuming that all proof obligations are discharged). Consider REQ-9:

REQ-9	The lights for pedestrians and cars must never be "go" at the same time

We omit the declaration and definition of the phenomena for brevity, and go straight to the rewritten requirement:

REQ-9-1	**car_go** and **ped_go** must never be **TRUE** at the same time

This can be traced using a "realizes" trace to the following invariant:

```
Formal representation of REQ-9-1
¬ (cars_go = TRUE ∧ peds_go = TRUE)
```

3.3 Traceability and Data Refinement

In Section 3.1 we introduced tl_cars and in Section 3.2 we introduced car_go. These two variables are connected through REQ-10, and we can realize this connection through refinement in Event-B. This is also depicted in Figure 4.

REQ-10	"go" means green for pedestrians and green or yellow for cars.

This requirement can be rewritten using the previously introduced names for the phenomena in question:

REQ-10-1	**peds_go = TRUE** means **GREEN** is active for **tl_ped**

REQ-10-2	**cars_go = TRUE** means **GREEN** or **YELLOW** is active for **tl_cars**.

The phenomena relating to the colors would be introduced in a machine that refines the one that introduced stop and go. Thus, the relationships (and thus REQ-10-1 and REQ-10-2) are realized through gluing invariants:

Meaning of Colors for pedestrians
peds_go = TRUE ⇔ { GREEN } ⊆ tl_peds

Meaning of Colors for cars
cars_go = TRUE ⇔ { GREEN } ⊆ tl_cars ∨   { YELLOW } ⊆ tl_cars

REQ-10-1 and REQ-10-2 and their gluing invariants are connected via explicit traces. The Event-B model contains a number of relevant implicit relationships that ensure that the model is consistent. For instance, the event that modifies peds_go has a corresponding event in the refinement that modifies tl_peds. Due to the gluing invariant, we can only discharge all proof obligations if the refinement preserves the properties of the abstract model. The corresponding Event-B is depicted in Figure 4.

3.4 Structuring Requirements Using Refinement

Some requirements are difficult to model as invariants. Consider the following:

REQ-12	The pedestrian light always follows the sequence red – green

REQ-12 is difficult to express as an invariant due to its temporal nature. We realize it by refining the event pedLight into two distinct events, pedsRed-ToGreen and pedsGreenToRed. This is the point where the traffic light is forced to behave differently from a "disco light". We can verify by inspection, model checking or animation whether the formal model reflects the requirement. In this particular case, we could animate the refinement (e.g. using ProB for Rodin [17]) to convince ourselves that red follows green and green always follows red. (This could also be stated in temporal logic, see Section 4.1).

Formal representation of REQ-12

```
event pedsRedToGreen refines pedLight
where
  ¬({GREEN} ⊆ tl_cars ∨ {YELLOW} ⊆ tl_cars)
  tl_peds = { RED }
with @c c = { GREEN }
then tl_peds := { GREEN }

event pedsGreenToRed refines pedLight
where
  ¬({GREEN} ⊆ tl_cars ∨ {YELLOW} ⊆ tl_cars)
  tl_peds = { GREEN }
with @c c = { RED }
then tl_peds := { RED }
```

This is an example where the model must be changed in various places. By using a dedicated refinement for this requirement, the changes in the model are comprehensible. Thus, we would establish an explicit trace to this Event-B machine, and we would not make any other changes to this refinement.

3.5 Requirements Outside the Formal Model

Some requirements are very hard to model in Event-B. Consider the following requirement REQ-16:

REQ-16	The length of the green phase of the pedestrian light has a specified duration.

Due to the temporal nature of the requirement, this requirement is hard to express in the formalism we chose. One option would be to introduce the concept of "ticks" that progress time on a regular basis. But even if we do that, it is not clear how long a tick is. We could also leave this requirement completely out of the model, leaving an aspect of the system that is not accounted for in the formal model. In our approach, this would manifest as a requirement without a trace to the formal model. Such untraced requirements are easily identified and must then be accounted for by other means, typically by providing for them directly in the implementation.

4   Related Work

The issue of traceability has been analyzed in depth by Gotel et. al. [10]. Our research falls into the area of post-requirements specification traceability.

Abrial [2] recognizes the problem of the transition from informal user requirements to a formal specification. He suggests to construct a formal model for the user requirements, but acknowledges that such a model would still require informal requirements to get started. He covers this approach in [3].

The WRSPM reference model [11] was attractive, because it deliberately left enough room to be tailored to specific needs, as opposed to more concrete methods like Problem Frames [14] or KAOS [9]. It is also more formal and complete than the functional-documentation model [20], another well-known approach.

The idea of the WRSPM reference model has been advanced in current research. In [19], the authors introduce a model of formal verification based on non-monotonic refinement that incorporates aspects of WRSPM. Problem Frames [14] could be useful for identifying phenomena and for improving the natural language requirements that we start out with, thereby complementing our approach. In [18], the authors show how Event-B and Problem Frames are being applied to an industrial case study. We drew some inspiration from this work, especially with regard to the relation between WRSPM and Event-B.

Some ideas in this paper are related to KAOS [9], a method for requirements engineering that spans from high-level goals all the way down to a formal model. KAOS requires the building of a data model in a UML-like notation, and it allows the association of individual requirements with formal real-time temporal expressions. Our approach distinguishes itself from KAOS by being very lightweight: KAOS uses many more model elements and relationships. KAOS also covers many more aspects of the system development process than our approach, which results in an "all or nothing" decision. We believe that our approach can easily be integrated into existing workflows and processes.

Reveal [22] is an engineering method based on Michael Jackson's "World and the Machine" model, which is compatible with WRSPM. Therefore we believe that our approach could be integrated nicely with Reveal.

4.1 Other Formalisms

Rather than using Event-B to model all artifacts, nothing is preventing us from choosing different formalisms. We demonstrate this in the following, where we model a requirement using linear temporal logic (LTL). LTL can actually be understood as an extension to Event-B, complementing its standard proof obligations.

LTL consist of path formulas with the temporal operators X (next), F (future), G (global), U (until) and R (release). Expressions between curly braces are B predicates which can refer to the variables of the Event-B model.

REQ-11	The traffic light for the cars always follows the sequence: green → yellow → red → red/yellow

REQ11 Sequence of car-lights (LTL)
$G(\{tl\_cars = \{green\}\} \implies (\{tl\_cars = \{green\}\}\ U\{tl\_cars = \{yellow\}\})) \wedge$ $G(\{tl\_cars = \{yellow\}\} \implies (\{tl\_cars = \{yellow\}\}\ U\{tl\_cars = \{red\}\})) \wedge$ $G(\{tl\_cars = \{red\}\} \implies (\{tl\_cars = \{red\}\}\ U\{tl\_cars = \{red, yellow\}\})) \wedge$ $G(\{tl\_cars = \{red, yellow\}\} \implies (\{tl\_cars = \{red, yellow\}\}\ U\{tl\_cars = \{green\}\}))$

This requirement can now be validated through model checking. Rodin can evaluate LTL expressions with the ProB model checker [21], which exists as a well-integrated Plug-in for Rodin.

5 Conclusion

In this paper, we presented an approach for building a formal model from natural language requirements. With our approach, the boundary between informal requirements and formal model is clearly defined by annotated chains of traces, which keep track of model evolution and explicit and implicit links. We present a number of approaches for modeling requirements and for providing traceability: Some requirements can be traced elegantly to invariants, and those that can not, can be structured using refinement. We can validate the traces in a systematic fashion and analyze the impact of changes in the requirements or the model.

In addition to the explicit traceability between requirements and model, we take advantage of the implicit traceability within the formal model to support us in verifying the model against the requirements. In particular, we take advantage of traceability through proof obligations: When all proof obligations are discharged, we know that the model is consistent. If we trust our traceability, then we have confidence that our requirements are consistent as well. Common identifiers can be used in the informal requirements and formal model. A supporting tool could support the user by pointing out matching identifiers.

We will also explore change management further. Requirements model and formal model are closely linked via the traceability information. Changes in either model will affect the other.

Our approach has proven successful with a number of small projects. In the near future, we will tackle bigger case studies; we will incorporate ongoing research like decomposition [8]. As of this writing the effort for building tool support within the Rodin platform is well under way[2].

Acknowledgements

The work in this paper is partly funded by Deploy[3]. Deploy is an European Commission Information and Communication Technologies FP7 project.

References

1. Abrial, J.-R.: The B-Book: Assigning Programs to Meanings. Cambridge University Press, Cambridge (2005)
2. Abrial, J.-R.: Formal Methods in Industry: Achievements, Problems, Future. In: Proc. of the 28th Int. Conf. on Software Engineering, pp. 761–768 (2006)

---

[2] http://www.pror.org
[3] http://www.deploy-project.eu

3. Abrial, J.-R.: Modeling in Event-B: System and Software Engineering. Cambridge University Press, Cambridge (2010)
4. Abrial, J.-R., Butler, M., Hallerstede, S., Voisin, L.: An open extensible tool environment for Event-B. In: Liu, Z., He, J. (eds.) ICFEM 2006. LNCS, vol. 4260, pp. 588–605. Springer, Heidelberg (2006)
5. Berry, D.M.: Formal Methods: The Very Idea – Some Thoughts About Why They Work When They Work. Science of Computer Programming 42(1), 11–27 (2002)
6. Bjørner, D.: From Domain to Requirements. In: Concurrency, Graphs and Models: Essays dedicated to Ugo Montanari on the Occasion of his 65th Birthday, pp. 278–300. Springer, Heidelberg (2008)
7. Börger, E., Stärk, R.: Abstract State Machines: A Method for High-Level System Design and Analysis. Springer, Heidelberg (2003)
8. Butler, M.: Decomposition Structures for Event-B. In: Leuschel, M., Wehrheim, H. (eds.) IFM 2009. LNCS, vol. 5423, pp. 20–38. Springer, Heidelberg (2009)
9. Darimont, R., Delor, E., Massonet, P., van Lamsweerde, A.: GRAIL/KAOS: An Environment for Goal-Driven Requirements Engineering. In: Proc. of the 19th Int. Conf. on Software Engineering, pp. 612–613. ACM, New York (1997)
10. Gotel, O., Finkelstein, A.: An Analysis of the Requirements Traceability Problem. In: Proc. of the First Int. Conf. on Requirements Engineering, pp. 94–101 (1994)
11. Gunter, C.A., Jackson, M., Gunter, E.L., Zave, P.: A Reference Model for Requirements and Specifications. IEEE Software 17, 37–43 (2000)
12. Hallerstede, S., Leuschel, M.: How to Explain Mistakes. In: Gibbons, J., Oliveira, J.N. (eds.) TFM 2009. LNCS, vol. 5846, pp. 105–124. Springer, Heidelberg (2009)
13. Hoare, C.A.R., He, J.: Unifying Theories of Programming. Prentice-Hall, Englewood Cliffs (1998)
14. Jackson, M.: Problem Frames: Analysing and Structuring Software Development Problems. Addison-Wesley/ACM Press (2001)
15. Jastram, M.: Requirements Traceability. Technical report, U. Southampton (2009)
16. Jones, C.B.: Systematic Software Development Using VDM. Prentice-Hall, Englewood Cliffs (1990)
17. Leuschel, M., Butler, M.: ProB: An Automated Analysis Toolset for the B Method. Int. Journal on Software Tools for Technology Transfer 10(2), 185–203 (2008)
18. Loesch, F., Gmehlich, R., Grau, K., Jones, C., Mazzara, M.: Report on Pilot Deployment in Automotive Sector. Technical Report D7, DEPLOY Project (2010)
19. Marincic, J., Wupper, H., Mader, A.H., Wieringa, R.J.: Obtaining Formal Models Through Non-Monotonic Refinement (2007)
20. Parnas, D.L., Madey, J.: Functional Documents for Computer Systems. Science of Computer programming 25(1), 41–61 (1995)
21. Plagge, D., Leuschel, M.: Seven at One Stroke: LTL Model Checking for High-Level Specifications in B, Z, CSP, and More. Int. Journal on Software Tools for Technology Transfer (1) (2008)
22. Praxis: Reveal – A Keystone of Modern Systems Engineering. Technical report (2003)

Dafny Meets the Verification Benchmarks Challenge

K. Rustan M. Leino[1] and Rosemary Monahan[2]

[1] Microsoft Research, Redmond, WA, USA
leino@microsoft.com
[2] National University of Ireland, Maynooth, Co.Kildare, Ireland
Rosemary.Monahan@nuim.ie

Abstract. A suite of verification benchmarks for software verification tools and techniques, presented at VSTTE 2008 [12], provides an initial catalogue of benchmark challenges for the Verified Software Initiative. This paper presents solutions to these eight benchmarks using the language and verifier Dafny. A Dafny program includes specifications, code, inductive invariants, and termination metrics. Each of the eight programs is fed to the Dafny verifier, which without further user interaction automatically performs the verification in a few seconds.

1 The Challenge

The motivation from this work comes from the Verified Software Initiative [4] and the suite of eight purposefully designed, incremental benchmarks for tools and techniques to prove total correctness of sequential object-based and object-oriented software, as presented by Weide *et al.* at VSTTE 2008 [12]. A solution to part of the first benchmark is provided, while the main contribution of their paper is the provision of a benchmark suite that aims to support the assessment of verification tools and the assessment of techniques to prove total correctness of the functionality of software. The benchmark suite also aims to provide for the evaluation of the state-of-the-art and to provide a medium that allows researchers to illustrate and explain how proposed tools and techniques deal with known pitfalls and well-understood issues, as well as how they can be used to discover and attack new ones.

In this paper, we contribute to this assessment and evaluation by presenting our solutions to the benchmark problems using the language and verifier Dafny [8,7]. The full programs are available online at boogie.codeplex.com, located by browsing the source code to access the folder Test/VSI-Benchmarks.

The benchmarks include several requirements of potential solutions, and we believe we meet these:

- Our Dafny programs contain all formal specifications relevant to the benchmarks, including user-defined mathematical functions where needed. Externally to the programs themselves, they rely only on constructs that are part of the Dafny language, which include sets and sequences.
- The Dafny verifier produces verification conditions via the intermediate verification language Boogie 2 [10,6]. The Boogie program and the resulting verification conditions can be viewed by using, respectively, the /print and /proverLog switches of

G.T. Leavens, P. O'Hearn, and S.K. Rajamani (Eds.): VSTTE 2010, LNCS 6217, pp. 112–126, 2010.
© Springer-Verlag Berlin Heidelberg 2010

the Dafny verifier. For example, for the benchmark in the file `b3.dfy`, the command

`dafny b3.dfy /print:b3.bpl /proverLog:b3.sx`

writes out the intermediate Boogie program as `b3.bpl` and the theorem-prover input, in S-expression form, as `b3.sx`.

- The Dafny verification system is described in a conference paper [8] and some lecture notes [7].
- The Dafny verifier checks for total correctness (that is, including termination). It is (designed to be) sound, which means it only proves correct programs to be correct. The Dafny regression test suite (at `boogie.codeplex.com`) includes many examples of erroneous programs that, as expected, do not verify. Similarly, any change to any part of our Dafny solution programs that renders them incorrect will cause the verifier to no longer verify the programs.
- Dafny uses modular specifications and modular verification. That is, our solutions need not be re-verified when they are incorporated as components in larger programs.
- Finally, we have alerted the VSI repository of our solution programs (although we have not seen them formally enter the repository yet).

2 Dafny

Dafny is an imperative, sequential language that supports user-defined generic classes and algebraic datatypes [8,7]. The language includes specification constructs, like pre- and postconditions à la Eiffel [11], JML [5], and Spec#[2,9]. In addition to instance variables and methods, a class can define mathematical functions, which can be used in specifications. Also, the language allows variables to be defined as **ghost**, meaning they are used by the verifier but need not be present at run time.

The types supported by Dafny are booleans, mathematical integers, sets, sequences, as well as user-defined classes and algebraic datatypes. Classes can be instantiated, giving rise to object references (*i.e.*, pointers), which makes the language useful for many common applications. However, as an object-oriented language, Dafny does not support subclasses and inheritance, except that the built-in type **object** is a supertype of all class types. As such, the language Dafny could perhaps be construed as a more modern version of Pascal or Euclid, or as a safe version of C.

The specification of a method consists of preconditions (introduced by the keyword **requires**) and postconditions (keyword **ensures**), as well as a modification frame (keyword **modifies**), which specifies which objects the method may modify, and a termination metric (keyword **decreases**), which gives a well-founded ranking function (also known as a variant function) for proving termination. The specification of a function consists of preconditions, which specify the domain of the function, a dependency frame (keyword **reads**), which indicates on which objects the function's value may depend, and a termination metric.

The body of a method consists of an imperative statement, which includes standard constructs like assignments, field updates, object allocation, conditional statements, loops, and method calls. A loop can indicate an inductive loop invariant as well as a termination metric. The body of a function is an expression that defines the value of the function.

The Dafny verifier, whose basic operation is described in detail in Marktoberdorf lecture notes [7] and whose source code is available at boogie.codeplex.com, follows the standard approach of first translating the input program into a program in an intermediate verification language. In particular, it translates Dafny programs into Boogie 2 [10,6], from which the Boogie tool [1,10] generates first-order verification conditions. These verification conditions, in turn, are fed to an automatic satisfiability-modulo-theories (SMT) solver, namely Z3 [3]. If the SMT solver proves the given formula to be valid, then the Dafny program is correct; if it reports a counterexample, then the Dafny verifier will report an error message about the Dafny program.

3 Benchmarks Solutions in Dafny

In this section, we present our approach to verifying each of the eight benchmarks in Dafny. The problem requirements for each benchmark challenge and our solutions to each follow. In each benchmark, the program text with specifications and other annotations are fed to the Dafny verifier, which then verifies them automatically with no further user guidance.

3.1 Benchmark #1: Adding and Multiplying Numbers

Problem Requirements: *Verify an operation that adds two numbers by repeated incrementing. Verify an operation that multiplies two numbers by repeated addition, using the first operation to do the addition. Make one algorithm iterative, the other recursive.*

We present an iterative solution to addition and a recursive solution to multiplication in Fig. 1. The standard procedural programming constructs arise in these two modular pieces of code which add and multiply two mathematical integers respectively. In both methods, the postcondition is verified, as is termination. The iterative method also requires the verification of a loop invariant.

Our iterative solution to addition is similar to the solution presented in [12], which uses the RESOLVE language and the SplitDecision simplifier.

When we started answering the benchmarks, Dafny did not verify the absence of infinite method recursion. When this was implemented, we were both surprised and embarrassed, at a reported error that showed that we did not do the recursion properly in our initial recursive solution. The **decreases** clause in Fig. 1, which uses a lexicographic pair, is used by Dafny to prove termination.

Also, we found that many termination metrics for loops are boring, so we extended the Dafny verifier with a few simple heuristics for guessing a termination metric from the loop guard, in case the loop has no explicit **decreases** clause. This simple trick let us simplify the program text for several loops. For example, the termination metrics −n and n, respectively, for the two loops in method Add are found by the verifier.

3.2 Benchmark #2: Binary Search in an Array

Problem Requirements: *Verify an operation that uses binary search to find a given entry in an array of entries that are in sorted order.*

```
method Add(x: int, y: int) returns (r: int)
  ensures r = x+y;
{
  r := x;
  if (y < 0) {
    var n := y;
    while (n ≠ 0)
      invariant r = x+y-n ∧ 0 ≤ -n;
    {
      r := r - 1; n := n + 1;
    }
  } else {
    var n := y;
    while (n ≠ 0)
      invariant r = x+y-n ∧ 0 ≤ n;
    {
      r := r + 1; n := n - 1;
    }
  }
}
method Mul(x: int, y: int) returns (r: int)
  ensures r = x*y;
  decreases x < 0, x;
{
  if (x = 0) {
    r := 0;
  } else if (x < 0) {
    call r := Mul(-x, y); r := -r;
  } else {
    call r := Mul(x-1, y); call r := Add(r, y);
  }
}
```

Fig. 1. Benchmark #1: Adding and multiplying numbers

```
method BinarySearch(a: array<int>, key: int) returns (result: int)
  requires a ≠ null;
  requires (∀ i, j • 0 ≤ i ∧ i < j ∧ j < |a| ⟹ a[i] ≤ a[j]);
  ensures -1 ≤ result ∧ result < |a|;
  ensures 0 ≤ result ⟹ a[result] = key;
  ensures result = -1 ⟹ (∀ i • 0 ≤ i ∧ i < |a| ⟹ a[i] ≠ key);
```

Fig. 2. Benchmark #2: Binary search specification

```
invariant 0 ≤ low ∧ low ≤ high ∧ high ≤ |a|;
invariant (∀ i • 0 ≤ i ∧ i < low ⟹ a[i] < key);
invariant (∀ i • high ≤ i ∧ i < |a| ⟹ key < a[i]);
```

Fig. 3. Benchmark #2: Loop invariants supplied in the binary search method

The binary search algorithm is straightforward to specify, implement, and verify. We include the verified binary search method specification and the verified loop conditions in Fig. 2 and Fig. 3, respectively.

Improvements were made to Dafny, as a result of this exercise, as an error in the well-formedness of functions (in particular, the **requires** clause) was detected and corrected.

3.3   Benchmark #3: Sorting a Queue

Problem Requirements: *Specify a user-defined FIFO queue ADT that is generic (i.e., parameterized by the type of entries in a queue). Verify an operation that uses this component to sort the entries in a queue into some client-defined order.*

The specification of an integer FIFO queue ADT with standard methods is straightforward in Dafny. However, specifying the queue as a generic type (*i.e.*, Queue<T>) highlighted errors in the translation process from Dafny programs to its representation as a Boogie program. These errors were corrected and a generic queue was successfully specified as in Fig. 4.

```
class Queue<T> {
  var contents: seq<T>;

  method Init();
    modifies this;
    ensures |contents| = 0;

  method Enqueue(x: T);
    modifies this;
    ensures contents = old(contents) + [x];

  method Dequeue() returns (x: T);
    requires 0 < |contents|;
    modifies this;
    ensures contents = old(contents)[1..] ∧ x = old(contents)[0];

  function method Head(): T
    requires 0 < |contents|;
    reads this;
  { contents[0] }

  function method Get(i: int): T
    requires 0 ≤ i ∧ i < |contents|;
    reads this;
  { contents[i] }
}
```

Fig. 4. Benchmark #3: Queue specification

A method to sort the queue, by removing the minimum element in the input queue and inserting it in the output queue, was easily verified. In our solution in Fig. 5, the ghost out-parameter perm is used to specify that the Sort method's output queue is a permutation of its input queue. When we first attempted this benchmark, ghost variables were not supported in Dafny. The complicated postconditions for the Sort method say that the output queue is sorted, that perm is a permutation of the input queue, and that perm describes the relationship between the input and output queues. Corresponding

```
method Sort(q: Queue<int>) returns (r: Queue<int>, ghost perm: seq<int>)
  requires q ≠ null;
  modifies q;
  ensures r ≠ null ∧ fresh(r);   // return a newly allocated Queue object
  ensures |r.contents| = |old(q.contents)|;
  ensures (∀ i, j • 0 ≤ i ∧ i < j ∧ j < |r.contents| ⟹ r.Get(i) ≤ r.Get(j));
  // perm is a permutation
  ensures |perm| = |r.contents|;
  ensures (∀ i • 0 ≤ i ∧ i < |perm| ⟹ 0 ≤ perm[i] ∧ perm[i] < |perm| );
  ensures (∀ i, j • 0 ≤ i ∧ i < j ∧ j < |perm| ⟹ perm[i] ≠ perm[j]);
  // the final Queue is a permutation of the input Queue
  ensures (∀ i • 0 ≤ i ∧ i < |perm| ⟹ r.contents[i] = old(q.contents)[perm[i]]);
{
  r := new Queue<int>;
  call r.Init();
  ghost var p := [];
  var n := 0;
  while (n < |q.contents|)
    invariant n ≤ |q.contents| ∧ n = |p|;
    invariant (∀ i • 0 ≤ i ∧ i < n ⟹ p[i] = i);
  {
    p := p + [n]; n := n + 1;
  }
  perm := [];
  ghost var pperm := p + perm;
  while (|q.contents| ≠ 0)
    invariant |r.contents| = |old(q.contents)| - |q.contents|;
    invariant (∀ i, j • 0 ≤ i ∧ i < j ∧ j < |r.contents| ⟹
                 r.contents[i] ≤ r.contents[j]);
    invariant (∀ i, j • 0 ≤ i ∧ i < |r.contents| ∧ 0 ≤ j ∧ j < |q.contents| ⟹
                 r.contents[i] ≤ q.contents[j]);
    // pperm is a permutation
    invariant pperm = p + perm ∧ |p| = |q.contents| ∧ |perm| = |r.contents|;
    invariant (∀ i • 0 ≤ i ∧ i < |perm| ⟹ 0 ≤ perm[i] ∧ perm[i] < |pperm|);
    invariant (∀ i • 0 ≤ i ∧ i < |p| ⟹ 0 ≤ p[i] ∧ p[i] < |pperm|);
    invariant (∀ i, j • 0 ≤ i ∧ i < j ∧ j < |pperm| ⟹ pperm[i] ≠ pperm[j]);
    // the current array is that permutation of the input array
    invariant (∀ i • 0 ≤ i ∧ i < |perm| ⟹ r.contents[i] = old(q.contents)[perm[i]]);
    invariant (∀ i • 0 ≤ i ∧ i < |p| ⟹ q.contents[i] = old(q.contents)[p[i]]);
  {
    call m,k := RemoveMin(q);
    perm := perm + [p[k]]; // adds index of min to perm
    p := p[k+1..] + p[..k]; // remove index of min from p
    call r.Enqueue(m);
    pperm := pperm[k+1..|p|+1] + pperm[..k] + pperm[|p|+1..] + [pperm[k]];
  }
  assert (∀ i • 0 ≤ i ∧ i < |perm| ⟹ perm[i] = pperm[i]); // lemma needed to trigger axiom
}
```

Fig. 5. Benchmark #3: Implementation of a method to sort the elements of a queue. For space reasons, we have omitted method RemoveMin.

invariants are required to verify the postcondition and while this leads to a high amount of annotations, Dafny verifies these automatically. We could have existentially quantified over perm, but chose simply to return the witness of that existential quantification.

When we first attempted the benchmarks, Dafny had (immutable) mathematical sequences, but no (mutable) arrays. In our initial versions of Benchmarks #2 and #3, we therefore coded up an Array class, which we specified in terms of a sequence. When arrays were subsequently added to Dafny, we changed our code to use them directly, as shown here.

Unfortunately, we were unable to sort a generically typed queue. The problem is that a generic comparable type could not be used, as Dafny has no way of specifying that the comparable type's AtMost function (as in Fig. 6) is total and transitive. An alternative solution would be to make the Sort operation generic, to pass the instantiation type and its comparison operator in as parameters, and to use a precondition to specify the transitive and reflective properties of the comparison operator. However, this is not possible in Dafny either, so we simply sort the generic queue that is instantiated with integers into increasing order.

```
class Comparable {
function AtMost(c: Comparable): bool;
  reads this, c;
}
```

Fig. 6. Benchmark #3: Comparable class

3.4   Benchmark #4: Layered Implementation of a Map ADT

Problem Requirements: *Verify an implementation of a generic map ADT, where the data representation is layered on other built-in types and/or ADTs.*

A generic map ADT may be specified using sequences of keys and values where a key stored at position i in the sequence of keys has its corresponding value stored at position i in the sequence of values. These are defined as **ghost** fields as illustrated in Fig. 7, which means they are part of the specification but not part of the compiled program. Built-in equality is used to compare keys. It would be nice to use a user-supplied comparison operator, but Dafny does not have support for that (*cf.* the discussion about operation AtMost in Benchmark #2).

An important part of the specification is to say which pieces of the program state are allowed to be changed. This is called *framing* and is specified in Dafny by a **modifies** clause. Frames in Dafny are at the granularity of objects with a dynamic frame (called Repr in Fig. 7) maintained as the set of objects that are part of the receiver's representation.

The consistency of an object is often specified using a class invariant [11], but Dafny does not have a class-invariant construct. Instead, consistency is specified using a function (called Valid in Fig. 7) that is systematically incorporated in method pre- and postconditions (see also [7,8]).

We implement the generic map ADT using a linked-list of nodes, where each node contains a key, its value, and a reference to the next node in the linked list as shown in Fig. 8. Verification of methods to initialise the mapping, find a value given a key, add a key/value pair, remove a key, and find the index at which a key is stored, are provided. We show two of the methods in Fig. 7.

```dafny
class Map<Key,Value> {
  ghost var Keys: seq<Key>;
  ghost var Values: seq<Value>;
  ghost var Repr: set<object>;

  var head: Node<Key,Value>;
  ghost var nodes: seq<Node<Key,Value>>;

  function Valid(): bool
    reads this, Repr;
  { this in Repr ∧
    |Keys| = |Values| ∧ |nodes| = |Keys| + 1 ∧ head = nodes[0] ∧
    (∀ i • 0 ≤ i ∧ i < |Keys| ⟹
        nodes[i] ≠ null ∧ nodes[i] in Repr ∧
        nodes[i].key = Keys[i] ∧ nodes[i].key ∉ Keys[i+1..] ∧
        nodes[i].val = Values[i] ∧ nodes[i].next = nodes[i+1]) ∧
        nodes[|nodes|-1] = null
  }

  method Init()
    modifies this;
    ensures Valid() ∧ fresh(Repr - {this}) ∧ |Keys| = 0;
  {
    Keys := [];
    Values := [];
    Repr := {this};
    head := null;
    nodes := [null];
  }

  method Add(key: Key, val: Value)
    requires Valid();
    modifies Repr;
    ensures Valid() ∧ fresh(Repr - old(Repr));
    ensures (∀ i • 0 ≤ i ∧ i < |old(Keys)| ∧ old(Keys)[i] = key ⟹
                |Keys| = |old(Keys)| ∧ Keys[i] = key ∧ Values[i] = val ∧
                (∀ j • 0 ≤ j ∧ j < |Values| ∧ i ≠ j ⟹
                    Keys[j] = old(Keys)[j] ∧ Values[j] = old(Values)[j]));
    ensures key ∉ old(Keys) ⟹ Keys = [key] + old(Keys);
    ensures Values = [val] + old(Values);
  {
    call p, n, prev := FindIndex(key);
    if (p = null) {
      var h := new Node<Key,Value>;
      h.key := key;  h.val := val;  h.next := head;
      head := h;
      Keys := [key] + Keys;  Values := [val] + Values;
      nodes := [h] + nodes;
      Repr := Repr + {h};
    } else {
      p.val := val;
      Values := Values[n := val];
    }
  }
  // ...
}
```

Fig. 7. Benchmark #4: Extract of the map ADT implementation

```
class Node<Key,Value> {
  var key: Key;
  var val: Value;
  var next: Node<Key,Value>;
}
```

Fig. 8. Benchmark #4: Node class used in the implementation of the map ADT

3.5   Benchmark #5: Linked Implementation of a Queue ADT

Problem Requirements: *Verify an implementation of the queue type specified for Benchmark #3, using a linked data structure for the representation.*

An implementation of the queue specified in Benchmark #3 is provided in terms of a set of nodes, references to the head and the tail node, and a sequence of values recording the queue contents.

In our solution, which we adapted from an example in the Marktoberdorf lecture notes on Dafny [7], the queue elements stored in nodes are generically typed. Elements are added to the queue by dynamically creating a new node, storing the element to be added in that node, and linking the queue's tail node to the new node that contains the element to be added. Other queue operations are implemented in a similar manner with

```
class Collection<T> {
  var Repr: set<object>;
  var elements: seq<T>;

  function Valid():bool
    reads this, Repr;
  { this in Repr }

  method GetCount() returns (c:int)
    requires Valid();
    ensures 0 ≤ c;
  { c := |elements|; }

  method Init()
    modifies this;
    ensures Valid() ∧ fresh(Repr - {this});
  {
    elements := []; Repr := {this};
  }

  method GetIterator() returns (iter:Iterator<T>)
    requires Valid();
    ensures iter ≠ null ∧ iter.Valid();
    ensures fresh(iter.Repr) ∧ iter.pos = -1;
    ensures iter.c = this;
  {
    iter := new Iterator<T>;
    call iter.Init(this);
  }

  // ...
}
```

Fig. 9. Sample collection class for use in Benchmark #6

Dafny's built-in set and sequence data types providing the underlying data structures that allow our solution to be automatically verified.

3.6   Benchmark #6: Iterators

Problem Requirements: *Verify a client program that uses an iterator for some collection type, as well as an implementation of the iterator.*

The implementation of both a collection class and an iterator class was necessary to meet this benchmark in Dafny. A generic collection class was implemented as a sequence of generic types with methods to initialise the collection, return an item, add an item, and get an iterator on collections. See Fig. 9 for an extract of the code. While we acknowledge that our solution does not meet the original challenge problem[1], which requires that an iterator be invalidated whenever its associated collection is updated, our solution does address the challenge as presented in the Weide *et al.* benchmark suite.

```
class Iterator<T> {
  var c: Collection<T>;
  var pos: int;
  var Repr: set<object>;

  function Valid():bool
    reads this, Repr;
  { this in Repr ∧ c ≠ null ∧ -1 ≤ pos ∧ null ∉ Repr }

  method Init(coll:Collection<T>)
    requires coll ≠ null;
    modifies this;
    ensures Valid() ∧ fresh(Repr - {this}) ∧ pos = -1;
    ensures c = coll;
  {
    c := coll;
    pos := -1;
    Repr := {this};
  }

  method MoveNext() returns (b:bool)
    requires Valid();
    modifies Repr;
    ensures fresh(Repr - old(Repr)) ∧ Valid();
    ensures pos = old(pos) + 1 ∧ b = HasCurrent() ∧ c = old(c);
  {
    pos := pos+1;
    b := pos < |c.elements|;
  }

  // ...
}
```

Fig. 10. Sample implementation of the iterator class for benchmark #6

Our client program uses an iterator over this collection type. This program stores the elements of the collection in a sequence and we verify that the iterator returns the correct elements. We also verify that the iterator does not destroy the collection that it iterates over.

---

[1] Issued at SAVCBS 2006.

3.7 Benchmark #7: Input and Output Streams

Problem Requirements: *Specify simple input and output capabilities such as character input streams and output streams. Verify an application program that uses them in conjunction with one of the components from the earlier benchmarks.*

Our specification of streams is implemented as a stream of integers with methods to create a stream for writing, open a stream, write an integer to a stream, read an integer from a stream, check for the end of a stream, and close a stream. Sample method implementations are presented in Fig. 11.

A client program that reads integers, stores them in a Queue (specified in Benchmark #3), sorts them (using the algorithm from Benchmark #3) and writes them to a stream, is verified using Dafny. Note that we assume finite streams and that if we were required to prove termination, then we would need some way to signal the end of a stream.

```
class Stream {
  var Repr: set<object>;
  var stream: seq<int>;
  var isOpen: bool;

  function Valid(): bool
    reads this, Repr;
  { null ∉ Repr ∧ this in Repr ∧ isOpen }

  method GetCount() returns (c:int)
    requires Valid();
    ensures 0 ≤ c;
  { c := |stream|; }

  method Create() //writing
    modifies this;
    ensures Valid() ∧ fresh(Repr - {this});
    ensures stream = [];
  {
    stream := [];
    Repr := {this};
    isOpen:= true;
  }

  method Open() //reading
    modifies this;
    ensures Valid() ∧ fresh(Repr - {this});
  {
    Repr := {this};
    isOpen :=true;
  }

  method PutChar(x: int)
    requires Valid();
    modifies Repr;
    ensures Valid() ∧ fresh(Repr - old(Repr));
    ensures stream = old(stream) + [x];
  { stream:= stream + [x]; }
}
```

Fig. 11. Benchmark #7: Sample implementation of input and output streams

3.8 Benchmark #8: An Integrated Application

Problem Requirements: *Verify an application program with a concisely stated set of requirements, where the particular solution relies on the integration of at least a few of the previous benchmarks.*

The application program that we verify implements a dictionary as a mapping between words and sequences of words. To set up the dictionary, we read a stream of words (adapting code from Benchmark #7) and put them into a mapping where the first word in the stream is the term to be defined. The subsequent words on the same line in the stream form that terms definition. Reading the stream again provides the next term followed by its definition and so on until nothing remains to be read. The map ADT used in this application is that verified in Benchmark #4. The sort method and the queue data type verified in Benchmark #3, are used to sort the words into alphabetical order. Some sample code is provided in Fig. 12.

```
var rs := new ReaderStream;
call rs.Open();
var glossary := new Map<Word,seq<Word>>;
call glossary.Init();
var q := new Queue<Word>;
call q.Init();

while (true)
  invariant rs.Valid() ∧ fresh(rs.Repr);
  invariant glossary.Valid();
  invariant glossary ∉ rs.Repr;
  invariant null ∉ glossary.keys;
  invariant (∀ d • d in glossary.values ⟹ null ∉ d);
  invariant q ∉ rs.Repr;
  invariant q.contents = glossary.keys;
  decreases *;  // we leave out the decreases clause - unbounded stream
{
  call term,definition := readDefinition(rs);
  if (term = null) {
    break;
  }
  call present, d := glossary.Find(term);
  if (¬present) {
    call glossary.Add(term,definition);
    call q.Enqueue(term);
  }
}
call rs.Close();
call q,p := Sort(q);
```

Fig. 12. Sample code verified in the solution to Benchmark #8

For this benchmark, we were unsure about how much would be reasonable to specify. For example, would one want to go as far as to say the output is a stream of characters that, interpreted as HTML and rendered by a standard web browser, provides a list of words with clickable hyperlinks that lead to other words on the page, and all words and definitions shown are those from the input? We chose a specification closer to the other end of the spectrum, namely to specify just enough to prove the absence of run-time errors in the code.

4   Dafny Success

The performance measures of the proofs, all of which are completed automatically, are presented in Fig. 13. Evidence that the tool automatically detects an incorrect solution can be generated by simple edits to the Dafny implementations. As noted in the presentation of our solutions, some errors in Dafny were detected as a result of attempting to verify our benchmark solutions. These errors were corrected while other Dafny features were added or improved.

Benchmark #	# of Verifications	Time (in seconds)
1	10	3.5
2	6	3.7
3	10	8.0
4	11	4.9
5	22	7.8
6	21	3.9
7	23	3.9
8	42	5.1

Fig. 13. Performance measurements of program verifications. Times shown take the average of 3 runs. For some of the benchmarks, these times also include some client code we added to the program files.

Notable enhancements to Dafny, since our first attempt at these benchmarks, include support for verifying recursion termination, heuristics that eliminate the need for many **decreases** clauses, the addition of ghost variables, the addition of arrays, and the redesign of the encoding of generics. This redesign includes improvements to the encoding of built-in types **set** and **seq** (see Boogie/Binaries/DafnyPrelude.bpl on codeplex.boogie.com). The syntax of Dafny has improved with additions such as the ⊄ operator, introduced on sets and sequences, and the Dafny **call** statement which now automatically declares left-hand sides as local variables, if they were not already local variables.

In early versions of our benchmark solutions, we often needed to supply lemmas to assist the automatic verification of sequence properties. Such a lemma is usually supplied as an **assert** statement, as shown in Fig. 5. The asserted expression, which is proved by the verifier, mentions terms that are relevant to the program's correctness, and the mention of these terms prompts the SMT solver to instantiate related axioms and other quantifications, as may be required in the proof. The treatment of sequences in Dafny has since been improved, allowing the verification to be completed mostly without the use of lemmas to trigger the proof.

In early versions of our benchmark solutions, we often needed to supply lemmas to assist the verifier in triggering the correct axioms to verify sequence properties. The treatment of sequences in Dafny has since been improved, allowing the verification to be completed mostly without the use of lemmas to trigger the proof.

We are aware that there are some limitation to our solutions. For example, Dafny uses mathematical integers, not the bounded integers found in most popular programming languages. This means that there is no issue of overflow in Dafny, which (is really a feature but) may be considered a limitation of what is verified. A more obvious shortcoming is in meeting Benchmark #3, where we couldn't sort a generic Queue into some client-defined order. However, this too is informative and will help us to compare Dafny with other tools that take up the benchmark challenges.

5   Conclusions

We have attempted to meet the given verification benchmarks using the language and verifier Dafny and are pleased with the results. We were not concerned about how the benchmarks themselves were designed, but tried to meet their original specifications. Our experience was that it is often tempting to make the benchmark fit your tool rather than to try to solve the benchmark itself. We hope that ongoing discussions with the benchmark authors, and discussions with others who will write solutions for these benchmarks, will help shape future revisions of these and other benchmarks. In particular, we would like to see that the next revision of the benchmarks would make it easier to constrain solutions so that it is easier to compare language features and verification techniques. A more detailed framework for comparing languages and verifiers, to be used in conjunction with the benchmarks, is also desirable. Further benchmarks that we hope to explore include the original iterator and the composite problems[2] which would help compare Dafny to other verifiers based on the dynamic framing paradigm.

The exercise allowed us to explore the strengths and weaknesses of Dafny and contributed towards improving both the syntax of the language and the verification process. We strongly encourage others to take up the verification challenge as this will help the community to compare and improve existing languages and tools. Having a number of problems solved in different languages will also assist researchers in learning about another's favourite language and how it compares to their own.

Acknowledgments. We thank the authors of [12] and their research students for feedback on our initial attempts at these verification benchmarks. We also thank the anonymous referees, for their thoughtful and helpful comments.

References

1. Barnett, M., Chang, B.-Y.E., DeLine, R., Jacobs, B., Leino, K.R.M.: Boogie: A modular reusable verifier for object-oriented programs. In: de Boer, F.S., Bonsangue, M.M., Graf, S., de Roever, W.-P. (eds.) FMCO 2005. LNCS, vol. 4111, pp. 364–387. Springer, Heidelberg (2006)
2. Barnett, M., Leino, K.R.M., Schulte, W.: The Spec# programming system: An overview. In: Barthe, G., Burdy, L., Huisman, M., Lanet, J.-L., Muntean, T. (eds.) CASSIS 2004. LNCS, vol. 3362, pp. 49–69. Springer, Heidelberg (2005)

---

[2] Presented at SAVCBS 2006 and SAVCBS 2008, respectively.

3. de Moura, L., Bjørner, N.: Z3: An efficient SMT solver. In: Ramakrishnan, C.R., Rehof, J. (eds.) TACAS 2008. LNCS, vol. 4963, pp. 337–340. Springer, Heidelberg (2008)
4. Hoare, C.A.R., Misra, J., Leavens, G.T., Shankar, N.: The verified software initiative: A manifesto. ACM Computing Surveys 41(4), 22:1–22:8 (2009)
5. Leavens, G.T., Baker, A.L., Ruby, C.: Preliminary design of JML: A behavioral interface specification language for Java. ACM SIGSOFT Software Engineering Notes 31(3), 1–38 (2006)
6. Leino, K.R.M.: This is Boogie 2. Manuscript KRML 178 (2008), http://research.microsoft.com/~leino/papers.html
7. Leino, K.R.M.: Specification and verification of object-oriented software. In: Broy, M., Sitou, W., Hoare, T. (eds.) Engineering Methods and Tools for Software Safety and Security. NATO Science for Peace and Security Series D: Information and Communication Security, vol. 22, pp. 231–266. IOS Press, Amsterdam (2009) (Summer School Marktoberdorf 2008 lecture notes)
8. Leino, K.R.M.: Dafny: An automatic program verifier for functional correctness. In: LPAR 16 (to appear, 2010)
9. Leino, K.R.M., Müller, P.: Using the Spec# language, methodology, and tools to write bug-free programs. In: Müller, P. (ed.) LASER Summer School 2007/2008. LNCS, vol. 6029, pp. 91–139. Springer, Heidelberg (2010)
10. Leino, K.R.M., Rümmer, P.: A polymorphic intermediate verification language: Design and logical encoding. In: Esparza, J., Majumdar, R. (eds.) TACAS 2010. LNCS, vol. 6015, pp. 312–327. Springer, Heidelberg (2010)
11. Meyer, B.: Object-oriented Software Construction. Series in Computer Science. Prentice-Hall International, Englewood Cliffs (1988)
12. Weide, B.W., Sitaraman, M., Harton, H.K., Adcock, B., Bucci, P., Bronish, D., Heym, W.D., Kirschenbaum, J., Frazier, D.: Incremental benchmarks for software verification tools and techniques. In: Shankar, N., Woodcock, J. (eds.) VSTTE 2008. LNCS, vol. 5295, pp. 84–98. Springer, Heidelberg (2008)

Specifying Reusable Components*

Nadia Polikarpova, Carlo A. Furia, and Bertrand Meyer

Chair of Software Engineering, ETH Zurich, Switzerland
{nadia.polikarpova,carlo.furia,bertrand.meyer}@inf.ethz.ch

Abstract. Reusable software components need expressive specifications. This paper outlines a rigorous foundation of *model-based contracts*, a method to equip classes with strong contracts that support accurate design, implementation, and formal verification of reusable components. Model-based contracts conservatively extend the classic Design by Contract approach with a notion of model, which underpins the precise definitions of such concepts as abstract object equivalence and specification completeness. Experiments applying model-based contracts to libraries of data structures suggest that the method enables accurate specification of practical software.

1 Introduction

The rationale for precise software specifications involves several well-known arguments; in particular, specifications help understand the problem before building a solution, and they are necessary for verifying implementations. In the context of reusable software components, there is another essential application of specifications: providing client programmers with an accurate description of the API. Design by Contract techniques [9] enable authors of reusable modules to equip them with specification elements known as "contracts" (routine pre and postconditions, class invariants).

While specification methods primarily intended for formal verification typically use notations based on mathematics, Design by Contract approaches, such as Eiffel [9], JML [8] and Spec# [2], rely instead on an assertion language embedded in the programming language. This adds a significant benefit: assertions can be *evaluated* during execution. As a consequence, contracts have played a major role in testing, especially for Eiffel, where an advanced testing environment, AutoTest [10], takes advantage of executable specifications for automatic test generation. More generally, Eiffel programmers routinely rely on runtime contract evaluation for testing and debugging. Another practical benefit of Design by Contract is approachability: programmers do not need to learn a separate notation for specifications.

These advantages of contracts have traditionally come at a price: expressiveness. The lack of an advanced mathematical notation makes it harder to express the full specification of components (see examples in Section 2). An extensive study [3] indicates that in practice Eiffel classes contain many contracts, but they cover only part of the intended functional properties.

Can we get all the advanced benefits of expressive formal specifications while retaining an executable specification language that does not introduce complex notation? The

* This research has been funded in part by Hasler Stiftung, ManCom project, grant # 2146.

G.T. Leavens, P. O'Hearn, and S.K. Rajamani (Eds.): VSTTE 2010, LNCS 6217, pp. 127–141, 2010.

present paper proposes a positive answer, based on the idea of *models*. Specifications, in this approach, are expressed in terms of the abstract model of a class, defined through one or more *model queries*. Model queries return instances of *model classes*: direct translations of mathematical concepts (such as sets or sequences) into the programming language.

The idea of using model classes and model queries in contracts is not new; our previous work [13,12] and, among others, JML [8] introduced the concepts and provided libraries of model classes. Two main contributions of the present paper are developing a *rigorous and systematic approach* to model-based specifications and confirming the applicability of the approach through two realistic *case studies*.

Section 3 shows how the interface of a class defines unambiguously a notion of *abstract object space* that determines the class model. Section 3 also outlines precise guidelines for writing contracts that refer to model queries. The guidelines come with a definition of specification *completeness* (with respect to the model). The definition is formal, yet amenable to informal reasoning; it is practically useful in assessing whether a contract is sufficiently detailed or is likely omitting some important details.

Section 4 describes two case studies applying model-based contracts to Eiffel-Base [4], Eiffel's standard collection of fundamental data structures, and to the development of EiffelBase2, intended to replace EiffelBase and to contribute to the Verified Software Repository [14]. The results show that the method is successful in delivering well-engineered components with expressive — usually complete — specifications. Most advantages of standard Design by Contract are retained, while pushing a more accurate evaluation of design choices and an impeccable definition of interfaces. The executability of most model classes supports the reuse of Eiffel's AutoTest infrastructure with more expressive contracts, which boosts the effectiveness of automated testing in finding defects in production software.

For lack of space, the rest of the paper omits some examples and references, which are available in an extended version [11].

2   Motivation and Overview

Design by Contract uses the same notation for expressions in the implementation and in the specification. This restriction ultimately impedes the formalization and verification of full functional correctness, as demonstrated below on two examples from the EiffelBase library [4].

Lines 1–13 in Figure 1 show a portion of class LINKED_LIST. Features (members) *count* and *index* record respectively the number of elements stored in the list and the position of the internal cursor. The routine *put_right* inserts an element, *v*, to the right of the cursor. The precondition of the routine (**require**) demands that the cursor not be after the last element. The postcondition (**ensure**) asserts that inserting an element increments *count* by one but does not change *index*. This is correct, but it does not capture the essence of the insertion semantics: in particular, it doesn't prevent the implementation from changing elements that were in the list before.

Expressing such complex properties is impossible or exceedingly complicated with the standard assertion language; as a result most specifications are *incomplete* in the

```
 1  class LINKED_LIST [G]
 2      put_right (v: G)
 3          −− Add 'v' to the right of cursor.
 4          require  0 ≤ index ≤ count
 5          do  ...
 6          ensure
 7              count = old count + 1
 8              index = old index
 9          end
10
11      count: INTEGER −− Number of elements
12      index: INTEGER −− Current cursor position
13  end
14
15  class TABLE [G, K]
16      put (v: G ; k: K)
17          −− Associate value 'v' with key 'k'.
18          require  ...
19          deferred
20          end
21  end
```

Fig. 1. Snippets from the EiffelBase classes LINKED_LIST (lines 1–13) and TABLE (lines 15–21)

sense that they fail to capture precisely the semantics of routines. Specification weakness hinders formal verification in two ways. First, establishing weak postconditions is simple, but confidence in the full functional correctness of a verified routine will be low. Second, weak contracts affect negatively verification modularity: it is impossible to establish what a routine r achieves, if r calls another routine s whose contract is not strong enough to document its effect within r precisely.

Weak assertions limit the potential of many other applications of Design by Contract. Specifications, for example, should document the abstract semantics of operations in deferred (abstract) classes. Incomplete contracts cannot fully do so; as a result, programmers have fewer safeguards to prevent inconsistencies in the design and fewer chances to make deferred classes useful to clients through polymorphism.

The feature *put* in class TABLE (lines 16–20 in Figure 1) is an example of such a phenomenon. It is unclear how to express the abstract semantics of *put* with standard contracts. In particular, the absence of a postcondition leaves it undefined what should happen when an element is inserted with a key that is already present: should *put* replace the existing element with the new one or leave the table unchanged? Indeed, some child classes of TABLE, such as class ARRAY, implement *put* with a replacement semantics, while others, such as class HASH_TABLE, disallow overriding of preexisting mappings with *put*. HASH_TABLE even introduces another feature *force* that implements the replacement semantics. This obscures the behavior of routines to clients and makes it questionable whether *put* has been introduced at the right point in the inheritance hierarchy.

Enhancing Design by Contract with Models. This paper presents an extension of Design by Contract that addresses the aforementioned problems. The extension conservatively enhances the standard approach with *model classes*: immutable classes representing mathematical concepts that provide for more expressive specifications. Wrapping mathematical entities with classes supports richer contracts without any need to extend the Design by Contract notation, familiar to programmers. Contracts using model classes are called *model-based contracts*.

Figure 2 shows an extensions of the examples in Figure 1 with model-based contracts. LINKED_LIST is augmented with a query *sequence* that returns an instance of class MML_SEQUENCE, a model class representing a mathematical sequence; the implementation, omitted for brevity, builds *sequence* according to the actual content of the list. The meta-annotation **note** declares the two features *sequence* and *index* as the model

```
 1 note model: sequence, index
 2 class LINKED_LIST [G]
 3     sequence: MML_SEQUENCE [G]
 4         −− Sequence of elements
 5         do ... end
 6
 7     index: INTEGER −− Current cursor position
 8
 9     put_right (v: G)
10         −− Add 'v' to the right of cursor.
11         require  0 ≤ index ≤ count
12         do ...
13         ensure
14             sequence = old ( sequence.front (index).
15                 extended (v) + sequence.tail (index + 1) )
16             index = old index
17         end
18 end
```

```
19 note model: map
20 class TABLE [G, K]
21     map: MML_MAP [G, K]
22         −− Map of keys to values
23         deferred end
24
25     put (v: G ; k: K)
26         −− Associate value 'v' with key 'k'.
27         require map.domain [k]
28         deferred
29         ensure
30             map = old map.replaced_at (k, v)
31         end
32 end
```

Fig. 2. Classes LINKED_LIST (left) and TABLE (right) with model-based contracts

of the class; all contracts will be written in terms of them. In particular, the postcondition of *put_right* can precisely describe the effect of the routine: the new *sequence* is the concatenation of the **old** *sequence* up to *index*, extended with element *v*, with the tail of the **old** *sequence* starting after *index*. We can assert that the new postcondition — including the clause about *index* — is *complete* with respect to the model of the class, because it defines the effect of *put_right* on the abstract model unambiguously. This notion of completeness is a powerful guide to writing accurate specification that makes for well-defined interfaces and verifiable classes.

The mathematical notion of a *map* — encapsulated by the model class MML_MAP — is a natural model for the class TABLE. Feature *map* cannot have an implementation yet, because TABLE is deferred and hence it is not committed to any representation of data. Nonetheless, availability of the model makes it possible to write a complete postcondition of *put* already at this abstract level, which in turn requires to commit to a specific semantics for insertion. The example in Figure 2 chooses the replacement semantics; correspondingly, all children of TABLE will have to conform to this semantics, guaranteeing a coherent reuse of TABLE throughout the class hierarchy.

3   Foundations of Model-Based Contracts

3.1   Specifying Classes with Models

Interfaces, References, and Objects. A class C denotes a collection of objects. Expressions such as $o : C$ define o as a reference to an object of class C; the notation is overloaded for conciseness, so that occurrences of o can denote the object it references or the reference itself, according to the context. Each class C defines a notion of *reference* equality $\equiv_C$ and of *object* equality $\overset{\circ}{=}_C$; both are equivalence relations. Two references $o_1, o_2 : C$ can be *reference equal* (written $o_1 \equiv_C o_2$) or *object equal* (written $o_1 \overset{\circ}{=}_C o_2$). Reference equality is meant to capture whether o_1 and o_2 are aliases for the same memory location, whereas object equality is meant to hold for (possibly) distinct copies of the same actual content.

```
 1 note model: sequence, index              11   duplicate (n: INTEGER): LINKED_LIST [G]
 2 class LINKED_LIST [G]                     12       −− A copy of at most 'n' elements
 3 . . .                                     13       −− starting at cursor position
 4   item: G                                 14    require n ≥ 0
 5        −− Value at cursor position        15    do . . .
 6    require sequence.domain [index]         16    ensure
 7    do . . .                               17       Result.sequence = sequence.interval (index, index + n − 1)
 8    ensure                                 18       Result.index = 0
 9       Result = sequence [index]           19    end
10    end                                    20 end
```

Fig. 3. Snippets of class LINKED_LIST with model-based contracts (continued from Figure 2)

The principle of information hiding prescribes that each class define an interface [9]. It is good practice to partition features into queries and commands; queries are functions of the object state, whereas commands modify the object state but do not return any value. $I_C = Q_C \cup M_C$ denotes the interface of a class C partitioned in queries Q_C and commands M_C.[1] It is convenient to partition all queries into *value-bound* queries and *reference-bound* queries. Value-bound queries create fresh objects to return (or more generally objects that were unknown to the client before calling the query), whereas reference-bound queries give the client direct access, through a reference, to preexisting objects. In other words, clients of a value-bound query should not rely on the identity of its result. The classification in value-bound and reference-bound extends naturally to *arguments* of features.

Example 1. Query *item* of class LINKED_LIST (Figure 3) is reference-bound, as the client receives a reference to the same memory location that was earlier inserted in the list. Query *duplicate* is instead value-bound, as it returns a copy of a portion of the list.

Abstract Object Space. The interface I_C induces an equivalence relation $\asymp_C$ over objects of class C called *abstract equality* and defined as follows: $o_1 \asymp_C o_2$ holds for $o_1, o_2 : C$ iff for any applicable sequence of calls to commands $m_1, m_2, \ldots \in M_C$ and a query $q \in Q_C$ returning objects of some class T, the qualified calls $o_1.m_1; o_1.m_2; \cdots$ and $o_2.m_1; o_2.m_2; \cdots$ (with identical actual arguments where appropriate) drive o_1 and o_2 in states such that if q is reference-bound then $o_1.q \equiv_T o_2.q$, and if q is value-bound then $o_1.q \overset{\circ}{=}_T o_2.q$. Intuitively, two objects are equivalent with respect to $\asymp_C$ if a client cannot distinguish them by any sequence of calls to public features. Abstract equality defines an *abstract object space*: the quotient set $A_C = C/\asymp_C$ of C by $\asymp_C$. As a consequence, two objects are equivalent w.r.t. $\asymp_C$ iff they have the same *abstract (object) state*. Any concrete set that is isomorphic to A_C is called a *model* of C.

Example 2. Consider a class implementing a *queue*. If the *remove* operation were not part of the interface, no element in the queue would be accessible to clients but the one that was enqueued first; the model of such a class would be $\mathbb{N} \times G$: a set of pairs recording the number of elements and the head element of generic type G. Including *remove* in the interface, as it usually is the case for queues, allows clients to access all the elements in the order of insertion. Hence, two queues with full interfaces are

---

[1] Constructors need no special treatment and can be modeled as queries returning new objects.

indistinguishable iff they have all the same elements in the same order, which makes G^* (sequences of elements) a model for queues.

Model Classes. The model of a class C is expressed as a tuple $D_C = D_C^1 \times D_C^2 \times \ldots \times D_C^n$ of *model classes*. Model classes are immutable classes designed for specification purposes; essentially, they are wrappers of rigorously defined mathematical entities: elementary sorts such as Booleans, integers, and object references, as well as more complex structures such as sets, bags, relations, maps, and sequences. The Mathematical Model Library (MML) [12] provides a variety of such model classes, equipped with features that correspond to common operations on the mathematical structures they represent, including first-order quantification. For example, class MML_SET models sets of elements of homogeneous type; it includes features such as membership test and quantification.

Model Queries. Every class C provides a collection of public *model queries* $S_C = s_C^1, s_C^2, \ldots, s_C^n$, one for each component model class in D_C. Each model query s_C^i returns an instance of the corresponding model class D_C^i that represents the current value of the i-th component of the model. Clauses in the class invariant can constrain the values of the model queries to match precisely the abstract object space. Consider, for example, the model of LINKED_LIST (Figure 2): model query *index*: INTEGER returning the cursor position should be constrained by an invariant clause $0 \leq index \leq sequence.count + 1$. A meta-annotation **note** model: $s_C^1, s_C^2, \ldots$ lists all model queries of the class.

It is likely that some model queries (such as *index* in the example above) are already used in the implementation before models are added explicitly; additional model queries (such as *sequence*) return the remaining components of the model for specification purposes. Our approach prefers to implement such additional model queries as functions rather than attributes. This choice facilitates a purely descriptive usage of references to model queries in specifications. In other words, instead of augmenting routine bodies with bookkeeping instructions that update model attributes, routine postconditions are extended with clauses that describe the new value returned by model queries in terms of the old one. This has the advantage of enforcing a cleaner division between implementation and specification, while better modularizing the latter at routine level (properties of model attributes are typically gathered in the class invariant).

Model-Based Contracts. Let C be a class equipped with model queries and let its interface I_C be partitioned into queries Q_C and commands M_C. Q_C now includes the model queries $S_C \subseteq Q_C$ together with other queries $R_C = Q_C \setminus S_C$. The rest of the section contains guidelines to writing model-based contracts for commands in M_C and queries in R_C.

The *precondition* of a feature is a constraint on the abstract states of its value-bound arguments and, possibly, on the actual references to its reference-bound arguments. The target object, in particular, can be considered an implicit value-bound argument. For example, the precondition *map.domain* [k] of feature *put* in class TABLE (Figure 2), refers to the abstract state of the target object, given by the model query *map*, and to its actual reference-bound argument k.

Postconditions should refer to abstract states only through model queries. This emphasizes the components of the abstract state that a feature modifies or relies upon, which in turn facilitates understanding and reasoning on the semantics of a feature.

The *postcondition of a command* defines a relation between the prestate and the poststate of its arguments and the target object. More precisely, the postcondition mentions only abstract values of its value-bound arguments and possibly the actual references to its reference-bound arguments; the target object is considered value-bound both in the prestate and in the poststate.

It is common that a command only affects a few components of the abstract state and leaves all the others unchanged. Accordingly, the *closed world assumption* is convenient: the value of any model query $s \in S_C$ that is not mentioned in the postcondition is assumed not to be modified by the command, as if $s = \mathbf{old}\ s$ were a clause of the postcondition. When the closed world assumption is wrong, explicit clauses in the postcondition should establish the correct semantics.

The *postcondition of a query* defines the result as a function of its arguments and the target object (with the usual discipline of mentioning only abstract values of value-bound arguments and target object and possibly actual references to reference-bound arguments). Value-bound queries define the abstract state of the result, whereas reference-bound queries describe an actual reference to it. For example, compare the postcondition of the reference-bound query *item* from class LINKED_LIST (Figure 3) with the postcondition of the value-bound query *duplicate* in the same class.

A clear-cut separation between queries and commands assumes *abstract purity* for all queries: executing a query leaves the abstract state of all its arguments and of the target object unchanged.

Inheritance and Model-Based Contracts. A class C' that inherits from a parent class C may or may not re-use C's model queries to represent its own abstract state. For every model query $s_C \in S_C$ of the parent class that is not among the child's model queries $S_{C'}$, C' should provide a *linking invariant*: a formula that defines the value returned by s_C in terms of the values returned by the model queries $S_{C'}$ of the inheriting class. This guarantees that the new model is indeed a specialization of the previous model, in accordance with the notion of sub-typing inheritance.

A properly defined linking invariant ensures that every inherited feature has a definite semantics in terms of the new model. However, the new semantics may be weaker; that is, incompleteness is introduced (see Section 3.2).

Example 3. Consider class COLLECTION in Figure 4, a generic container of elements whose model is a bag. Class DISPENSER inherits from COLLECTION and specializes it by introducing a notion of insertion order; correspondingly, its model is a sequence. The linking invariant of DISPENSER defines the value of the inherited model query *bag* in terms of the new model query *sequence* and ensures that the semantics of features *is_empty* and *wipe_out* is unambiguously defined also in DISPENSER. At the same time, the model-based contract of command *put* in COLLECTION and the linking invariant are insufficient to characterize the effects of *put* in DISPENSER, as the position within the sequence where the new element is inserted is irrelevant for the bag.

```
 1 note model: bag
 2 class COLLECTION [G]
 3   bag: MML_BAG [G]
 4
 5   is_empty: BOOLEAN
 6     ensure Result = bag.is_empty end
 7
 8   wipe_out
 9     ensure bag.is_empty end
10
11   put (v: G)
12     ensure bag = old bag.extended (v) end
13 end
```

```
14 note model: sequence
15 class DISPENSER [G]
16 inherit COLLECTION [G]
17
18   sequence: MML_SEQUENCE [G]
19
20   invariant
21     bag.domain = sequence.range
22     bag.domain.for_all ( agent (x: G): BOOLEAN
23                             bag [x] = sequence.occurrences (x) )
24 end
```

Fig. 4. Snippets of classes COLLECTION (left) and DISPENSER (right) with model-based contracts

3.2   Completeness of Contracts

The notion of *completeness* for the specification of a class gives an indication of how accurate the contracts are with respect to the model of that class. An incomplete contract does not fully capture the effects of a feature, suggesting that the contract may be more detailed or, less commonly, that the model of the class — and hence its interface — is not abstract enough. A dual notion of soundness is definable along the same lines; for brevity, this section only presents the more interesting notion of completeness.

Completeness of a Model-Based Contract. The specification of a feature f of class C denotes two predicates $\mathbf{pre}_f$ and $\mathbf{post}_f$. $\mathbf{pre}_f$ represents the set of objects of class C that satisfy the precondition[2]. If f is a command, $\mathbf{post}_f$ has signature $C \times C$ and denotes the pairs of target objects before and after executing the command. If f is a query with return type T, $\mathbf{post}_f$ has signature $C \times T$; it denotes the pairs of target and returned objects for value-bound queries; and the pairs of target object and returned reference for reference-bound queries. In both cases $\mathbf{post}_f$ does not refer to the target object after executing the query because all queries are assumed to be abstractly pure.

- The *postcondition of a command* m is *complete* iff: for every $o, o'_1, o'_2 : C$ such that $\mathbf{pre}_m(o)$, $\mathbf{post}_m(o, o'_1)$, and $\mathbf{post}_m(o, o'_2)$ it is $o'_1 \asymp_C o'_2$.
- The *postcondition of a value-bound query* q is *complete* iff: for every $o : C$ and $t_1, t_2 : T$ such that $\mathbf{pre}_q(o)$, $\mathbf{post}_q(o, t_1)$, and $\mathbf{post}_q(o, t_2)$ it is $t_1 \asymp_T t_2$.
- The *postcondition of a reference-bound query* q is *complete* iff: for every $o : C$ and $t_1, t_2 : T$ such that $\mathbf{pre}_q(o)$, $\mathbf{post}_q(o, t_1)$, and $\mathbf{post}_q(o, t_2)$ it is $t_1 \equiv_T t_2$.

A postcondition is complete if all the pairs of objects that satisfy it are equivalent (according to the right model of equivalence). This means that the complete postcondition of a command defines its effect as a mathematical *function* (as apposed to a relation) from A_C to A_C. Similarly, the complete postcondition of a query defines the result as a *function* from A_C to A_T if the query is value-bound and to the set of references if the query is reference-bound.

---

[2] For simplicity, the following definitions do not mention feature arguments; introducing them is, however, straightforward.

Example 4. The contracts of features *is_empty*, *wipe_out*, and *put* in class COLLECTION (Figure 4) are complete; the postcondition of *put*, in particular, is complete as it defines the new value of *bag* uniquely. In the child class DISPENSER, however, the inherited postcondition of *put* becomes incomplete: the linking invariant does not uniquely define *sequence* from *bag*, hence inequivalent sequences (for example, one with *v* inserted at the beginning and another one with *v* at the end) satisfy the postcondition.

Completeness in Practice. As the previous example suggests, reasoning informally — but precisely — about completeness of model-based contracts is often straightforward and intuitive, especially if the guidelines of Section 3.1 have been followed. Completeness captures the uniqueness of the (abstract) state described by a postcondition, hence postconditions in the form **Result** = *exp* and similar, where *exp* is a side-effect free expression, are painless to check for completeness.

Example 5. Consider the following example, from class ARRAY whose model is a map.

```
1   fill (v: G ; l, u: INTEGER) —— Put 'v' at all positions in ['l', 'u'].
2      require map.domain [l] and map.domain [u]
3      ensure map.domain = old map.domain
4         ( map | {MML_INT_SET} [[l, u]] ).is_constant (v)
5         ( map | (map.domain − {MML_INT_SET} [[l, u]]) ) =
6                  old ( map | (map.domain − {MML_INT_SET} [[l, u]]) )
7      end
```

The following reasoning shows that the postcondition is complete: a map is uniquely defined by its domain and by a value for every key in the domain. The first clause of the postcondition (line 3) defines the domain completely. Then, let k be any key in the domain. If $k \in [l, u]$ then the second clause (line 4) defines *map* $(k) = v$; otherwise $k \notin [l, u]$, and the third clause (lines 5–6) postulates *map*(k) unchanged.

How useful is completeness in practice? As a norm, completeness is a valuable yardstick to evaluate whether the contracts are sufficiently detailed. This is not enough to guarantee that the contracts are correct — and meet the original requirements — but the yardstick is serviceable methodologically to focus on what a routine really achieves and how that is related to the abstract model. As a result, inconsistencies in specifications are less likely to occur, and the impossibility of systematically writing complete contracts is a strong indication that the model is incorrect, or the implementation is faulty. Either way, a warning is available before attempting a correctness proof.

While complete postconditions should be the norm, there are recurring cases where incomplete postconditions are unavoidable or even preferable. Two major sources of benign incompleteness are:

– inherently *nondeterministic or stochastic* specifications and
– usage of *inheritance* to factor out common parts of (complete) specifications.

As an example of the latter consider class DISPENSER in Figure 4, a common parent of STACK and QUEUE. Based on the interface, its model has to be isomorphic to a sequence, but the postcondition of feature *put* cannot define the exact position of the

```
1 note mapped_to: "Sequence G"            9 type Sequence T = [int] T ;
2 class MML_SEQUENCE [G]                  10 function Sequence.extended ⟨T⟩ (Sequence T, T)
3   extended (x: G): MML_SEQUENCE[G]      11    returns (Sequence T);
4     -- Current sequence extended with 'x' at the end   12 axiom (∀ ⟨T⟩ s: Sequence T, x:T •
5     note mapped_to: "Sequence.extended(Current, x)"   13    Sequence.extended(s, x) =s[Sequence.count(s)+1 := x]) ;
6     do ... end                         14 axiom (∀ ⟨T⟩ s: Sequence T, x: T •
7 ...                                     15    Sequence.count(Sequence.extended(s, x)) =
8 end                                     16          Sequence.count(s)+1);
                                          17 ...
```

Fig. 5. Snippets from class MML_SEQUENCE (left) and the corresponding Boogie theory (right)

new element in that sequence: a choice compatible with the semantics of STACK will be incompatible with QUEUE and vice versa.

In such cases, reasoning about completeness is still likely to improve the understanding of the classes and to question constructively the choices made for interfaces and inheritance hierarchies.

3.3 Verification: Proofs and Runtime Checking

This subsection outlines the main ideas behind using model-based contracts for verification with formal correctness proofs and with runtime checking for automated testing. Its goal is not to detail any particular proof or testing technique, but rather to sketch how to express the semantics of model-based contracts within standard verification frameworks.

Proofs. The *axiomatic* treatment of model classes [12] is quite natural: the semantics of a model class is defined directly in terms of a theory expressed in the underlying proof language, rather than with "special" contracts. The mapping often has the advantage of reusing theories that are optimized for effective usage with the proof engine of choice. In addition, the immutability (and value semantics) of model classes makes them very similar to mathematical structures and facilitates a straightforward translation into mathematical theories.

We are currently developing an accurate mapping of model classes and model-based contracts into Boogie [2]. First, the mapping introduces axiomatic definitions of MML model classes as Boogie theories; annotations in the form **note** mapped_to connect MML classes to the corresponding Boogie types (see Figure 5 for an example). Then, each model query in a class with model-based contracts maps to a Boogie function that references a representation of the heap. For example, the model query *sequence* in LINKED_LIST becomes **function** LinkedList. *sequence*(HeapType, *ref*) **returns** (Sequence *ref*). Axioms that connect the value returned by the function to the attributes of the translated class are generated from the postconditions of model queries. The issue of providing such postconditions (*abstraction functions*) is outside the scope of current paper as here we are only concerned with interface specifications. Finally, model-based contracts are translated into Boogie formulas according to the mapped_to annotations in model classes.

Runtime Checking and Testing. Most model classes represent *finite* mathematical objects, such as sets of finite cardinality, sequences of finite length, and so on. All these classes can have an implementation of their operations which is executable in finite time; this supports the runtime checking of assertions that reference these model classes.

Testing techniques can leverage runtime checkable contracts to fully automate the testing process: generate objects by randomly calling constructors and commands; check the precondition of a routine on the generated objects to filter out valid inputs; execute the routine body on a valid input and check the validity of the postcondition on the result; any postcondition violation on a valid input is a fault in the routine.

This approach to contract-based testing has proved very effective at uncovering plenty of bugs in production code [10], hence it is an excellent "lightweight" precursor to correctness proofs. Contract-based testing, however, is only as good as the contracts are; the weak postconditions of traditional Design by Contract, in particular, leave many real faults undetected. Runtime checkable model-based contracts can help in this respect and boost the effectiveness of contract-based testing by providing more expressive specifications. Section 4 describes some testing experiments that support this claim.

4   Model-Based Contracts at Work

This section describes experiments in developing model-based contracts for real object-oriented software written in Eiffel. The experiments target two non-trivial case studies based on data-structure libraries (described in Section 4.1) with the goal of demonstrating that deploying model-based contracts is feasible, practical, and useful. Section 4.2 discusses the successes and limitations highlighted by the experiments.

4.1   Case Studies

The first case study targeted EiffelBase [4], a library of general-purpose data structures widely used in Eiffel programs; EiffelBase is representative of mature Eiffel code exploiting extensively traditional Design by Contract. We selected 7 classes from EiffelBase, for a total of 304 features (254 of them are public) over more that 5700 lines of code. The 7 classes include 3 widely used container data structures (ARRAY, ARRAYED_LIST, and LINKED_LIST) and 4 auxiliary classes. Our experiments systematically introduced models and conservatively augmented the contracts of all public features in these 7 classes with model-based specifications.

The second case study developed EiffelBase2, a new general-purpose data structure library. The design of EiffelBase2 is similar to that of its precursor EiffelBase; EiffelBase2, however, has been developed from the start with expressive model-based specifications and with the ultimate goal of proving its full functional correctness — backward compatibility is not one of its primary aims. This implies that EiffelBase2 rediscusses and solves any deficiency and inconsistency in the design of EiffelBase that impedes achieving full functional correctness or hinders the full-fledged application of formal techniques. EiffelBase2 provides containers such as arrays, lists, sets, tables, stacks, queues, and binary trees; iterators to traverse these containers; and comparator objects to parametrize containers with respect to arbitrary equivalence and order relations on their elements. The current version of EiffelBase2 includes 46 classes with 460 features (403 of them are public) totaling about 5800 lines of code; these figures make

EiffelBase2 a library of substantial size with realistic functionalities. The latest version of EiffelBase2 is available at `http://eiffelbase2.origo.ethz.ch`.

4.2 Results and Discussion

How Many Model Classes? Model-based contracts for EiffelBase used model classes for Booleans, integers, references, (finite) sets, relations, and sequences. EiffelBase2 additionally required (finite) maps, bags, and infinite maps and relations for special purposes (such as modeling comparator objects). This suggests that a moderate number of well-understood mathematical models suffices to specify a general-purpose library of data structures.

Determining to what extent this is generalizable to software other than libraries of general-purpose data structures is an open question which belongs to future work. Some problem domains may indeed require domain-specific model classes (e.g., real-valued functions, stochastic variables, finite-state machines), and application software that interacts with a complex environment may be less prone to accurate documentation with models. However, even if writing model-based contracts for such systems proved exceedingly complex, some formal model is required if the goal is formal verification. In this sense, focusing model-based contracts on library software is likely to have a great payoff through extensive reuse: the many clients of the reusable components can rely on expressive contracts not only as detailed documentation but also to express their own contracts and interfaces by combining a limited set of well-understood, highly dependable components.

Another interesting remark is that the correspondence between the limited number of model classes needed in our experiments and the classes using these model classes is far from trivial: reusable data structures are often more complex than the mathematical structures they implement. Consider, for example, class SET: EiffelBase2 sets are parameterized with respect to an equivalence relation, hence the model of SET is a pair of a mathematical set and a relation; correspondingly, the postcondition of feature *has* relies on the model by defining **Result** = **not** (*set* ∗ *relation.image_of* (*v*)).*is_empty*. Another significant example is BINARY_TREE: instead of introducing a new model class for trees or graphs, BINARY_TREE concisely represents a tree as a map of paths to values, where paths are encoded as sequences of Booleans.

How Many Complete Contracts? Reasoning informally, but rigorously, about the completeness of postconditions — along the lines of Section 3.2 — proved to be straightforward in our experiments. Only 18 (7%) out of 254 public features in Eiffel-Base with model-based contracts and 17 (4%) out of 403 public features in EiffelBase2 have incomplete postconditions. All of them are examples of "intrinsic" incompleteness mentioned at the end of Section 3.2; EiffelBase2, in particular, was designed trying to minimize the number of features with intrinsically incomplete postconditions.

These results indicate that model-based contracts make it feasible to write systematically complete contracts; in most cases this was even relatively straightforward to achieve. Unsurprisingly, using model-based contracts dramatically increases the completeness of contracts in comparison with standard Design by Contract. For example, 42 (66%) out of 64 public features of class LIST in the original version of EiffelBase (without model-based contracts) have incomplete postconditions, including 20 features (31%) without any postcondition.

Contract-Based Testing with Model-Based Contracts. The standard EiffelBase library has been in use for many years and has been extensively tested, both manually and automatically. Are the expressive contracts based on models enough to boost automated testing finding new, subtle bugs? While preliminary, our experiments seem to answer in the affirmative. Applying the AutoTest testing framework [10] on EiffelBase with model-based contracts for 30 minutes discovered 3 faults; none of them would have been detectable with standard contracts. Running these tests did not require any modification to AutoTest or model classes, because the latter include an executable implementation.

The 3 faults reveal subtle mistakes that have gone undetected so far. For example, consider an implementation of routine *merge_right* in LINKED_LIST (not shown for brevity); the routine merges a linked list *other* into the current list at the cursor position by modifying references in the chain of elements. The routine deals in a special way with the case when the cursor in the current list is *before* the first element; in this case the *first_element* reference is attached directly to the first element of the other list. This is not sufficient, as the routine should also link the end of the other list to the front of the current one, otherwise all elements in the current list become inaccessible. The original contract does not detect this fault; in particular the postcondition clause $count =$ **old** $count$ + **old** $other.count$ is satisfied as the attribute $count$ is updated correctly, but its value does not reflect the actual content of the new list. On the contrary, the clause $sequence =$ **old** ($sequence.front$ ($index$)+ $other.sequence + sequence.tail$ ($index + 1$)) of the complete model-based postcondition specifies the desired configuration of the list after executing the command, which leads to easily detecting the error.

5   Related Work

Hoare pioneered the usage of mathematical models to define and prove correctness of data type implementations [7]. This idea spawned much related work; the following paragraphs shortly summarize a few significant representatives, with particular focus on the approaches that are closest to the one in the present paper.

Algebraic Notations. Algebraic notations formalize classes in terms of (uninterpreted) functions and axioms that describe the mutual relationship among the functions. The most influential work in algebraic specifications is arguably Guttag and Horning's [6] and Gougen et al.'s [5], which gave a foundation to much derivative work. The former also introduced a notion of *completeness*. Algebraic notations emphasize the calculational aspect of a specification. This makes them very effective notations to formalize and verify data types at a high level of abstraction, but does not integrate as well with real programming languages to document implementations in the form of pre and post-conditions.

Descriptive Notations. Descriptive notations formalize classes in terms of simpler types — ultimately grounded in simple mathematical models such as sets and relations — and operations defined as input/output relations. Descriptive notations can be used in isolation to build language-independent models, or to give a formal semantics to concrete implementations. Languages and methods such as B [1] pursue the former approach; other specification languages and tools such as Jahob [15] are examples of the latter approach. Descriptive notations are apt to develop correct-by-construction designs and to accurately document implementations, often with the goal of verifying functional correctness; using them in contracts, however, introduces a new notation on top of the programming language, which requires additional effort and expertise from the programmer. This weakness is shared by algebraic notations alike.

Design by Contract Approaches. Design by Contract [9] introduces formal specifications in programs using the same notation for implementation and annotations, in an attempt to make writing the contracts as congenial as possible to programmers. The Eiffel programming language epitomizes the Design by Contract methodology, together with many similar solutions for other languages such as Spec$^\#$ [2] for C$^\#$. As we discussed also in the rest of the paper, using a subset of the programming language in annotations often does not provide enough expressive power to formalize (easily) "complete" functional correctness.

Model-Based Annotation Languages. The Java Modeling Language (JML) [8] is likely the approach that shares the most similarities with ours: JML annotations are based on a subset of the Java programming language and the JML framework provides a library of model classes mapping mathematical concepts. While sharing a common outlook, the approaches in JML and in the present paper differ in several details. At the technical level, JML prefers model variables while our method leverages model queries; each approach has its merits, but model queries have some advantages (discussed in Section 3.1). A notational difference is that JML extends Java's expressions with notations for logic operators, while our method reuses Eiffel notation such as agents to express quantifications and other aspects. In terms of scope, our approach strives to be more methodological and systematic, with the primary target of fully contracting complete libraries of data structures, while keeping the additional effort required to the programmer to a minimum. The present paper extends in scope the previous work of ours on model-based contracts [13,12], and systematically applies the results to the redesign and re-implementation of a rich library of data structures. The experience gained in this practical application also prompted us to refine and rethink aspects of the previous approach, as we discussed at length in the rest of the paper.

6   Conclusions and Future Work

The present work introduces a method to write strong interface specifications for reusable object-oriented components. The method is soundly based on the concept of model and features a notion of specification completeness which is formal, yet easy to reason about. The application of the method to the development of a library of general-purpose data structures demonstrates its practicality and its many uses in analysis, design, and verification.

Future work includes short- and long-term goals. Among the former, we plan to apply model-based contracts to more real-life examples, including application software from diverse domains. A user study will try to confirm the preliminary evidence that model-based contracts are easy to write, understand, and reason about informally. Longer term work envisions integrating model-based contracts within a comprehensive verification environment.

Acknowledgements. To Marco Piccioni, Stephan van Staden, and Scott West for comments on a draft of this paper.

References

1. Abrial, J.-R.: The B-book. Cambridge University Press, Cambridge (1996)
2. Barnett, M., DeLine, R., Fähndrich, M., Jacobs, B., Leino, K.R.M., Schulte, W., Venter, H.: The Spec$^{\#}$ programming system: Challenges and directions. In: Meyer, B., Woodcock, J. (eds.) VSTTE 2005. LNCS, vol. 4171, pp. 144–152. Springer, Heidelberg (2008)
3. Chalin, P.: Are practitioners writing contracts? In: Rigorous Development of Complex Fault-Tolerant Systems, pp. 100–113 (2006)
4. http://freeelks.svn.sourceforge.net
5. Gougen, J.A., Thatcher, J.W., Wagner, E.G.: An initial algebra approach to the specification, correctness, and implementation of abstract data types. In: Current Trends in Programming Methodology, pp. 80–149. Prentice-Hall, Englewood Cliffs (1978)
6. Guttag, J.V., Horning, J.J.: The algebraic specification of abstract data types. Acta Inf. 10, 27–52 (1978)
7. Hoare, C.A.R.: Proof of correctness of data representations. Acta Inf. 1, 271–281 (1972)
8. Leavens, G.T., Cheon, Y., Clifton, C., Ruby, C., Cok, D.R.: How the design of JML accommodates both runtime assertion checking and formal verification. Sci. Comput. Program. 55(1-3), 185–208 (2005)
9. Meyer, B.: Object-oriented software construction, 2nd edn. Prentice Hall, Englewood Cliffs (1997)
10. Meyer, B., Fiva, A., Ciupa, I., Leitner, A., Wei, Y., Stapf, E.: Programs that test themselves. Computer 42(9), 46–55 (2009)
11. Polikarpova, N., Furia, C.A., Meyer, B.: Specifying reusable components, Extended version, http://arxiv.org/abs/1003.5777
12. Schoeller, B.: Making classes provable through contracts, models and frames. PhD thesis, ETH Zurich (2007)
13. Schoeller, B., Widmer, T., Meyer, B.: Making specifications complete through models. In: Architecting Systems with Trustworthy Components, pp. 48–70 (2004)
14. http://vsr.sourceforge.net/
15. Zee, K., Kuncak, V., Rinard, M.C.: Full functional verification of linked data structures. In: PLDI 2008, pp. 349–361. ACM, New York (2008)

Reusable Verification of a Copying Collector

Magnus O. Myreen

Computer Laboratory, University of Cambridge, UK

Abstract. Garbage collectors are very hard to implement correctly due to their low-level manipulation of memory. In this paper, we construct a copying garbage collector which we have proved to be functionally correct. Our verification proof is structured as a sequence of refinements to aid clarity and proof reuse; it is the first to map implementations into three different machine languages and, unlike some noteworthy published proofs, our verified implementations of memory allocation handle termination and the 'out-of-memory' case properly. The work presented here has been developed in the HOL4 theorem prover.

1   Introduction

Garbage collectors are important cornerstones of any implementation of a functional programming language and most object-oriented programming languages. They are hard to implement correctly due to their low-level manipulation of memory and very hard to test for faults since the property of a correct execution is rather abstract: every execution must produce a heap which is,

- isomorphic to the original heap, i.e. must be equivalent to the original heap modulo renaming of addresses, and
- minimal in the sense that it must not contain unnecessary heap elements, i.e. elements that are not reachable from root addresses.

In this paper we present the construction of a copying collector that we have proved formally correct, i.e. for which we know that the above properties hold for every possible execution of the verified code. A sample of the verified ARM, x86 and PowerPC code is listed in Figure 6.

There are numerous publications on the topic of garbage collector verification and some very impressive recent work on proving the correctness of assembly and C-like implementations of copying garbage collectors. These proofs, which we will describe in Section 2, are unfortunately tied to specific programming logics and mix reasoning for why the algorithm is correct (how heap isomorphism is achieved) with implementation specific details (such as how specific heap elements are represented in memory). As a result published proofs are cumbersome to adapt to new settings.

This paper attempts to remedy these shortcomings by presenting a verification proof which has been carefully designed to be reusable for any stop-the-world copying collector. The main contributions of this paper are as follows:

G.T. Leavens, P. O'Hearn, and S.K. Rajamani (Eds.): VSTTE 2010, LNCS 6217, pp. 142–156, 2010.

- We present a verification proof which is sufficient for proving low-level implementations correct and at the same time independent of any particular programming logic. The proof cleanly separates reasoning about the correctness of the core algorithm from all implementation specific details.
- Data refinement is used to map our proofs down to the level of verified ARM, x86 and PowerPC machine code. This is the first paper to construct garbage collectors that have been proved correct with respect to realistic models of machine languages.
- These collectors are the first verified collectors to be used as mere building blocks in a much larger verification effort: our verified garbage collectors are part of verified implementations of Lisp.[1]
- Our verified implementations of allocation handle the 'out-of-memory' case properly. They terminate with an error message in case there is an insufficient amount of memory available after a full garbage collection. This is in contrast to noteworthy published work [3,12] which only prove partial correctness of code that diverges in the 'out-of-memory' case.

The work presented here has been developed inside the HOL4 theorem prover.[2]

2   Related Work

There are number of publications on the topic of specification and verification of garbage collection routines, e.g. [5,6,7,11,16]. However, few have proved copying collectors correct with respect to detailed models of realistic execution environments. Notable exceptions are work by Birkedal et al. [3], McCreight et al. [12], and Hawblitzel and Petrank [9].

Birkedal et al. used a version of separation logic to verify, on paper it seems, the correctness of a C-like program implementing the Cheney algorithm for a stop-the-world copying collector. McCreight et al. developed a general framework for collector proofs, in Coq, and verified MIPS-like code for several different collector algorithms, including two copying collector, one of which was incremental. The allocators verified by McCreight et al. and Birkedal et al. enter an infinite loop in case the heap is full after a complete collection cycle. In contrast, the allocators verified here have been proved to terminate: they terminate in the 'out-of-memory' case by jumping to code that can produce an appropriate error message.

In some very impressive recent work by Hawblitzel and Petrank, a copying collector and a mark-and-sweep collector, with competitive real-world performance, were verified mechanically. They did not use a theorem prover, instead they used the Boogie verification generator which links to the Z3 SMT solver. This system proved their x86-like implementations correct automatically given low-level code decorated with a substantial amount of annotations. They did

---

[1] Our work on verified Lisp interpreters has been published before [13], but the proof of its garbage collectors is published here for the first time.

[2] Our proofs are available at hol.sf.net in SVN under HOL/examples/machine-code

not prove termination but were able to run a suite of benchmarks which showed that their collectors have competitive performance compared with other collectors. Similar proofs might be possible in theorem provers in the future, even in LCF-style provers, as their support for SMT solvers is starting to mature [4].

None of the above mentioned verified copying collectors have been used as a building block inside a verified run-time, i.e. it has not been tried whether the resulting correctness theorems are usable as components in further formal developments. Our verified garbage collectors have been used inside verified Lisp interpreters [13]. However, these Lisp interpreters fall short of being practically useful at present due to the restrictive subset of Lisp which they implement. As far as we know, the VLISP project [8] is the only project which has successfully built a usable verified run-time which included a verified garbage collector. The VLISP verification consists of lengthy pen-and-paper-style proofs.

Novel work by Benton on specification and verification of a memory allocator [1] should also be mentioned. Benton verified, using Coq, an implementation of an allocator in an invented assembly language. Instead of using conventional unary predicates for describing program properties, he used quantified binary relations and stated program properties in terms of contextual equivalence. This allowed him to show that his allocator transfers ownership of memory states to the client program and that the client program is parametrised by the allocator. The allocator specification presented here does not provide such clean logical separation, instead the allocator always 'owns' the allocated memory and the client is forced to view the heap as an abstraction of the real memory. However, it remains unclear whether the cost of adding these extra features to the specifications is worth the effort since Benton's proofs seem to have been frustratingly hard work, as he commented in a separate note [2]. However, this might have been caused the fact that this was the first time Benton seriously used a theorem prover, instead of any feature in his approach that might have made it ill-suited for the automation provided by modern theorem provers.

3 Method

This paper presents verified garbage collectors which have been constructed through a sequence of refinements, starting from a high-level specification and going down to concrete machine code. We use the following refinement layers.

L1. We start with a specification which states what a full garbage collection is to achieve, namely, to remove unreachable heap elements and rename addresses in a consistent manner. At this level of abstraction, which we call L1, garbage collection is a single transition.

L2. At the second level of abstraction, we provide an abstract implementation of L1 as the transitive closure of a step relation. We prove that any complete execution of these steps implements L1. This proof, which is only 300 lines long, verifies the core idea behind the correctness of copying collection.

L3. At the third level of abstraction, we refine the non-deterministic implementation from L2 into a deterministic function which operates over a more concrete notion of memory: heap elements now have sizes and temporary reference cells are stored in memory alongside heap elements.

L4. At the next level, we introduce actual implementation types, e.g. addresses become real machine addresses (aligned 32-bit words). We also subdivide memory accesses into individual 32-bit memory reads and writes.

L5. At the lowest level of abstraction, we have the concrete ARM, x86 and PowerPC machine code. These implementations are automatically synthesised from the L4 implementation using a previously developed compiler which produces a proof of correspondence for each compilation.

Each refinement is proved correct with respect to the layers above it. The sizes of the manual proofs are approximately 300, 800 and 700 lines for L1/L2, L2/L3 and L3/L4, respectively. In total these proofs are less than half of the length of the proofs described in McCarthy et al. [12].

3.1   Specification – L1

We start by formalising what we mean by garbage collection in terms of a heap represented as a finite partial ($\rightharpoonup$) mapping h where addresses are natural numbers. The domain of h is a finite subset of $\mathbb{N}$ and the codomain of h consists of pairs (as, d) where as is a list of addresses and d is some data. The type of heap h is defined as the following using two type variables $null$ and $data$. We let null pointers be of arbitrary type so that later refinements can store data inside null pointers, which is often done in practice.

$$\mathbb{N} \quad \rightharpoonup \quad (\mathbb{N} + null) \; \text{list} \times data$$

We define the set of reachable addresses as the smallest inductively defined set such that a is reachable whenever a is a root or a is pointed to by some reachable element b. Let set as be the set of non-null addresses in the list as.

$$\frac{a \in \text{set } roots}{a \in \text{reach } (h, roots)} \qquad \frac{a \in \text{set } as \; \wedge \; h(b) = (as, data) \; \wedge \; b \in \text{reach } (h, roots)}{a \in \text{reach } (h, roots)}$$

The most abstract notion of garbage collection can now simply be defined as a function filter which restricts ($\downharpoonright$) the domain of a heap mapping h to only elements reachable from the root nodes.

$$\text{filter } (h, roots) \; = \; (h{\downharpoonright}(\text{reach } (h, roots)), roots)$$

In this paper we consider the verification of a copying garbage collector, i.e. one which must also have the right to rearrange heap elements. For this we define a function rename which updates all addresses in h by a given function $f : \mathbb{N} \to \mathbb{N}$. Let map f update all non-null addresses of a list by application of f.

$$\text{domain } (\text{rename } f \; h) = \text{image } f \; (\text{domain } h)$$
$$(\text{rename } f \; h)(f(x)) = (\text{map } f \; as, d) \qquad \text{whenever } h(x) = (as, d)$$

Using rename, we define a valid rearrangement as a relation $\xrightarrow{\text{translate}}$ which relates two heaps whenever one heap can be converted into the other by applying a global swap function f, i.e. a function such that $f \circ f = \text{id}$.

$$\frac{f \circ f = \text{id}}{(h, roots) \xrightarrow{\text{translate}} (\text{rename } f \ h, \text{map } f \ roots)}$$

We can now define that a garbage collection is a relation $\xrightarrow{\text{gc}}$, which filters out unreachable heap elements and renames the addresses.

$$x \xrightarrow{\text{gc}} y \quad = \quad (\text{filter } x) \xrightarrow{\text{translate}} y$$

3.2   Abstract Implementation – L2

Our first refinement is to split the single-step implementation of garbage collection from L1 into a sequence of small step updates, and prove that the transitive closure of this step update implements L1. The step relation $\xrightarrow{\text{step}}$ is defined, below, using three rules that operate over a state which consists of:

h — the heap, a finite partial mapping, mentioned above for L1,
x — address set: completely processed heap elements,
y — address set: moved elements with pointers to not-yet-moved elements,
z — address set: elements that are still to be moved,
f — a function which records where elements have been moved: $\mathbb{N} \to \mathbb{N}$

The main operation performed by the collector is to move an element $a \in z$ to a new unused location $b \notin \text{domain } h$. The source and target location must not have been part of earlier move operations, i.e. we must have $f(a) = a \wedge f(b) = b$. The new address b is inserted into the set of moved but not complete elements y, the addresses as stored at $h(a)$ are inserted into the set of addresses to be moved z and the swap of addresses $a \leftrightarrow b$ is recorded in function f.

$$\frac{a \in z \ \wedge \ b \notin \text{domain } h \ \wedge \ f(a) = a \ \wedge \ f(b) = b \ \wedge \ h(a) = (as, d)}{(h, x, y, z, f) \xrightarrow{\text{step}} (h[b \mapsto (as, d)] - \{a\}, x, y \cup \{b\}, z \cup \text{set } as, f[a \mapsto b][b \mapsto a])}$$

Addresses a that have been moved, i.e. for which $f(a) \neq a$, but which are still in the set of addresses that are to be moved z can be deleted from set z.

$$\frac{a \in z \ \wedge \ f(a) \neq a}{(h, x, y, z, f) \xrightarrow{\text{step}} (h, x, y, z - \{a\}, f)}$$

Once all of the addresses as, stored at some heap location $a \in y$, have been removed from set z, i.e. set $as \cap z = \{\}$, then we can finalise this heap element $h(a)$ by updating the addresses as with mapping f and moving address a from set y to set x.

$$\frac{a \in y \ \wedge \ h(a) = (as, d) \ \wedge \ \text{set } as \cap z = \{\}}{(h, x, y, z, f) \xrightarrow{\text{step}} (h[a \mapsto (\text{map } f \ as, d)], x \cup \{a\}, y - \{a\}, z, f)}$$

Correctness. The formal connection between L1 and L2 is summed up in the following theorem, which states that any execution of the transitive closure of the step relation $\xrightarrow{\text{step}}{}^{*}$, which starts with $x = y = \{\}$ and z initialised to the root addresses and ends in a state $y = z = \{\}$, is in fact a correct execution of the garbage collector $\xrightarrow{\text{gc}}$ defined for L1. The domain of the resulting heap h_2 is restricted to the set of moved addresses x, i.e. $h_2 \lfloor x$.

$$\forall h\ h_2\ roots\ x\ f.$$
$$(h, \{\}, \{\}, \text{set } roots, \text{id}) \xrightarrow{\text{step}}{}^{*} (h_2, x, \{\}, \{\}, f) \wedge \text{ok\_heap}\ (h, roots) \implies$$
$$(h, roots) \xrightarrow{\text{gc}} (h_2 \lfloor x, \text{map } f\ roots)$$

$$\text{where}\quad \text{ok\_heap}\ (h, roots) = \text{pointers } h \cup \text{set } roots \subseteq \text{domain } h$$
$$\text{pointers } h = \{\ x \mid \exists a\ as\ d.\ x \in \text{set } as \wedge h(a) = (as, d)\ \}$$

Invariant. Instead of delving into the details of our proof, we present the invariant inv which allows us to prove the above theorem.

$$\forall x\ s\ t.\ \text{inv } x\ s\ \wedge\ s \xrightarrow{\text{step}} t \implies \text{inv } x\ t$$

The full definition of our invariant is shown in Figure 1. It took approximately one week to get this invariant completely right. We believe that this invariant is sufficiently independent of the lower-level implementations L3, L4, L5 to be of use also in verification proofs of significantly different versions of L3, L4 and L5. A complete understanding of the invariant is not necessary to follow the rest of this paper. However, for those who are interested: line 0 defines an abbreviation *old* to denote the set of addresses that were originally the domain of h; line 1 states that x and y are disjoint and that f must be its own inverse; line 2 states that all pointers from within h restricted to addresses x must point to heap elements in x or y; line 3 ensures that all pointers outside of h restricted to x, i.e. inside h restricted to the complement of x, are in the set of *old* addresses; line 4 guarantees that elements from x, y and z are reachable; lines 5-6 state

$$\text{inv } (h_0, roots)\ (h, x, y, z, f) =$$

0	let $old = (\text{domain } h \cup \{\ a \mid f(a) \neq a\ \}) - (x \cup y)$ in
1	$(x \cap y = \{\}) \wedge (f \circ f = \text{id}) \wedge$
2	pointers $(h \lfloor x) \subseteq x \cup y \wedge$
3	pointers $(h \lfloor x^c) \subseteq old \wedge$
4	pointers $(h \lfloor y) \cup \text{set } roots \subseteq \text{image } f\ (x \cup y) \cup z \subseteq \text{reach } (h_0, roots) \wedge$
5	$(\forall a.\ a \in z \implies \text{if } f(a) = a \text{ then } a \in old \text{ else } f(a) \in x \cup y) \wedge$
6	$(\forall a.\ f(a) \neq a \implies \neg(a \in x \cup y \iff f(a) \in x \cup y)) \wedge$
7	$(\forall a.\ a \in x \cup y \iff f(a) \neq a \wedge a \in \text{domain } h) \wedge$
8	domain $h = \text{image } f\ (\text{domain } h_0) \wedge$
9	$(\forall a\ as\ d.\ f(a) \in \text{domain } h \wedge h(f(a)) = (as, d) \implies$
	$\qquad h_0(a) = \text{if } f(a) \in x \text{ then } (\text{map } f\ as, d) \text{ else } (as, d)$

Fig. 1. The invariant used for proving a connection between L1 and L2

when f is allowed to point into $x \cup y$; line 7 states that $x \cup y$ is the set of new addresses; lines 8-9 ensure that f relates h to h_0.

Our proofs using this invariant are relatively small, the proof connecting L1 and L2 is approximately 300 lines long. We achieve this brevity by stating the invariant in terms of sets and set operations, which leads to subgoals that are easily discharged using a standard first-order prover [10].

3.3   Implementation with Memory – L3

The next refinement introduces a memory which makes the memory layout concrete. At this level of abstraction intermediate reference cells, called Ref elements, keep a record of renaming function f in memory alongside data stored in Block elements. The memory, we call it m, is a mapping from $\mathbb{N}$ to a data-type with type constructors:

Block (as, l, d) — a block of length l which contains addresses as and data d
Ref a — a reference cell containing the address a
Emp — an empty location or 'don't care'

Memory m is a correct representation of h and f whenever, for any a:

$$
\begin{aligned}
m(a) &= \text{Block } (h(a)) && \text{if } a \in \text{domain } h \\
m(a) &= \text{Ref } (f(a)) && \text{if } a \notin \text{domain } h \text{ and } f(a) \neq a \\
m(a) &= \text{Emp} && \text{if } a \notin \text{domain } h \text{ and } f(a) = a
\end{aligned}
$$

Here the type variable $data$ in the type of h has been instantiated to $\mathbb{N} \times data$ to make $h(a)$ a triple of type: $(\mathbb{N} + null) \text{ list} \times \mathbb{N} \times data$. We will refer to the above relation between m, h and f as ref_mem (h, f, m).

As mentioned above, each $m(a) = \text{Block } (as, l, data)$ stores a length l. Based on this we have a well-formedness criteria which states that the next l memory locations $m(a+1), m(a+2), \ldots, m(a+l)$ must be Emp.

$$\text{empty } (a, l) \ m \ = \ \forall i \in \mathbb{N}. \ i < l \implies m(a + i + 1) = \text{Emp}$$

We formalise this criterion as an inductively defined relation part_heap $(a, b) \ m \ k$ which states that the memory locations in the range $a...b$ (we write $a...b$ to mean $\{ n \in \mathbb{N} \mid a \leq n \wedge n < b \}$) form a well-formed heap containing blocks of data that have a combined length of k.

$$\frac{}{\text{part\_heap } (a, a) \ m \ 0}$$

$$\frac{m(a) = \text{Block } (as, l, data) \ \wedge \ \text{empty } (a, l) \ m \ \wedge \ \text{part\_heap } (a + l + 1, b) \ m \ k}{\text{part\_heap } (a, b) \ m \ (l + 1 + k)}$$

$$\frac{(m(a) = \text{Ref } i \ \vee \ m(a) = \text{Emp}) \ \wedge \ \text{part\_heap } (a + 1, b) \ m \ k}{\text{part\_heap } (a, b) \ m \ k}$$

Finally, the memory is split into two disjoint spaces, the so called *to-space* and *from-space*. During execution heap blocks are moved from the from-space into

```
move (RHS n, j, m) = (RHS n, j, m)
move (LHS a, j, m)  = case m(a) of
                        Ref i → (LHS i, j, m)
                        | Block (as, l, d) →
                            let m = m[a ↦ Ref j] in
                            let m = m[j ↦ Block (as, l, d)] in
                            (LHS j, j + l + 1, m)

move_roots ([], j, m) = ([], j, m)
move_roots (r::rs, j, m) =
    let (r, j, m) = move (r, j, m) in
    let (rs, j, m) = move_roots (rs, j, m) in
    (r::rs, j, m)

readBlock (Block x) = x
cut (i, j) m = λk. if i ≤ k ∧ k < j then m j else Emp

loop (i, j, m) =
    if i = j then (i, m) else
    let (as, l, d) = readBlock (m i) in
    let (as, j, m) = move_list (as, j, m) in
    let m = m[i ↦ Block (as, l, d)] in
    loop (i + l + 1, j, m)

     collector (roots, b, i, e, b₂, e₂, m) =
1       let (b₂, e₂, b, e) = (b, e, b₂, e₂) in
2       let (roots, j, m) = move_list (roots, b, m) in
3       let (i, m) = loop (b, j, m) in
4       let m = cut (b, i) m in
        (roots, b, i, e, b₂, e₂, m)
```

Fig. 2. Implementation at level L3

the to-space. The to-space consists of locations $b...e$ and the from-space are at locations $b_2...e_2$.

Our implementation of copying collection is listed in Figure 2. The top-level function is called collector. We give a brief overview of how it works here. Line 1 flips the meaning of the to-space and the from-space, i.e. what used to be the to-space is now the from-space. All elements are assumed to lie within the from-space at this stage. Line 2 then moves all heap elements pointed to by root addresses into the to-space. Line 3 starts a loop which moves all other reachable elements from the from-space into the to-space. Finally line 4 overwrites the entire from-space with 'don't care' elements Emp.

Correctness. We have proved that our implementation at level L3, listed in Figure 2, is correct with respect to our definition at level L1, via L2. In order to state this formally, we define ok_mem_heap to assert what suffices as a valid initial/final state of memory as follows. Line 1: the heap must be split into two disjoint semi-heaps, $b \ldots e$ and $b_2 \ldots e_2$, of equal size, with an index i into heap $b \ldots e$. Line 2: the memory inside of $b \ldots i$ must form a well-formed heap and all other parts of the heap are empty. And line 3: the memory m must be related to some well-formed heap h according to ref_mem and ok_heap.

$$\text{ok\_mem\_heap } (h, roots) \ (b, i, e, b_2, e_2, m) =$$

1     $b \leq i \leq e \ \wedge \ b_2 \leq e_2 \ \wedge \ e_2 - b_2 = e - b \ \wedge \ (e < b_2 \vee e_2 < b) \ \wedge$
2     $(\exists k. \ \text{part\_heap } (b, i) \ m \ k) \ \wedge \ (\forall a. \ a \notin b \ldots i \implies m(a) = \text{Emp}) \ \wedge$
3     $\text{ref\_mem } (h, \text{id}) \ m \ \wedge \ \text{ok\_heap } (h, roots)$

The guarantee for the final state is slightly stronger: the final state satisfies part_heap $(b, i) \ m \ (i - b)$. Let precise $(b, i, \ldots, m) = \text{part\_heap } (b, i) \ m \ (i - b)$.

The correctness of our L3 implementation is now stated as the following theorem: for any valid initial state x, which is related to high-level state $(h, roots)$, an execution of collector produces a state y, for which there exists a corresponding abstract heap h_2 such that our top-level definition of garbage collection ($\xrightarrow{\text{gc}}$) relates the initial heap h to the new heap h_2.

$\forall h \ roots \ roots_2 \ x \ y.$
    $\text{ok\_mem\_heap } (h, roots) \ x \ \wedge \ \text{collector } (roots, x) = (roots_2, y) \implies$
    $\exists h_2. \ \text{ok\_mem\_heap } (h_2, roots_2) \ y \ \wedge \ (h, roots) \xrightarrow{\text{gc}} (h_2, roots_2) \ \wedge \ \text{precise } y$

The presence of precise y is important for proving allocation correct, Section 4.

Invariant. We will again not go into details of the correctness proof, but instead only explain the invariant which was used for the proof. Our invariant, called mem_inv, was used for proving the following property of the main loop:

$\text{mem\_inv } (h_0, roots_0, h, f) \ (b, i, j, e, b_2, e_2, m, \text{pointers } (h \!\downarrow\! (i \ldots j))) \ \wedge$
$\text{loop } (i, j, m) = (i_2, m_2) \implies$
$\exists h_2 \ f_2. \ \text{mem\_inv } (h_0, roots_0, h_2, f_2) \ (b, i_2, i_2, e, b_2, e_2, m_2, \{\}) \ \wedge$
$\qquad j \leq i_2 \wedge \forall a. \ f(a) \neq a \implies f_2(a) = f(a)$

The definition of our invariant mem_inv is listed in Figure 3. The main idea behind this invariant should be clear from lines 5 and 6. They state that memory m is a refinement of (h, f) and that (h, f) is related, through the reflexive-transitive closure of $\xrightarrow{\text{step}}$, to an initial state $(h_0, roots_0)$ which satisfies ok_heap. Lines 2–4 are less interesting; they ensure that the memory is correctly organised. Line 1 states that the heap is split into two semi-heaps, and that i and j are indexes in the to-heap.

3.4   Implementation with Concrete Types – L4

The previous refinements layer, called L3, produced an implementation with memory and concrete memory layout of the heap. However, L3 made no commitment to how memory elements, Block and Ref, are to be represented in actual memory. In this layer, called L4, we make all types concrete: addresses and data

$\mathsf{mem\_inv}\ (h_0, roots_0, h, f)\ (b, i, j, e, b_2, e_2, m, z) =$

1   $b \le i \le j \le e \wedge (e < b_2 \vee e_2 < b)\ \wedge$

2   $(\forall a.\ a \notin b_2...e_2 \cup b...j \implies m(a) = \mathsf{Emp})\ \wedge$

3   $\mathsf{part\_heap}\ (b, i)\ m\ (i - b) \wedge \mathsf{part\_heap}\ (i, j)\ m\ (j - i)\ \wedge$

4   $(\exists k.\ \mathsf{part\_heap}\ (b_2, e_2)\ m\ k \wedge k \le e - j)\ \wedge$

5   $\mathsf{ref\_mem}\ (h, f)\ m \wedge \mathsf{ok\_heap}\ (h_0, roots_0)\ \wedge$

6   $(h_0, \{\}, \{\}, \mathsf{set}\ roots_0, \mathsf{id}) \xrightarrow{\mathsf{step}} * (h, \mathsf{domain}\ h \cap (b...i), \mathsf{domain}\ h \cap (i...j), z, f)$

Fig. 3. The invariant which relates implementations L3 with L2

are bit strings and memory is a partial function from machine addresses (aligned 32-bit words) to 32-bit words.

We choose to represent each Block as a sequence of 32-bit words. The header word contains a 22-bit number n which contains the length of the payload (a list of 32-bit words: $w_1, w_2, \ldots, w_n$), an 8-bit field for data called the *tag*, and a 1-bit field b which indicates whether the payload consists of data, in case $b = 0$, or addresses, in case $b = 1$. The header is followed by the payload.

$$[n.tag.1.b], \quad [w_1], \quad [w_2], \quad [w_3], \quad \ldots, \quad [w_n]$$

We also allow data to be stored into 'null-addresses'. A 32-bit word appearing in the place of an address but which is not word-aligned (i.e. not a multiple of four) is considered to be data. The reason for why this works with the abstraction layers above is that we left the type of null addresses as a type variable *null*, as mentioned at the start.

Our garbage collector is implemented at level L4 as a functional program which uses only concrete machine types. An extract of the lengthy implementation is listed in Figure 4, which shows the L4 implementation mx_move of the function move from level L3 (i.e. the code which copies a Block element from the from-heap to the to-heap). The first test, $r_2 \& 3 \ne 0$, tests whether the address is a real address (not a null-address). The second test, $r_4 \& 3 = 0$, checks whether the word that was read from memory is a header of a Block element or a references cell Ref. If the first word is the header of a Block element then we copy over the payload using the tail-recursive function mc_move_loop.

Correctness. The correctness of the L4 implementation is stated concisely in the following theorem: if level L3 state y is related to level L4 state z then an execution of the L3 function collector on y is related to L4 function mc_collector applied to z. The definition of ok_mc_heap will be presented below.

$$\forall x\ y\ z.\ \mathsf{ok\_mc\_heap}\ x\ y\ z \implies \mathsf{ok\_mc\_heap}\ x\ (\mathsf{collector}\ y)\ (\mathsf{mc\_collector}\ z)$$

Invariant. In order to keep our statements and proofs clean and concise even at this low-level of abstraction, we will use some light-weight separation logic [15]

$$\mathsf{mc\_move\_loop}\ (r_2, r_3, r_4, g) =$$
if $r_4 = 0$ then (r_2, r_3, r_4, g) else
let $r_5 = g(r_2)$ in
let $r_4 = r_4 - 1$ in
let $r_2 = r_2 + 4$ in
let $g = g[r_3 \mapsto r_5]$ in
let $r_3 = r_3 + 4$ in
$\quad\mathsf{mc\_move\_loop}\ (r_2, r_3, r_4, g)$

$$\mathsf{mc\_move}\ (r_1, r_2, r_3, g) =$$
if $(r_2 \,\&\, 3 \neq 0)$ then (r_1, r_3, g) else
let $r_4 = g(r_2)$ in
if $r_4 \,\&\, 3 = 0$ then
$\quad$let $g = g[r_1 \mapsto r_4]$ in
$\quad(r_1, r_3, g)$
else
$\quad$let $g = g[r_1 \mapsto r_3]$ in
$\quad$let $g = g[r_3 \mapsto r_4]$ in
$\quad$let $g = g[r_2 \mapsto r_3]$ in
$\quad$let $r_4 = r_4 \gg 10$ in
$\quad$let $r_3 = r_3 + 4$ in
$\quad$let $r_2 = r_2 + 4$ in
$\quad$let $(r_2, r_3, r_4, g) = \mathsf{mc\_move\_loop}\ (r_2, r_3, r_4, g)$ in
$\quad(r_1, r_3, g)$

Fig. 4. The invariant used for proving a connection between L1 and L2

for memory assertions. We need the separating conjunction $*$, which we define over sets: $p * q$ is true for set s if s can be partitioned into two sets t and u such that p holds for t and q holds for u.

$$(p * q)\ s \quad = \quad \exists t\ u.\ p\ t\ \wedge\ q\ u\ \wedge\ t \cup u = s\ \wedge\ t \cap u = \{\}$$

Now let fun2set map a partial function to a set of pairs, let one (x, y) assert the value of a pair in such a set, and let emp assert that the set is empty:

$$
\begin{aligned}
\mathsf{fun2set}\ g &= \{\ (a, g(a)) \mid a \in \mathsf{domain}\ g\ \} \\
\mathsf{one}\ (x, y) &= \lambda s.\ (s = \{(x, y)\}) \\
\mathsf{emp} &= \lambda s.\ (s = \{\}) \\
\langle b \rangle &= \lambda s.\ (s = \{\}) \wedge b
\end{aligned}
$$

With these we can define ref, in Figure 5, which allows us to state that segments of L3 memory m are present in L4 memory g, e.g. the following line states that memory locations $b...e$ and $b_2...e_2$ from memory m are represented correctly in L4 memory g, i.e. both halves of the heap are correctly represented.

$$(\mathsf{ref}\ (b, e)\ m\ *\ \mathsf{ref}\ (b_2, e_2)\ m\ *\ p)\ (\mathsf{fun2set}\ g)$$

$$\text{ref\_heap\_addr (RHS } n) \; = \; 2 \times n + 1$$
$$\text{ref\_heap\_addr (LHS } a) \; = \; 4 \times a$$

$$\text{one\_list } a \; [] \; = \; \text{emp}$$
$$\text{one\_list } a \; (x :: xs) \; = \; \text{one } (a, x) \; * \; \text{one\_list } (a{+}4) \; xs$$

$$\text{header } (n, b, tag) \; = \; 1024 \times n + 4 \times tag + 2 + (\text{if } b \text{ then } 1 \text{ else } 0)$$

$$\text{ref\_aux } a \; \text{Emp} \; = \; \exists x. \; \text{one } (a, x)$$
$$\text{ref\_aux } a \; (\text{Ref } n) \; = \; \text{one } (a, 4 \times n)$$
$$\text{ref\_aux } a \; (\text{Block } (xs, l, (tag, b, ys))) \; =$$
$$\quad \text{let } zs = (\text{if } b \text{ then map ref\_heap\_addr } xs \text{ else } ys) \text{ in}$$
$$\qquad \text{one } (a, \text{header } (\text{length } zs, b, tag)) \; * \; \text{one\_list } (a{+}4) \; zs$$

$$\text{ref\_inc } a \; \text{Emp} \; = \; 1$$
$$\text{ref\_inc } a \; (\text{Ref } n) \; = \; 1$$
$$\text{ref\_inc } a \; (\text{Block } (xs, l, d)) \; = \; 1 + l$$

$$\text{ref } (a, e) \; m \; =$$
$$\quad \text{if } e \leq a \text{ then } \langle a = e \rangle \text{ else}$$
$$\qquad \text{ref\_aux } (4 \times a) \; (m(a)) \; * \; \text{ref } (a{+}\text{ref\_inc } (m(a)), e) \; m$$

Fig. 5. Part of the invariant which relates L3 to L4

The main part of each proof is to show that this type of ref-relationship is maintained between m and g throughout execution of the two implementations.

There is still a further well-formedness criteria for memory m that needs to be mentioned: all lists in Block elements must be of reasonable size and the length field l must correspond to the actual payload:

$$\text{ok\_memory } m =$$
$$\quad \forall a \; l \; xs \; b \; t \; ys.$$
$$\qquad m(a) = \text{Block } (xs, l, (b, t, ys)) \implies$$
$$\qquad\quad \text{length } ys < 2^{22} \wedge \text{length } xs < 2^{22} \wedge$$
$$\qquad\quad \text{if } t \text{ then } l = \text{length } xs \text{ else } l = \text{length } ys \wedge xs = []$$

3.5   Machine-Code Implementations – L5

The final leap from low-level functional implementations (L4) to concrete machine code (L5) would be very tedious to prove manually. To avoid a manual proof we use a previously developed compiler to produce correct machine code automatically from the functional implementation at level L4.

Our compiler is not verified, but instead produces a proof for each compilation run, i.e. the compiler steers the theorem prover to a proof which certifies that the input function is correctly executed by the generated machine code. For example, the following theorem is produced when the compiler compiles function mc_move from Figure 4 into ARM machine code. This theorem certifies that any execution of the machine code which starts at a state where (r_1, r_2, r_3, g) describes the values of registers 1, 2, 3 and memory, terminates in a state where

```
        tst r2, #3              test ecx, 3            andi. 0, 2, 3
        bne L0                  jne L0                 bne L0
        ldr r4, [r2]            mov ebx, [ecx]         lwz 4, 0(2)
        tst r4, #3              test ebx, 3            andi. 0, 4, 3
        streq r4, [r1]          jne L2                 bne L2
        beq L0                  mov [eax], ebx         stw 4, 0(1)
        str r3, [r1]            jmp L0                 b L0
        str r4, [r3]        L2: mov [eax], edx     L2: stw 3, 0(1)
        str r3, [r2], #4        mov [edx], ebx         stw 4, 0(3)
        mov r4, r4, LSR #10     mov [ecx], edx         stw 3, 0(2)
        add r3, r3, #4          shr ebx, 10            srawi 4, 4, 10
    L1: cmp r4, #0              add edx, 4             addi 3, 3, 4
        beq L0                  add ecx, 4             addi 2, 2, 4
        ldr r5, [r2]        L1: cmp ebx, 0         L1: cmplwi 4,0
        sub r4, r4, #1          je L0                  beq L0
        add r2, r2, #4          mov edi, [ecx]         lwz 5, 0(2)
        str r5, [r3]            dec ebx                addi 4, 4, -1
        add r3, r3, #4          add ecx, 4             addi 2, 2, 4
        b L1                    mov [edx], edi         stw 5, 0(3)
    L0:                         add edx, 4             addi 3, 3, 4
                                jmp L1                 b L1
                            L0:                    L0:
```

Fig. 6. Verified ARM, x86 and PowerPC code, respectively, for mc_move from Figure 4

mc_move (r_1, r_2, r_3, g) accurately describes the value of registers 1, 3 and memory. This is stated in terms of a machine-code Hoare triple [14], and conditioned on an automatically generated precondition mc_move_pre.

$\forall r_1 \ r_2 \ r_3 \ g \ p.$
    mc_move_pre $(r_1, r_2, r_3, g) \implies$
    { r1 r_1 * r2 r_2 * r3 r_3 * r4 _ * r5 _ * memory g * s * pc p }
    p : E3120003 1A000010 E5924000 E3140003 05814000 0A00000C E5813000
        E5834000 E5823000 E1A04524 E2833004 E2822004 E3540000 15925000
        12444001 12822004 15835000 12833004 1AFFFFF8
    { let (r_1, r_3, g) = mc_move (r_1, r_2, r_3, g) in
      r1 r_1 * r2 _ * r3 r_3 * r4 _ * r5 _ * memory g * s * pc $(p+76)$ }

We have used our proof-producing compiler to compile the top-level L4 function mc_collector into ARM, x86 and PowerPC code. Each of the resulting certificate theorems are conditioned on a precondition mc_collector_pre. This precondition simply asserts that each memory access was done properly, no load/store to unaligned addresses. We have proved that these preconditions are always met:

$$\forall x \ y \ z. \ \text{ok\_mc\_heap} \ x \ y \ z \implies \text{mc\_collector\_pre} \ z$$

4 Using the Verified Garbage Collectors

In this section we will briefly explain how the verified garbage collectors have been used as components in the construction of verified interpreters for Lisp [13].

For our Lisp case study, we define allocation of a cons cell as follows at abstraction level L3. Note that it is tempting to define allocate_cons as recursive function to avoid writing has_space twice, but that would result in an unsatisfactory infinite loop when allocation runs out of memory (and allow for a trick if only partial correctness is to be proved).

$$\text{has\_space } (roots, b, i, e, b_2, e_2, m) \;=\; 3 \le e - i$$
$$\text{alloc\_fail } (r_1 :: r_2 :: roots, b, i, e, b_2, e_2, m) \;=\; (\text{nil} :: r_2 :: roots, b, i, e, b_2, e_2, m)$$
$$\text{alloc\_ok } (r_1 :: r_2 :: roots, b, i, e, b_2, e_2, m) \;=$$
$$(\text{LHS } i :: r_2 :: roots, b, i{+}3, e, b_2, e_2, m[i \mapsto \text{Block } ([r_1, r_2], 2, (\text{T}, 0, []))])$$

$$\text{allocate\_cons } state \;=$$
$$\quad \text{if has\_space } state \text{ then alloc\_ok } state \text{ else}$$
$$\quad\quad \text{let } state = \text{collector } state \text{ in}$$
$$\quad\quad\quad \text{if has\_space } state \text{ then alloc\_ok } state \text{ else alloc\_fail } state$$

We write a similar L4 implementation and from these generate L5 implementations. The correctness theorems used in the Lisp case study for cons allocation are stated as follows. The following theorems use a heap assertion lisp which states that Lisp s-expressions $v_1 \ldots v_6$ are stored in a heap with a capacity for l cons cells. Allocation of a new cons cell is guaranteed to be successful if the size of the six root s-expressions is strictly less than the heap limit l:

$$\text{size } v_1 + \text{size } v_2 + \text{size } v_3 + \text{size } v_4 + \text{size } v_5 + \text{size } v_6 < l \;\Rightarrow$$
$$\{ \text{ lisp } (v_1, v_2, v_3, v_4, v_5, v_6, l) * \text{pc } p \}$$
$$p : \text{E50A3018 E50A4014 E50A5010 E50A600C } \ldots \text{ E51A8004 E51A7008}$$
$$\{ \text{ lisp } (\text{cons } v_1\, v_2, v_2, v_3, v_4, v_5, v_6, l) * \text{pc } (p + 324) \}$$

We also have a different theorem describing all executions: all executions of the allocator will terminate either in a successful state, or jump to a special program point (lisp_out_of_memory) which generates an error message.

$$\{ \text{ lisp } (v_1, v_2, v_3, v_4, v_5, v_6, l) * \text{pc } p \}$$
$$p : \text{E50A3018 E50A4014 E50A5010 E50A600C } \ldots \text{ E51A8004 E51A7008}$$
$$\{ \text{ lisp } (\text{cons } v_1\, v_2, v_2, v_3, v_4, v_5, v_6, l) * \text{pc } (p + 324) \vee \text{lisp\_out\_of\_memory} \}$$

5 Conclusions and Future Work

We aimed for a clear, understandable and reusable verification. By structuring the verification as a sequence of refinements, our work separates reasoning about the algorithm from implementation level details and as a result made each part of the proof (refinement step) clearly focused on separate aspects of the verification. The fact that only the lowest level of abstraction (L5) is tied to specific programming logics and program semantics ought to aid proof reuse.

Why did we not verify a generational garbage collector? The short answer is that we did not need one. However, we believe a generational collector is only a refinement step away (from implementation L3): the idea is to treat all pointers to previous generations as if they were pure data stored in null pointers.

Acknowledgements. I would like to thank Mike Gordon and the anonymous reviewers for helpful suggestions regarding presentation. This work was partially supported by EPSRC Research Grant EP/G007411/1.

References

1. Benton, N.: Abstracting allocation: The new new thing. In: Ésik, Z. (ed.) CSL 2006. LNCS, vol. 4207, pp. 182–196. Springer, Heidelberg (2006)
2. Benton, N.: Machine obstructed proof (abstract). In: ACM SIGPLAN Workshop on Mechanizing Metatheory (2006)
3. Birkedal, L., Torp-Smith, N., Reynolds, J.: Local reasoning about a copying garbage collector. In: Principles of programming languages (POPL). ACM, New York (2004)
4. Böhme, S., Weber, T.: Fast LCF-style proof reconstruction for Z3. In: Theorem Proving in Higher Order Logics (TPHOLs), Springer, Heidelberg (to appear, 2010)
5. Dijkstra, E.W., Lamport, L., Martin, A.J., Scholten, C.S., Steffens, E.F.M.: On-the-fly garbage collection: an exercise in cooperation. Commun. ACM 21(11), 966–975 (1978)
6. Gonthier, G.: Verifying the safety of a practical concurrent garbage collector. In: Alur, R., Henzinger, T.A. (eds.) CAV 1996. LNCS, vol. 1102, pp. 462–465. Springer, Heidelberg (1996)
7. Gries, D.: An exercise in proving parallel programs correct. Commun. ACM 20(12), 921–930 (1977)
8. Guttman, J., Ramsdell, J., Wand, M.: VLISP: A verified implementation of Scheme. Lisp and Symbolic Computation 8(1/2), 5–32 (1995)
9. Hawblitzel, C., Petrank, E.: Automated verification of practical garbage collectors. In: Principles of Programming Languages (POPL). ACM, New York (2009)
10. Hurd, J.: First-order proof tactics in higher-order logic theorem provers. In: Design and Application of Strategies/Tactics in Higher Order Logics (STRATA 2003), NASA/CP-2003-212448 in NASA Technical Reports, pp. 56–68 (2003)
11. Jackson, P.B.: Verifying a garbage collection algorithm. In: Grundy, J., Newey, M. (eds.) TPHOLs 1998. LNCS, vol. 1479, pp. 225–244. Springer, Heidelberg (1998)
12. McCreight, A., Shao, Z., Lin, C., Li, L.: A general framework for certifying garbage collectors and their mutators. In: Programming Language Design and Implementation (PLDI), pp. 468–479. ACM, New York (2007)
13. Myreen, M.O., Gordon, M.J.C.: Verified LISP implementations on ARM, x86 and PowerPC. In: Urban, C. (ed.) TPHOLs 2009. LNCS, vol. 5674, pp. 359–374. Springer, Heidelberg (2009)
14. Myreen, M.O., Slind, K., Gordon, M.J.C.: Machine-code verification for multiple architectures – An application of decompilation into logic. In: Formal Methods in Computer Aided Design (FMCAD). IEEE, Los Alamitos (2008)
15. Reynolds, J.: Separation logic: A logic for shared mutable data structures. In: Logic in Computer Science (LICS). IEEE Computer Society, Los Alamitos (2002)
16. Russinoff, D.M.: A mechanically verified incremental garbage collector. Formal Asp. Comput. 6(4), 359–390 (1994)

To `Goto` Where No Statement Has Gone Before

Mike Barnett and K. Rustan M. Leino

Microsoft Research, Redmond, WA, USA
{mbarnett,leino}@microsoft.com

Abstract. This paper presents a method for deriving an expression from the low-level code compiled from an expression in a high-level language. The input is the low-level code represented as blocks of code connected by goto statements, *i.e.*, a control flow graph (CFG). The derived expression is in a form that can be used as input to an automatic theorem prover. The method is useful for program verification systems that take as input both programs and specifications after they have been compiled from a high-level language. This is the case for systems that encode specifications in an existing programming language and do not have a special compiler. The method always produces an expression, unlike the heuristics for decompilation which may fail. It is efficient: the resulting expression is linear in the size of the CFG by maintaining all sharing of subgraphs.

0   Introduction

A program verifier checks that a given program satisfies its specifications. Some programming languages such as Eiffel [16], Java with JML [12], or Spec# [3] provide the programmer a nice syntax for writing the specifications in the source text. This has many advantages, *e.g.*, that programmers are immediately aware of the relationship between their code and its specification. However, in a multi-language platform like .NET, one would like to have one program verifier that works for any language, regardless of what special syntax, if any, each language may provide. In this paper, we consider one issue that arises in such a multi-language setting.

Code Contracts for .NET [1] is a library-based framework for writing specifications in .NET code. Programmers use the methods from the contract library to write specifications within their program (written in any .NET language, like C#, Visual Basic, or F#) as stylized method calls at the beginning of a method's body. For example, Figure 0 shows a method with a postcondition, expressed as a call to `Contract.Ensures`. The regular .NET compiler for the source program is invoked to produce bytecode. Code Contracts then has several tools which operate on the resulting bytecode, for example the runtime checker rewrites the bytecode to move the evaluation of postconditions to all of the method body's exit points.

We are connecting an existing program verifier to the Code Contracts framework by translating the compiled bytecode into an intermediate verification language, Boogie 2 [0,15,13], and then generating verification conditions for a theorem prover (we primarily use the SMT solver Z3 [7]). Source-program uses of Code Contracts show up in the bytecode as calls to the contract methods, preceded by a snippet of code that evaluates the arguments. For the example in Figure 0, the bytecode computes the postcondition and then passes that boolean value as the argument to `Contract.Ensures`.

G.T. Leavens, P. O'Hearn, and S.K. Rajamani (Eds.): VSTTE 2010, LNCS 6217, pp. 157–168, 2010.
© Springer-Verlag Berlin Heidelberg 2010

Therefore, *expressions* in the source language become *code*. In general, the code is a linearized form of a DAG, with a high degree of sharing.

The problem is that the verification conditions needed by the theorem prover must be first-order formulas. While there are various contexts in which this can be avoided, the body of a quantifier *must* be a genuine expression, not code.

We propose to convert the code representing a boolean expression back into a genuine expression in two steps. First, our program verifier identifies the code snippets in the bytecode and converts them into *code expressions* of the form

$$\{\{ \quad \textbf{var } b; \ S \ ; \ \textbf{return } e \quad \}\}$$

where S denotes some code in the intermediate verification language, e denotes the value returned by the code expression, and b denotes a list of local variables that may be used in S and e. Defining code expressions in the intermediate verification language has the advantage that we can make use of facilities in the intermediate verification language that expect expressions, like pre- and postconditions and bodies of logical quantifiers.

Second, we define the meaning of a code expression in terms of a first-order formula. We show how to construct this formula from the code expression. The resulting formula is "efficient": it maintains the sharing in the DAG, and is thus linear in the size of the control-flow graph of the code expression.

In this paper, we also give some healthiness conditions for what it means to interpret code as a genuine expression.

1   The Starting Point

An example program in the C# programming language using Code Contracts is shown in Figure 0. The example shows a simple method that has a postcondition (encoded using the method `Contract.Ensures`). It states that the return value (encoded with `Contract.Result`) has the same length as the parameter A and that each element is the division of k by the corresponding element of A, except in the case that the element is zero[0]. In order to state that, it uses a quantifier: the method `Contract.Forall` is given three arguments, an inclusive lower bound, an exclusive upper bound, and an *anonymous delegate*. The latter is the .NET form for a *lambda expression*, *i.e.*, a functional value. The type of `Forall` restricts the function to take a single argument of type **int** and return a boolean[1]. In the example, the function's parameter is named i. In traditional notation, the function would be written as $(\lambda \, i : int \, . \, A[i] \neq 0 \Rightarrow result[i] = k/A[i])$. Anonymous delegates are lexically scoped and "capture" references, such as to the method's parameter A.

---

[0] The method `Contract.Result` is generic and must be instantiated since its type cannot be inferred from its arguments because it is a nullary method (hence the open-close parentheses). Type instantiation is indicated by referring to the return type of the method, **int[]**, within angled brackets. This shows why it is so nice to have a language provide surface syntax for specifications!

[1] There is another version of `Forall` that allows a more general predicate.

```
using System.Diagnostics.Contracts;
public class C {

  public int[] M(int[] A, int k) {
    Contract.Ensures(
      Contract.Result<int[]>().Length == A.Length &&
      Contract.ForAll(
        0, Contract.Result<int[]>().Length,
        i => A[i] == 0 || Contract.Result<int[]>()[i] == k/A[i]
      )
    );
    ...
  }
}
```

Fig. 0. A portion of a C# program using Code Contracts

The source-language compiler (in this case the C# compiler) is used to compile the program to MSIL. Since we do not have control over the C# compiler, the specifications are compiled into MSIL just as the "real" program is. In particular, short-circuit boolean expressions are compiled into *code expressions*. These are a linearized DAG of basic blocks with assignment statements and goto statements where the value of the boolean expression is left on the stack. For the current example, Figure 1 shows the MSIL that the anonymous delegate in Figure 0 compiles into. A more readable form written in C# is:

```
bool Anonymous(int i) {
  bool b;
  if (A[i] == 0) goto L_0024;
  if (result[i] == k/A[i]) goto L_0024;
  b := false;
  goto L_0028;
  L_0024: b := true;
  L_0028: return b;
}
```

2   The Midpoint: Boogie

An intermediate verification language serves a purpose analogous to that of an intermediate representation in a compiler: it separates the concerns of defining source-language semantics from the concerns of generating formulas for a theorem prover. Many program verifiers are built around an architecture that uses an intermediate verification language (*e.g.*, [0,10,5]).

```
.method public hidebysig instance bool <M>b__0(int32 i) cil managed
{
  .maxstack 4
  .locals init (
    [0] bool CS$1$0000)
  L_0000: ldarg.0
  L_0001: ldfld int32[] C/<>c__DisplayClass1::A
  L_0006: ldarg.1
  L_0007: ldelem.i4
  L_0008: brfalse.s L_0024
  L_000a: call !!0 [Microsoft.Contracts]System.Diagnostics.Contracts.Contract::Result<int32[]>()
  L_000f: ldarg.1
  L_0010: ldelem.i4
  L_0011: ldarg.0
  L_0012: ldfld int32 C/<>c__DisplayClass1::k
  L_0017: ldarg.0
  L_0018: ldfld int32[] C/<>c__DisplayClass1::A
  L_001d: ldarg.1
  L_001e: ldelem.i4
  L_001f: div
  L_0020: ceq
  L_0022: br.s L_0025
  L_0024: ldc.i4.1
  L_0025: stloc.0
  L_0026: br.s L_0028
  L_0028: ldloc.0
  L_0029: ret
}
```

Fig. 1. The bytecode compiled from the body of the anonymous delegate in Figure 0. The labels on each line are the byte offsets of the instructions. The code from offset 0x0 to 0x7 represents the left disjunct $A[i] == 0$. The right disjunct, Contract.Result<**int**[]>()[i] == k/A[i], is computed in the code from offset 0x0a to 0x20. "arg 0" refers to **this**, the implicit receiver and "arg 1" refers to the parameter i. There is an implicit receiver because the captured variables in an anonymous delegate become fields on a compiler-generated class in order to retain the necessary state in between invocations. In this case, there are fields for A and k.

2.0   Previously...

We reiterate the language from [2], which forms the core of the Boogie intermediate verification language:

$$
\begin{array}{lll}
\textit{Program} & ::= & \textit{Block}^+ \\
\textit{Block} & ::= & \textit{BlockId} \; : \; \textit{Stmt} \; ; \; \textit{Goto} \\
\textit{Stmt} & ::= & \textit{VarId} := \textit{Expr} \mid \textbf{havoc } \textit{VarId} \\
& & \mid \; \textit{Stmt} \; ; \; \textit{Stmt} \mid \textbf{skip} \\
& & \mid \; \textbf{assert } \textit{Expr} \mid \textbf{assume } \textit{Expr} \\
\textit{Goto} & ::= & \textbf{goto } \textit{BlockId}^*
\end{array}
$$

In our core language, a program consists of a set of basic blocks, where the unstructured control flow between blocks is given by goto statements. A goto with multiple target labels gives rise to a non-deterministic choice; a goto with no target labels gives rise to normal termination. The *BlockId*'s listed in a goto statement are the *successors* of the block.

The semantics of the core language is defined over *traces*, *i.e.*, sequences of program states. Each finite trace either terminates normally or ends in an error. There are two assignment statements: $x := e$ sets variable x to the value of expression e, and **havoc** x sets x to an arbitrary value. Semi-colon is the usual sequential composition of statements, and **skip**, which is the unit element of semi-colon, terminates normally without changing the state. The assert statement **assert** e behaves as **skip** if e evaluates to *true*; otherwise, it causes the trace to end in an error (we say the trace *goes wrong*). The assume statement **assume** e is a *partial command* [18]: it behaves as **skip** if e evaluates to *true*; otherwise, it leads to no traces at all. The assume statement is thus used to describe which traces are feasible.

The normally terminating traces of a block are extended with the traces of the block's successors.

Note that the core language does not have a method call as a primitive statement; a method call is encoded as a sequence of statements that assert the method's precondition, use havoc statements to set the locations that the method may modify to an arbitrary value, and then assume the method's postcondition.

Verification condition generation proceeds by first converting the program into *passive form*, where loops are cut (see [2]) and where all assignment statements are replaced by assumptions expressed over a single-assignment form of the program variables [11]. For example, a statement

$$x := y \; ; \; x := x + y \; ; \; \textbf{assert } y < x$$

is converted into a passive form like

$$\textbf{assume } x_1 = y_0 \; ; \; \textbf{assume } x_2 = x_1 + y_0 \; ; \; \textbf{assert } y_0 < x_2$$

where y_0, x_1, and x_2 are fresh variables.

The passive program is turned into a formula via *weakest preconditions* [9]. For any passive statement S and any predicate Q characterizing a set of post-states of S, $wp[\![S, Q]\!]$ is a predicate that characterizes those pre-states from which execution of S will not go wrong and will end in a state described by Q. The weakest-precondition equations for passive statements are as follows:

$$
\begin{array}{lcl}
wp[\![\textbf{skip}, Q]\!] & = & Q \\
wp[\![S \; ; \; T, \; Q]\!] & = & wp[\![S, wp[\![T, Q]\!]]\!] \\
wp[\![\textbf{assert } e, Q]\!] & = & e \wedge Q \\
wp[\![\textbf{assume } e, Q]\!] & = & e \Rightarrow Q
\end{array}
$$

In each of the last two equations, the occurrence of e on the left-hand side is an expression in Boogie, whereas its occurrence on the right-hand side must be an expression in the input language of the theorem prover. These expressions are usually so similar that we do not mind glossing over this difference; however, for code expressions this makes an important difference.

To deal with (unstructured) control flow, we introduce a variable A_{ok} for every block labeled A, and we define A_{ok} to be *true* iff no execution from A goes wrong [2]. In particular, for any block A with body S and successors $Succ(A)$, we define

$$A_{ok} \;=\; wp[\![S, \bigwedge_{B \in Succ(A)} B_{ok}]\!]$$

2.1 Adding Code Expressions to Boogie

We extend the core language to include code expressions. Previously [2], we left implicit the definition of *Expr* (and its implementation did not allow code expressions). Now, we explicitly extend the definition of *Expr* to include them:

Expr	::=	*Expr op Expr* | *MethodCall* | *CodeExpr*
CodeExpr	::=	{{ *LocalDecl* CodeBlock$^+$* }}
LocalDecl	::=	*VarId* : *Type*
CodeBlock	::=	*BlockId* : *Stmt* ; *Transfer*
Transfer	::=	*Goto* | *Return*
Return	::=	**return** *Expr*

We need each code expression to be a self-contained unit. In order to achieve that, we assume that each code expression is *well-formed* by meeting the following conditions:

- A *transfer command* comprising a goto statement has at least one successor.
- All successors are other blocks within the code expression.
- No block in a code expression is a successor of any block not in the code expression.
- The graph induced on the blocks by the successor relation is acyclic.
- All paths within the code expression end with a block whose transfer command comprises a return statement.

We also assume each code expression has a first block labeled "*Start*", which is the entry point to the code expression.

2.2 When Is Code an Expression?

It is one thing to syntactically allow code expressions in Boogie, but we still must consider when a code expression really does represent a genuine expression, *i.e.*, when we are justified in using the same semantics for them as for genuine expressions. Thus the question of this section: when can we look at a chunk of code and consider it a genuine expression?

It must meet four requirements:

0. It must be deterministic. (All branches are mutually exclusive.)
1. It must be total in terms of not being a partial command.
2. It must be total, in the "expression sense". That is, its execution does not go wrong (*i.e.*, failing an assertion, like dereferencing *null* or dividing by zero).
3. It must not have any side effects (on variables other than the local variables it introduces).

In our setting, the first two requirements are satisfied since our code expressions are the output of a .NET compiler. That is, .NET bytecode (IL) obeys Dijkstra's "Law of the Excluded Miracle" [9] and does not contain any non-deterministic features. (If we were to allow code expressions to contain partial commands, then our scheme derives the value *true* in states where the partiality comes into play.)

We enforce the third requirement by omitting all assertions within a code expression. Such *definedness checks*, *e.g.*, that a divisor is non-zero, are enforced by many verifiers [14] for expressions separately from the expressions themselves by inserting extra checks which guarantee that the expression is total.

The fourth requirement is enforced by making sure that all assignment statements within a code expression are to its local variables and that all method calls are to *pure methods*, *i.e.*, methods whose Boogie encoding do not have any modifies clauses.

3   The Endpoint: Deriving an Expression from Code

But now we have a mismatch: we have code expressions in places where they need to be translated to expressions in the prover's language. We either need a new definition for the weakest precondition when an expression is a code expression or we need a translation scheme that produces a genuine expression from a code expression.

We take the latter approach and, for now, restrict ourselves to *boolean* code expressions, *i.e.*, the value they return is a boolean. For boolean code expressions that meet the requirements in Section 2.2, we compute an equivalent boolean expression (that does not contain any code expressions). For the code expression

$$\{\{ \quad \textbf{var } b; \quad S \; ; \quad \textbf{return } e \quad \}\}$$

the equivalent boolean expression is

$$(\forall b \bullet \; wp[\![S, e]\!] \,) \tag{0}$$

This presumes that S is a structured command, *i.e.*, control flows from S to the return statement. When the code expression is unstructured, then we form the block equations as in Section 2.0. The only difference is that for any block A whose transfer statement comprises a return statement **return** e, we define the block equation as:

$$A_{ok} \quad = \quad wp[\![S, e]\!]$$

Because code expressions are acyclic, we can avoid having to quantify over the block variables by defining them via let-expressions. (Z3 supports the SMT-LIB format [19], which allows let-expressions in the verification condition.)

So the body of the anonymous delegate can be represented in Boogie as:

```
{{  b : bool;
Start : skip ; goto L0, L1;
L0 : assume A[i] = 0 ; goto L2;
L1 : assume A[i] ≠ 0 ; goto L3, L4;
L2 : b := true ; goto L5;
L3 : assume result[i] = k/A[i] ; goto L2;
L4 : assume result[i] ≠ k/A[i] ; b := false ; goto L5;
L5 : skip ; return b;  }}
```

We first convert it into passive form by introducing a new *incarnation* of a variable each time it is assigned. Join points (*e.g.*, $L5$) also produce a new incarnation with equations pushed into each predecessor relating the value of the variable in that branch with that of the join point's incarnation.

$\{\{\ b:$ **bool**;
$Start$: **skip** ; **goto** $L0, L1$;
$L0$: **assume** $A[i] = 0$; **goto** $L2$;
$L1$: **assume** $A[i] \neq 0$; **goto** $L3, L4$;
$L2$: **assume** $b_0 = true$; **assume** $b_2 = b_0$; **goto** $L5$;
$L3$: **assume** $result[i] = k/A[i]$; **goto** $L2$;
$L4$: **assume** $result[i] \neq k/A[i]$; **assume** $b_1 = false$; **assume** $b_2 = b_1$; **goto** $L5$;
$L5$: **skip** ; **return** b_2; $\}\}$

Then the block equations, written as let-expressions, are:

$$
\begin{array}{llll}
\textbf{let } L5_{ok} & = & wp[\![\textbf{skip}, b_2]\!] & \textbf{in} \\
\textbf{let } L2_{ok} & = & wp[\![\textbf{assume } b_0 = true \text{ ; } \textbf{assume } b_2 = b_0, L5_{ok}]\!] & \textbf{in} \\
\textbf{let } L3_{ok} & = & wp[\![\textbf{assume } result[i] = k/A[i], L2_{ok}]\!] & \textbf{in} \\
\textbf{let } L4_{ok} & = & wp[\![\textbf{assume } result[i] \neq k/A[i] \text{ ; } \textbf{assume } b_1 = false \text{ ;} & \\
& & \textbf{assume } b_2 = b_1, L5_{ok}]\!] & \textbf{in} \\
\textbf{let } L1_{ok} & = & wp[\![\textbf{assume } A[i] \neq 0, L3_{ok} \wedge L4_{ok}]\!] & \textbf{in} \\
\textbf{let } L0_{ok} & = & wp[\![\textbf{assume } A[i] = 0, L2_{ok}]\!] & \textbf{in} \\
\textbf{let } Start_{ok} & = & wp[\![\textbf{skip}, L0_{ok} \wedge L1_{ok}]\!] & \textbf{in} \\
& & Start_{ok}
\end{array}
$$

After simplifying[2] the expression is equivalent to:

$$
\begin{array}{llll}
\textbf{let } L5_{ok} & = & b_2 & \textbf{in} \\
\textbf{let } L2_{ok} & = & b_0 = true \Rightarrow b_2 = b_0 \Rightarrow L5_{ok} & \textbf{in} \\
\textbf{let } L3_{ok} & = & \textbf{result}[i] = k/A[i] \Rightarrow L2_{ok} & \textbf{in} \\
\textbf{let } L4_{ok} & = & \textbf{result}[i] \neq k/A[i] \Rightarrow b_1 = false \Rightarrow b_2 = b_1 \Rightarrow L5_{ok} \ \textbf{in} \\
\textbf{let } L1_{ok} & = & A[i] \neq 0 \Rightarrow L3_{ok} \wedge L4_{ok} & \textbf{in} \\
\textbf{let } L0_{ok} & = & A[i] = 0 \Rightarrow L2_{ok} & \textbf{in} \\
\textbf{let } Start_{ok} & = & L0_{ok} \wedge L1_{ok} & \textbf{in} \\
& & Start_{ok}
\end{array}
$$

If we denote that entire expression by R, then the genuine expression which is equivalent to the body of the anonymous delegate is:

$$(\forall b_0, b_1, b_2 \bullet R)$$

and the entire postcondition of the method in Figure 0 is:

$$
\begin{array}{l}
\textbf{result}.Length = A.Length \ \wedge \\
(\forall i \bullet 0 \leq i < \textbf{result}.Length \Rightarrow (\forall b_0, b_1, b_2 \bullet R))
\end{array}
$$

---

[2] Yes, we realize it doesn't look particularly simple. We mean that we have applied the definition of the weakest-precondition.

Looking closely[3], one can see that the truth value of this expression is equivalent to the original postcondition.

We perform this translation in a depth-first traversal of the program, replacing each code expression from innermost to outermost.

4   Non-boolean Code Expressions

In this section, we extend our translation of boolean code expressions to code expressions of any type. The basic idea is to distribute the non-boolean code expression to a context where its value can be stated as a boolean antecedent.

Let $G[\cdot]$ denote an expression context with a "hole". That is, if we place an expression e in the hole, written $G[e]$, we get an expression with an occurrence of e as a subexpression. We assume bound variables in G are suitably renamed so as to always avoid name capture of the free variables of e.

Now, let e be a code expression of an arbitrary type (that is, not necessarily boolean), and let $VC[e]$ be the verification condition (in other words, the verification condition contains an occurrence of e). We now show how to transform expression $VC[e]$ to an equivalent expression that does not contain this occurrence of e but instead contains a boolean code expression. First, for any variable x occurring free in e and introduced in the verification condition by a let binding **let** $x = t$ **in** u, replace x by t in e. Then, consider any context G such that $G[e]$ is a boolean subexpression of $VC[e]$; that is, $G[e]$ is some subexpression of $VC[e]$ such that the free variables of e are also free variables of $G[e]$. Specifically, if e is contained in a quantifier, then $G[e]$ can be the body of the innermost such quantifier; if e is not contained in any quantifier, then $G[e]$ can simply be $VC[e]$.

Since $G[e]$ is boolean, it is equivalent to the expression

$$(\forall k \bullet\ k = e \Rightarrow G[k])$$

where k is a fresh variable. Considering that e is a code expression, we have:

$$
\begin{aligned}
&(\forall k \bullet\ k = \{\!\{\ \ \textbf{var}\ b;\ S\ ;\ \textbf{return}\ d\ \ \}\!\} \Rightarrow G[k]) \\
=\ &\{ \text{ distribute "}k =\text{" over the code expression } \} \\
&(\forall k \bullet\ \{\!\{\ \ \textbf{var}\ b;\ S\ ;\ \textbf{return}\ k = d\ \ \}\!\} \Rightarrow G[k])
\end{aligned}
$$

The transformation we have just showed can thus be used to replace non-boolean code expressions with boolean ones, after which the semantics that we have defined for boolean code expressions earlier in the paper can be used.

5   Related Work

An alternative means for recovering boolean expressions would be to *decompile* the MSIL back into a high-level expressions [6]. For the trivial example with which we have demonstrated our scheme, this clearly would be quite easy.

---

[3] Squinting helps too.

However, we believe all decompilers are heuristic and so may not always be able to successfully decompile an expression, certainly not without perhaps introducing the same redundancy as a tree-encoding of the DAG, compared to the linear size of our derived expression. Also, a decompiler's goal is to produce an expression which is "close" to a boolean expression that a programmer would write. We are not concerned with making the expression "readable", but instead just need to be able to communicate it to a theorem prover.

There are other approaches that derive a functional form, *i.e.*, an expression, from imperative code [17,4], but it isn't clear whether their results are more usable by an SMT solver than ours. It also isn't clear whether the sharing represented in the compiled CFG is preserved.

6   Conclusions

In Section 0, we noted that there are contexts in which code expressions do not need to be converted back into a genuine expression. For instance, Boogie encodes precon-ditions (respectively, postconditions) as assume (respectively, assert) statements in the Boogie program itself. Instead of forming the verification condition $P \Rightarrow wp[\![S, Q]\!]$ for a program S, precondition P, and postcondition Q, it computes the weakest precondi-tion with respect to *true* of the program:

$$\textbf{assume } P\ ;$$
$$S;$$
$$\textbf{assert } Q$$

This means that if P or Q are code expressions, they can be *in-lined* and the assume (assert) "distributed" so that any return statement in the code expression, **return** e, becomes an assertion (assumption) on e. Then, the definitions of wp in Section 2 will produce a first-order formula that is accepted by theorem provers.

But this cannot be done for quantifiers: instead they must be translated into an equiv-alent quantifier in the input language of the theorem prover, which does not include code expressions. Therefore, we need to perform our technique only for code expressions oc-curring within a quantifier. As we progress with the implementation of this scheme in Boogie, we will need to see if the introduction of the quantifier in Equation 0 leads to problems with triggering. (A trigger is the pattern a Simplify-like SMT solver requires before it instantiates a quantifier [8].)

The general form for a quantifier is:

$$(\, Q\, x : T\ |\ x \in D\ \bullet\ P(x)\,)$$

It has four parts that are defined by the specification language: Q, T, D, and P. The kind of the quantifier is Q, which is usually either universal or existential quantifica-tion. T is the type of the bound variable x. Different specification languages also may restrict the kind of domain, D, that a bound variable may be drawn from. For instance, Spec# restricts D to be a finite, computable set that has an interpretation at runtime. Our technique is concerned only with the fourth part: representing the body $P(x)$. The choices made for the other three are completely orthogonal.

In summary, in this paper, we have adapted our previous work on verification condition generation [2] to provide a scheme for turning code that represents an expression back into an expression in order for it to be easily translated into input for an automatic theorem prover. The scheme avoids decompilation and is efficient. We also outlined four healthiness conditions for ensuring that a code expression can be treated as a genuine expression.

Acknowledgements

We would like to thank Manuel Fähndrich, Francesco Logozzo, and Michał Moskal for valuable help and insight. Comments by the anonymous referees were also helpful.

References

0. Barnett, M., Chang, B.-Y.E., DeLine, R., Jacobs, B., Leino, K.R.M.: Boogie: A modular reusable verifier for object-oriented programs. In: de Boer, F.S., Bonsangue, M.M., Graf, S., de Roever, W.-P. (eds.) FMCO 2005. LNCS, vol. 4111, pp. 364–387. Springer, Heidelberg (2006)
1. Barnett, M., Fähndrich, M., Logozzo, F.: Embedded contract languages. In: ACM SAC - OOPS, March 2010. ACM, New York (2010)
2. Barnett, M., Leino, K.R.M.: Weakest-precondition of unstructured programs. In: PASTE 2005: The 6th ACM SIGPLAN-SIGSOFT workshop on Program analysis for software tools and engineering, pp. 82–87. ACM Press, New York (2005)
3. Barnett, M., Leino, K.R.M., Schulte, W.: The Spec# programming system: An overview. In: Barthe, G., Burdy, L., Huisman, M., Lanet, J.-L., Muntean, T. (eds.) CASSIS 2004. LNCS, vol. 3362, pp. 49–69. Springer, Heidelberg (2005)
4. Charguéraud, A.: Program verification through characteristic formulae. In: ACM SIGPLAN International Conference on Functional Programming (to appear, 2010)
5. Chatterjee, S., Lahiri, S.K., Qadeer, S., Rakamarić, Z.: A reachability predicate for analyzing low-level software. In: Grumberg, O., Huth, M. (eds.) TACAS 2007. LNCS, vol. 4424, pp. 19–33. Springer, Heidelberg (2007)
6. Cifuentes, C., John Gough, K.: Decompilation of binary programs. Software — Practice and Experience 25(7), 811–829 (1995)
7. de Moura, L., Bjørner, N.: Z3: An efficient SMT solver. In: Ramakrishnan, C.R., Rehof, J. (eds.) TACAS 2008. LNCS, vol. 4963, pp. 337–340. Springer, Heidelberg (2008)
8. Detlefs, D., Nelson, G., Saxe, J.B.: Simplify: a theorem prover for program checking. Journal of the ACM 52(3), 365–473 (2005)
9. Dijkstra, E.W.: A Discipline of Programming. Prentice Hall, Englewood Cliffs (1976)
10. Filliâtre, J.-C., Marché, C.: The Why/Krakatoa/Caduceus platform for deductive program verification. In: Damm, W., Hermanns, H. (eds.) CAV 2007. LNCS, vol. 4590, pp. 173–177. Springer, Heidelberg (2007)
11. Flanagan, C., Saxe, J.B.: Avoiding exponential explosion: Generating compact verification conditions. In: Conference Record of the 28th Annual ACM Symposium on Principles of Programming Languages, January 2001, pp. 193–205. ACM, New York (2001)
12. Leavens, G.T., Baker, A.L., Ruby, C.: JML: A notation for detailed design. In: Kilov, H., Rumpe, B., Simmonds, I. (eds.) Behavioral Specifications of Businesses and Systems, pp. 175–188. Kluwer Academic Publishers, Dordrecht (1999)

13. Rustan, K., Leino, M.: This is Boogie 2. Manuscript KRML 178 (2008),
    http://research.microsoft.com/~leino/papers.html
14. Leino, K.R.M.: Specification and verification of object-oriented software. In: Broy, M., Sitou, W., Hoare, T. (eds.) Engineering Methods and Tools for Software Safety and Security. NATO Science for Peace and Security Series D: Information and Communication Security, vol. 22, pp. 231–266. IOS Press, Amsterdam (2009) (Summer School Marktoberdorf 2008 lecture notes)
15. Leino, K.R.M., Rümmer, P.: A polymorphic intermediate verification language: Design and logical encoding. In: Esparza, J., Majumdar, R. (eds.) TACAS 2010. LNCS, vol. 6015, pp. 312–327. Springer, Heidelberg (2010)
16. Meyer, B.: Object-oriented Software Construction. Series in Computer Science. Prentice-Hall International, New York (1988)
17. Myreen, M.O., Gordon, M.J.C., Slind, K.: Machine-code verification for multiple architectures - an application of decompilation into logic. In: FMCAD, pp. 1–8 (2008)
18. Nelson, G.: A generalization of Dijkstra's calculus. ACM Transactions on Programming Languages and Systems 11(4), 517–561 (1989)
19. Ranise, S., Tinelli, C.: The SMT-LIB Standard: Version 1.2. Technical report, Department of Computer Science, The University of Iowa (2006), http://www.SMT-LIB.org

The Next 700 Separation Logics
(Invited Paper)

Matthew Parkinson

Microsoft Research Cambridge

Abstract. In recent years, separation logic has brought great advances in the world of verification. However, there is a disturbing trend for each new library or concurrency primitive to require a new separation logic. I will argue that we shouldn't be inventing new separation logics, but should find the right logic to reason about interference, and have a powerful abstraction mechanism to enable the library's implementation details to be correctly abstracted. Adding new concurrency libraries should simply be a matter of verification, not of new logics or metatheory.

Landin's seminal paper, The Next 700 Programming Languages [33], opens with:

> Most programming languages are partly a way of expressing things in terms of other things and partly a basic set of given things.

The same sentiment should be true for programming logics. There are some fundamental features that the logic must reason about directly; the other language features can be reasoned about in terms of these fundamental features. In this paper, I outline my perspective on how to achieve Landin's vision in the context of programming logics. Unfortunately, I am not in as strong a position as Landin was: I don't know exactly what the right core logic is, although recent work on deny-guarantee [17,15] suggests one route to this core.

Recently there have been many separation logics [27,48] developed to reason about different libraries, concurrency primitives and program constructs. For example, there have been extensions to separation logic to deal with statically allocated locks [38,9], dynamically allocated locks [22,26], reentrant locks [23], channels [25,2,54,55], and event driven programs [31]. Each separation logic provides the appropriate abstractions for a particular library or program feature. To reason about the feature the logics introduce new predicates to describe the state of this feature and ability to perform operations on this feature, for example, we may introduce a predicate representing the state of a channel, or a predicate for the ability to send messages on a channel. The problem with this proliferation of logics is that each logic requires a new soundness proof. Moreover, if we want a logic that deals with both locks and channels, then we will require a new logic that combines the previous ones. We are in effect building a new logic for each concurrency primitive or combination of concurrency primitives.

These language features can be implemented in terms of lower-level concepts. We should be able to mirror this implementation by realising the high-level

G.T. Leavens, P. O'Hearn, and S.K. Rajamani (Eds.): VSTTE 2010, LNCS 6217, pp. 169–182, 2010.
© Springer-Verlag Berlin Heidelberg 2010

reasoning principles in terms of the low-level principles, thus, deriving many of these separation logics. For example, a logic that supports dynamically allocated locks is required for reasoning about most concurrent programs, but the lock may be implemented in terms of hardware atomic instructions: for instance, a spin lock might use atomic Compare-And-Swap (CAS) and write instructions. If we have a logic to reason about these hardware atomic instructions, then we should be able derive the logic for dynamically allocated locks. After all, that is exactly what the programmer does. Our logics should provide at least the level of abstraction provided in our programming language.

Moreover, the module programmer actually isolates the client from the implementation details. They provide a high-level interface that does not require understanding of the precise implementation details. Thus, changes to the implementation should not affect the client. Similarly, the details of the verification should not be exposed to the client. There should be sufficient abstraction such that if the implementation of the lock is changed, then the verification of the client should not be affected. This means our logic requires a powerful abstraction mechanism that naturally mirrors the programmer's informal reasoning.

Some might take this paper to mean "no more separation logics, please". That is simply not my intent. The scientific method requires us to perform experiments, conjecture theories based on the experiments, and perform new experiments to test these theories. I view each separation logic as an experiment in verification, and what I am proposing is a more general theory that captures the results of these experiments, which we then need to validate against new programs and libraries. Deny-guarantee points the way to a more general theory.

Each of the logics mentioned above [38,9,22,26,23,25,2,54,55,31] requires the addition of axioms and new primitive predicates to the logic to deal with the infrastructure the feature provides. These additions hide the underlying interference or interaction, but in doing so, require this hiding to be proved sound. Deny-guarantee [17,15] takes a different approach. It enables interference to be directly described and even abstracted in the logic. The predicates that describe the language features, such as locks or channel ends, can be defined by the state changes they allow (changing the flag from locked to unlocked) and the possible current states. We do not need to resort to extending the logic with new bespoke predicates. We can simply define the predicates in the logic, and use abstract predicates to hide the details. We do not require a new soundness proof for each library.

The rest of the paper is a survey of the research that led to my search for a general logic. I will present a survey of research on separation logic focusing on abstraction and concurrency. I have included footnotes where possible to highlight additional related work that doesn't fit with the flow of the overall paper.

1   Separation

Let us begin with a brief overview of separation logic [27,48]. The core idea behind separation logic is *Local reasoning* [39], that is, verification should focus on what changes, not what doesn't change. To achieve this, separation logic takes a different starting point to Hoare logic: instead of pre- and post-conditions describing the (global) state, they just describe a part of the state. A pre-condition must describe the parts of memory that a command accesses, and everything not mentioned in a pre-condition is implicitly left unchanged. Intuitively, you can see the pre-condition as giving the command the abilities to access parts of the memory. More formally, the judgment $\vdash \{P\}\, C\{Q\}$ means: when executing the command C in a partial state satisfying the assertion P, the command will not access memory outside this partial state and, moreover, if it terminates, then the resulting partial state will satisfy Q. To capitalise on this property separation logic introduces a new logical connective: the separating conjunction $P * R$, that says the current (partial) state can be split into two disjoint parts, one satisfying P, and the other R. This connective enables the frame rule, which epitomises local reasoning:

$$\frac{\vdash \{P\}\, C\{Q\}}{\vdash \{P * R\}\, C\{Q * R\}} \qquad \text{(Frame)}$$

The frame rule says: anything disjoint from the pre-condition P of C is automatically preserved by the command. This rule captures the key insight in local reasoning: only describe what you access; the rest will stay the same. This leads to clean verification of sequential heap-manipulating programs.

Somewhat surprisingly it even extends naturally to concurrency [38,9]. We can reason about disjoint concurrency simply by saying the two threads must access disjoint memory.

$$\frac{\vdash \{P_1\}\, C_1\{Q_1\} \qquad \vdash \{P_2\}\, C_2\{Q_2\}}{\vdash \{P_1 * P_2\}\, C_1 \| C_2\{Q_1 * Q_2\}} \qquad \text{(DisjPar)}$$

If C_1 will only access the P_1 part of the memory, and C_2 the P_2 part, then they can happily execute side-by-side without interfering in a state satisfying $P_1 * P_2$.

Earlier in the semantics of judgments we used the phrase "will not access memory outside [the pre-condition]". You may think that only the overall effect on a location matters: writing to a location and then changing the value back to its original value would be okay. This is the case with normal *modifies* clauses in Hoare logic, but with separation logic it is not. The specification is capturing the abilities the command requires to execute, as well as its input/output behaviour.

In the parallel rule (DisjPar), the abilities C_1 requires are distinct from the abilities C_2 requires. Capturing the abilities required by a command is a key feature of separation logics, and is the crux of all that follows, as it will enable abstraction.

2   Hiding from Separation

The early ideas of modules developed by Hoare [24], Parnas [45] and others said the internal state of a module should be hidden from its clients, so that clients cannot depend on the internal details. Hoare's seminal paper [24] on data abstraction showed how to hide the internal state of a module. The difference between the internal and external views has been aptly named "Hoare's mismatch" by Naumann and Banerjee [37].

Separation logic supports hiding with the hypothetical frame rule [40]:

$$\frac{\{P_1\}f_1\{Q_1\},\ldots,\{P_n\}f_n\{Q_n\} \vdash \{P\}C\{Q\}}{\{P_1 * R\}f_1\{Q_1 * R\},\ldots,\{P_n * R\}f_n\{Q_n * R\} \vdash \{P * R\}C\{Q * R\}}$$
$$\text{(HypFrm)}$$

This says that if we can verify a program, C, which uses some procedures $f_1,\ldots,f_n$, then we can extend the specifications of these procedures with R and know that the client preserves R between each call to a procedure. The informal understanding is simple: to prove $\{P\}C\{Q\}$ we know the client code doesn't depend on any additional state, in particular R, so the code cannot affect the additional state. When we extend the specifications of the procedures, we know automatically that only the procedures will update this additional state.

A quintessential example of this reasoning is the specification of a memory manager. Typically it has an internal list of free blocks. Consider a simple memory manager that allocates two-word blocks, $x \mapsto \_, \_$. The client should use the specifications:

$$\{empty\}\, x := \text{malloc}()\{x \mapsto \_, \_\}$$
$$\{x \mapsto \_, \_\}\, \text{free}(x)\{empty\}$$

but the actual implementation of the library will be validated against the specifications:

$$\{\text{freelist}\}\, x := \text{malloc}()\{\text{freelist} * x \mapsto \_, \_\}$$
$$\{\text{freelist} * x \mapsto \_, \_\}\, \text{free}(x)\{\text{freelist}\}$$

The client code uses the simple specifications that do not mention the freelist. Using the hypothetical frame rule, we can extend the proof of a client to the actual specification of a memory manager with an internal freelist. Note the modules operations must all preserve the internal invariant.[1,2]

The hypothetical frame rule enables two views of a module, and thus the client code is independent of the internal invariant of the module, following Parnas's advice.

---

[1] The hypothetical frame rule has been extended to reason about both higher-order functions [5] and higher-order store [49], and even anti-frame rules that hide the internal state of a module that fits more naturally with type systems [46,50]. Naumann and Banerjee have provided a similar notion to the hypothetical frame rule in region logic [37].

[2] This form of reasoning can naturally be extended to a concurrent setting. Concurrent separation logic [38,9] uses the same principles to associate state to a lock, such that when the lock is acquired that state becomes available to the client. It carefully hides the internal interference of an algorithm from the external observers. It can be viewed as taking the hypothetical frame rule and adding a lock to the code. Whenever a lock is acquired, the thread gets more state. This has then been extended from statically allocated locks, to dynamically allocated locks [22,26] and even reentrant locks [23]. The invariant hides the details of the interaction, but the mechanism is tied directly to the implementation.

3 Being Opaque

The problem with the hypothetical frame rule is that it only deals with single instances of the hidden data structure. Hence, it cannot be used for many common forms of abstraction, including ADTs and classes, where we require multiple instances of the hidden resource. To deal with this in separation logic, Parkinson and Bierman took a different approach: abstract predicates [44,42,43].

Instead of hiding the internal state of the module it is abstracted. Intuitively, abstract predicates are used like abstract data types. Abstract data types have a name, a scope and a concrete representation. Operations defined within this scope can freely exchange the data type's name and representation, but operations defined outside the scope can only use the data type's name. Similarly abstract predicates have a name and a formula. The formula is scoped: code verified inside the scope can use both the predicates name and its body, while code verified outside the scope must treat the predicate atomically. We are just using the theory of abstract data types developed in the 80s [47,35] for reasoning in a program logic. Instead of using type variables to provide abstraction, we use predicate variables to provide abstraction.

The whole approach can be summarised by the following rule:

$$\frac{\Delta; \Gamma \vdash \{\,P\,\}\,C\{\,Q\,\}}{\Delta, \alpha(\overline{x}) \stackrel{\text{def}}{=} R; \Gamma \vdash \{\,P\,\}\,C\{\,Q\,\}} \qquad \text{(AbsIntro)}$$

We perform verification in a context of functions, Γ, and of predicate definitions Δ. At any point in a verification, we can specialise a predicate α to a precise definition R. The verification of C in the premise cannot depend on the definition of α, so we can specialise it to any definition soundly.

As an illustration, let us consider making our earlier malloc able to allocate arbitrary sized blocks. The standard specification [29] of free only requires it to deallocate blocks provided by malloc. It is undefined on all other arguments. Using abstract predicates we are able to provide an adequate specification. We can provide a predicate with each block allocated by malloc, and require that predicate in the pre-condition of free:

$$\{\,empty\,\}\,x := \text{malloc}(n)\{\,x \mapsto \_ * ... * (x + n - 1) \mapsto \_ * \text{MBlock}(x, n)\,\}$$
$$\{\,x \mapsto \_ * ... * (x + n - 1) \mapsto \_ * \text{MBlock}(x, n)\,\}\,\text{free}(x)\{\,empty\,\}$$

This is important, as without the MBlock predicate it is hard to see how much memory should be deallocated by free, since it does not take an explicit size parameter. MBlock can be seen as a module-specific ability to call free.

An actual implementation of malloc and free will have to realise this predicate in terms of some concrete state, for instance:

$$\text{MBlock}(x, n) \stackrel{\text{def}}{=} (x - 1) \mapsto n$$

The memory manager will use this definition to know how much memory has been returned by the client. The client will be verified independently of this definition, so cannot rely on the location before the block containing the length of the block, or even being allocated. Importantly, the client can only access things they have the ability to access. As they do not know what abilities MBlock gives them, they cannot use them. The client cannot use the implication

$$\mathrm{MBlock}(x, n) \Rightarrow (x - 1) \mapsto n$$

as they must treat the MBlock predicate as a variable. This implication is however, critical for the module to be able to meet its specification.[3]

4   Nobody Likes to Share

Separation provides an elegant abstraction. However, there are problems when we don't have separation. If we need to expose several independent properties of the same state to the clients, then we cannot achieve abstraction through separation. We have sharing, and thus no separation.[4]

The simplest example of this is read-sharing. In the standard model of separation logic it is not possible for the same location to be used in two threads, hidden in two invariants or predicates even if it will only be used in a read-only way. This difficulty led to fractional permissions in separation logic [8,6]. Here the notion of separation logic is adapted to enable locations to be split into fractions, the whole gives the ability to write, and any smaller non-zero fraction gives the ability to read. This deals with sharing where there is no mutation, but what if we want sharing when there is mutation?

Let us consider a slightly more complex memory manager that exhibits this problem [56]. The memory manager contains a list of all contiguous blocks, and a flag to say if the block is allocated or not. We illustrate the kind of arena below.

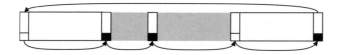

There is a cyclic list that goes through each block. Here we have two free blocks (white) and two allocated blocks (grey), and between each block a pointer to the next block, with a bit signifying if the block is allocated (black), or not (white). We would like the MBlock(x, n) predicate to signify that the block at x is reachable in the list from the start. For example, we might define it as

$$\mathrm{MBlock}(x, n) \stackrel{\mathrm{def}}{=} \mathrm{mlist}(\mathtt{start}, x - 1) * (x - 1) \mapsto n$$

---

[3] This form of reasoning has very natural connections with higher-order quantification as found in higher-order separation logic (HOSL) [4,3]. HOSL has been used to verify some design patterns abstractly [30], and a similar approach is taken in Hoare Type Theory (HTT) [36] to deal with abstraction of data types.

[4] I think we are a long way from having "nice" proofs of arbitrary sharing. There have been some proofs of graph algorithms [57,7] and garbage collectors [51,34]. Here I will only consider fairly simple sharing patterns.

That is, a list of malloc blocks starting at start going to $x - 1$ and then containing the length of the block n. Unfortunately, this requires many MBlock predicates to describe the same state, for instance, all of them will describe the contents of start. We cannot simply use this definition with our earlier specification of malloc and free.

Intuitively, the system works because freeing a block does not invalidate any other MBlock predicates. They are separate at an algorithmic level, but not in terms of the actual state that represents them. We would like the MBlock predicate to have sufficient knowledge of the other abilities to alter the list, so that it knows the block will remain in the list.

The situation worsens when we get to the concurrent setting. For example, we also get sharing when we consider implementations of locks. Many threads will all have access to the same piece of state, but once it is locked they know no one else will be able to acquire the lock. Again, we cannot directly abstract the sharing required for concurrency in separation logic. Hence, each concurrency primitive or concurrent library requires its own separation logic.

This is not a scalable solution. We need sufficient abstraction that a library can provide an illusion of separation.[5] The internal changes that are not externally visible need to be hidden from the client. We need to deal with the internal interference of the module directly.

5   Coping with Change

There has been a long line of research on dealing with the interference caused by concurrent threads, beginning with the Owicki-Gries method [41], which allows assertions about the global state of the program to be made. Each assertion must be checked against all the potential parallel commands to ensure it does not interfere with the assertion. For example, the command $x := x + 1$ interferes with assertion $x = 5$ but not with $x \geq 5$. If the latter is true and the command executes, it is still true. By using assertions that are unaffected by the context the proof is sound even in a concurrent setting.

However, checking each assertion against each command does not scale well, because the number of checks grows rapidly with the number of threads and commands. The rely-guarantee method [28] abstracts this approach. Instead of directly inspecting each command of the other threads, two relations are used to approximate the interference: the rely, R, the interference a thread can tolerate from the environment; and the guarantee, G, the interference that a command is allowed to cause. Each assertion about the shared state must be stable with respect to the rely, that is, closed under the relation. The reasoning is perhaps best expressed by the parallel composition rule:

---

[5] This illusion was perhaps first observed when trying to connect the high-level context logic reasoning about trees [11,12] to the low-level heap representations. To make this relationship precise one has to introduce a notion of crust [16], a context that is changed, but only in a superficial way, to preserve the data structure's internal invariant.

$$
\begin{array}{c}
G_2 \subseteq R_1 \\
G_1 \subseteq R_2 \\
R_1, G_1 \vdash \{\, P_1 \,\} \, C_1 \{\, Q_1 \,\} \\
R_2, G_2 \vdash \{\, P_2 \,\} \, C_2 \{\, Q_2 \,\} \\
\hline
R_1 \cap R_2, G_1 \cup G_2 \vdash \{\, P_1 \wedge P_2 \,\} \, C_1 \| C_2 \{\, Q_1 \wedge Q_2 \,\}
\end{array}
\qquad \text{(RGPar)}
$$

To compose two threads, the interference tolerated by the first thread R_1 must contain the interference caused by the second G_2, and similarly R_2 must contain G_1. The parallel composition can thus tolerate the interference expected by both threads $R_1 \cap R_2$, and the combination can cause the interference of either thread $G_1 \cup G_2$.

The concepts of rely-guarantee have been combined with separation logic, SAGL [19] and RGSep [52,53], to allow the manipulation of heap-based data structures using fine-grain or non-blocking concurrency control. Separation is used to restrict the effects of interference, and the interference is carefully described using relations as in rely-guarantee. Both approaches allow pre- and post-conditions to describe both local and shared heaps. For example, in RGSep, the assertion language allows assertions to be made about the shared state: $\boxed{P}$ means the shared state contains P. The separating conjunction then only separates the assertions about the local state, and just behaves like conjunction on the shared state. Interference only affects the shared state; the local state cannot be changed by other threads.

We can give the parallel rule from RGSep:

$$
\begin{array}{c}
G_2 \subseteq R_1 \\
G_1 \subseteq R_2 \\
R_1, G_1 \vdash \{\, P_1 \,\} \, C_1 \{\, Q_1 \,\} \\
R_2, G_2 \vdash \{\, P_2 \,\} \, C_2 \{\, Q_2 \,\} \\
\hline
R_1 \cap R_2, G_1 \cup G_2 \vdash \{\, P_1 * P_2 \,\} \, C_1 \| C_2 \{\, Q_1 * Q_2 \,\}
\end{array}
\qquad \text{(RGSepPar)}
$$

Note that it only differs by substitution of $*$ for $\wedge$ from the previous rule (RG-Par). Importantly, if the pre- and post-conditions only describe shared state then this degenerates to the (RGPar) rule, and if it only mentions the local state then it degenerates to the separation logic rule for disjoint concurrency (DisjPar).

Although these logics allow local reasoning about the *state* in a concurrent system, the *interference* is global. The interference of a library has to be considered by its clients: we don't get the same principles of information hiding as with the hypothetical frame rule. The rely and guarantee affect the whole proof. Feng has begun to address this problem, by allowing a more flexible structure to the relations, in local rely guarantee (LRG) [18]. However, it still cannot abstract internal interference for a library. As the interference in rely-guarantee is separate from the assertions there is no way to use abstract predicates to hide the details of the interference. If we could make the interference specification part of the assertion language, then we would be able to use abstract predicates.

6   Embracing Change

One observation we might make is that the guarantee is about ability to change, and similarly the separation logic assertions are about ability to change a part of the state. RGSep, SAGL and LRG all treat these as two different notions. Recently, a new logic, deny-guarantee [17,15], has emerged that alters the fundamental building block of separation logic to be no longer about state, but instead about action (state change).

In deny-guarantee, we have assertions that describe the ability to perform a state change. Earlier we mentioned read-permissions, an extension to separation logic to allow multiple readers single writer to a particular heap location. We can see this concept as really saying no one can change that location, that is, a *deny* on the changing that location in the state, e.g. a read permission $x \overset{r}{\mapsto} y$ could be defined as

$$x \overset{r}{\mapsto} y \overset{\text{def}}{=} \boxed{x \mapsto y} * \circledast_{o,n}. \ [x \mapsto o \rightsquigarrow x \mapsto n]_{\text{deny}}$$

That is, the shared state contains the location x with contents y, $\boxed{x \mapsto y}$; and we deny any change to that locations value. The assertion $[x \mapsto o \rightsquigarrow x \mapsto n]_{\text{deny}}$ means that we forbid changing x from containing o to n.[6] The quantifier $\circledast_{o,n}$ is $*$ iterated over all values of n and o.

Similarly we provide assertion that allow certain actions called a guarantee permission. Consider an increment permission, it might be defined as a deny on the location being decreased in value, and allowing the location to be increased in value, e.g.

$$x \overset{i}{\mapsto} y \overset{\text{def}}{=} \boxed{x \mapsto y} * \circledast_{o,n}. \ n < o \Rightarrow [x \mapsto o \rightsquigarrow x \mapsto n]_{\text{deny}}$$
$$\wedge \, n > o \Rightarrow [x \mapsto o \rightsquigarrow x \mapsto n]_{\text{guar}}$$

Our assertion language is defined over worlds that define both state and state change. We can extract the rely and guarantee from these worlds, and combine these worlds, written σ, with a commutative $*$ operation. This gives the $*$ in the logic by lifting it to sets. The $*$ is partial as we cannot combine a guarantee and a deny permission for the same action of state change. For example, the following logical implication holds,

$$[x \mapsto o \rightsquigarrow x \mapsto n]_{\text{deny}} * [x \mapsto o \rightsquigarrow x \mapsto n]_{\text{guar}} \Rightarrow \text{false}$$

This principle leads to the important property:

$$\sigma_1 * \sigma_2 \text{ defined} \Rightarrow \text{guarantee}(\sigma_2) \subseteq \text{rely}(\sigma_1)$$

---

[6] We have to associate permissions (fractions) to actions to ensure the underlying structure is cancellative. Without this we would not get a well behaved separation logic [13], see [17] for details. Note an operation $\oplus$ is cancellative if $m_1 \oplus m_3 = m_2 \oplus m_3$ implies $m_1 = m_2$.

Here you can see that the rely-guarantee parallel rule is captured directly by the $*$. The parallel rule in deny-guarantee is just the same as originally in separation logic.

$$\frac{\vdash \{\, P_1 \,\} \, C_1 \{\, Q_1 \,\} \quad \vdash \{\, P_2 \,\} \, C_2 \{\, Q_2 \,\}}{\vdash \{\, P_1 * P_2 \,\} \, C_1 \| C_2 \{\, Q_1 * Q_2 \,\}} \qquad \text{(DGPar)}$$

Now the $*$ captures the compatibility of interference inside the assertion language rather than as an additional context. We can also defined an assertion as stable, if it is closed under the interference it allows the environment to perform.

We can now use the abstract predicates from separation logic to hide both interference and state. Hence, the bespoke predicates that were added to the logic can now be defined in the logic. Consider the specification of dynamically allocated locks [22,26]:

$$\{\, \text{isLock}(x, P) \,\} \, \texttt{lock}(x) \{\, \text{Locked}(x, P) * \text{isLock}(x, P) * P \,\}$$
$$\{\, \text{Locked}(x, P) * P \,\} \, \texttt{unlock}(x) \{\, \text{empty} \,\}$$
$$\text{Locked}(x, P) * \text{Locked}(x, Q) \Rightarrow \text{false}$$

The predicate $\text{isLock}(x, P)$ holds of a location that can be used as a lock protecting a resource P.[7] Here, we specify that calling $\texttt{lock}$ returns the Locked predicate, and this is required to call $\texttt{unlock}$. We also specify that we cannot have the Locked predicate twice. Hence, only one person can hold the lock. This specification does not reveal any details about the implementation of the lock, just an abstract interface to use it. Both Hobor $et\ al.$ and Gotsman $et\ al.$ then provide a soundness proof of the logic extended with these predicates with respect to an operational semantics that assumes locks as a primitive command.

In deny-guarantee we can simply define these predicates in terms of the state changes they permit and the current state. For a spin lock, the $\text{Locked}(x)$ predicate says that the shared state at location x contains 1 and the local state contains the unique ability to change it from 1 to 0 while putting P in the shared state. The isLock predicate says the local state contains a non-exclusive ability to change the shared state from 0 to 1 while removing P from the shared state, and that either the shared state at x contains 0, the resource P and the ability to change it from 1 to 0 while putting P in the shared state, or the shared state contains 1. These predicates describe both the state and the ability to change it. The module can prove the definitions are self-stable: cannot be invalidated by the environment. Hence, the client does not need any knowledge of the internal interference. The client is independent of these definitions.

The specification is sufficiently abstract that we can prove other implementation meet this specification. For example, we have verified [15] a variant of Lamport's bakery algorithm [32] used in the Linux Kernel. This changes the internal interference and the representation in memory, but these changes are not visible to the client.

---

[7] We currently haven't published how to use higher-order parameters to predicates in deny-guarantee, and it isn't supported by the model presented in [15]. But it will be the subject of a forthcoming paper.

On top of this abstract specification of a lock we have verified two different implementations of a set that use the lock to deal with concurrency. The first uses a single lock to protect the set, while the second uses one lock per element in the set.

In deny-guarantee, we can build an abstraction of a concurrency primitive directly in the logic. To prove the soundness of the two lock libraries is simply a matter of verification not meta-theory.

7 Deny Everything?

We now almost have 700 programming languages.[8] But I don't think we will ever have 700 separation logics. The important point of this paper is that we should find the right core principles to verify libraries and provide abstract specifications of them, rather than using similar principles in many slightly different ways. By finding the right core logic, we can concentrate on the difficult problems.

With deny-guarantee we can begin to see a route to a solution. It has demonstrated that we can encode several concurrency primitives into it, and we do not have to perform arguments outside the program logic. We can remain in a single verification framework and use abstraction to hide the details. For any solution to be successful, we must consider many large examples, and push to see what can and cannot be achieved. This is an exciting time for verification.

Feng *et al.* [21] present a contrasting view to this paper. They propose a system for integrating a collection of different logics, where each logic is tailored to a specific problem. Their claim is code typically only has one or two difficult features, for instance, the boot loader deals with the mutation of code [10], but not system interrupts [20], and typically the scheduler doesn't have to deal with code mutation, but does have to deal with interrupts. I think there will be cases where the derivation approach I propose will be easier, and times when their many integrated logics will be easier.

One could view Dijkstra's language of guarded commands [14], and thus systems like Boogie [1], as approaching my aims for a core logic. Boogie has been used in many impressive verifications without needing extensions. However, language features like the heap and frame properties are encoded into Boogie by adding axioms. This means that metaproofs are required to ensure the soundness of the system. I like Boogie and the tools built on top of it: it shows how to architect a platform for verification that language features can be encoded onto. However, the correctness of these encodings typically require a research paper to support them. I want to be able to define language features simply by giving a low-level implementation and abstracting the details. This should just be done in the same logic; it shouldn't require metaproofs of the soundness of this library.

Ultimately separation logic has been a great inspiration to deny-guarantee. Separation logic provides a logical operation to split states. Deny-guarantee simply builds a logical operation to split state changes. This tiny shift has enabled more flexible reasoning and abstraction. What the right core logic is remains an

---

[8] Wikipedia listed 692 programming languages on June 2 2010,
   http://en.wikipedia.org/wiki/Alphabetical_list_of_programming_languages

open question. But hopefully we are a step closer to a situation in which adding new language features and concurrency primitives to a logic is simply a case of verifying their implementation rather than resorting to meta-theory. If you See What I Mean?

Acknowledgments

While I was at the University of Cambridge, this work was supported by an EP-SRC/RAEng fellowship and EPSRC grant F019394. I should like to thank my collaborators on the work in this paper Gavin Bierman, Richard Bornat, Thomas Dinsdale-Young, Mike Dodds, Xinyu Feng, Philippa Gardner, Alexey Gotsman, Peter O'Hearn, Viktor Vafeiadis, and John Wickerson. Further thanks go to Matko Botincan, Samin Ishtiaq and Neel Krishnaswami for feedback on this paper.

References

1. Barnett, M., Chang, B.-Y.E., Deline, R., Jacobs, B., Leino, K.R.M.: Boogie: A modular reusable verifier for object-oriented programs. In: de Boer, F.S., Bonsangue, M.M., Graf, S., de Roever, W.-P. (eds.) FMCO 2005. LNCS, vol. 4111, pp. 364–387. Springer, Heidelberg (2006)
2. Bell, C.J., Appel, A., Walker, D.: Concurrent separation logic for pipelined parallelization. In: The 17th Annual Static Analysis Symposium (2009)
3. Biering, B., Birkedal, L., Torp-Smith, N.: BI hyperdoctrines and higher-order separation logic. In: Sagiv, M. (ed.) ESOP 2005. LNCS, vol. 3444, pp. 233–247. Springer, Heidelberg (2005)
4. Biering, B., Birkedal, L., Torp-Smith, N.: Bi-hyperdoctrines, higher-order separation logic, and abstraction. ACM Trans. Program. Lang. Syst. 29(5) (2007)
5. Birkedal, L., Torp-Smith, N., Yang, H.: Semantics of separation-logic typing and higher-order frame rules for ALGOL-like languages. Logical Methods in Computer Science 2(5) (2006)
6. Bornat, R., Calcagno, C., O'Hearn, P., Parkinson, M.: Permission accounting in separation logic. In: POPL, pp. 259–270 (2005)
7. Bornat, R., Calcagno, C., O'Hearn, P.: Local reasoning, separation and aliasing. In: SPACE (2004)
8. Boyland, J.: Checking interference with fractional permissions. In: Cousot, R. (ed.) SAS 2003. LNCS, vol. 2694, Springer, Heidelberg (2003)
9. Brookes, S.: A semantics for concurrent separation logic. In: Gardner, P., Yoshida, N. (eds.) CONCUR 2004. LNCS, vol. 3170, pp. 16–34. Springer, Heidelberg (2004)
10. Cai, H., Shao, Z., Vaynberg, A.: Certified self-modifying code. In: PLDI, pp. 66–77 (2007)
11. Calcagno, C., Gardner, P., Zarfaty, U.: Context logic and tree update. In: POPL (2005)
12. Calcagno, C., Gardner, P., Zarfaty, U.: Local reasoning about data update. Festschrift Computation, Meaning and Logic: Articles dedicated to Gordon Plotkin, 172 (2007)
13. Calcagno, C., O'Hearn, P.W., Yang, H.: Local action and abstract separation logic. In: Symp. on Logic in Comp. Sci. (LICS 2007), pp. 366–378 (2007)
14. Dijkstra, E.W.: Guarded commands, nondeterminacy and formal derivation of programs. Commun. ACM 18(8), 453–457 (1975)

15. Dinsdale-Young, T., Dodds, M., Gardner, P., Parkinson, M., Vafeiadis, V.: Concurrent abstract predicates. In: ECOOP (2010)
16. Dinsdale-Young, T., Gardner, P., Wheelhouse, M.: Locality refinement. Technical Report DTR10-8, Imperial College London (2010)
17. Dodds, M., Feng, X., Parkinson, M., Vafeiadis, V.: Deny-guarantee reasoning. In: Castagna, G. (ed.) ESOP 2009. LNCS, vol. 5502, pp. 363–377. Springer, Heidelberg (2009)
18. Feng, X.: Local rely-guarantee reasoning. In: POPL (2009)
19. Feng, X., Ferreira, R., Shao, Z.: On the relationship between concurrent separation logic and assume-guarantee reasoning. In: De Nicola, R. (ed.) ESOP 2007. LNCS, vol. 4421, pp. 173–188. Springer, Heidelberg (2007)
20. Feng, X., Shao, Z., Dong, Y., Guo, Y.: Certifying low-level programs with hardware interrupts and preemptive threads. In: PLDI, pp. 170–182 (2008)
21. Feng, X., Shao, Z., Guo, Y., Dong, Y.: Combining domain-specific and foundational logics to verify complete software systems. In: Shankar, N., Woodcock, J. (eds.) VSTTE 2008. LNCS, vol. 5295, pp. 54–69. Springer, Heidelberg (2008)
22. Gotsman, A., Berdine, J., Cook, B., Rinetzky, N., Sagiv, M.: Local reasoning for storable locks and threads. In: Shao, Z. (ed.) APLAS 2007. LNCS, vol. 4807, pp. 19–37. Springer, Heidelberg (2007)
23. Haack, C., Huisman, M., Hurlin, C.: Reasoning about Java's Reentrant Locks. In: Ramalingam, G. (ed.) APLAS 2008. LNCS, vol. 5356, pp. 171–187. Springer, Heidelberg (2008)
24. Hoare, C.A.R.: Proof of correctness of data representations. Acta Inf. 1, 271–281 (1972)
25. Hoare, C.A.R., O'Hearn, P.W.: Separation logic semantics for communicating processes. Electr. Notes Theor. Comput. Sci. 212, 3–25 (2008)
26. Hobor, A., Appel, A.W., Nardelli, F.Z.: Oracle semantics for concurrent separation logic. In: Drossopoulou, S. (ed.) ESOP 2008. LNCS, vol. 4960, pp. 353–367. Springer, Heidelberg (2008)
27. Ishtiaq, S.S., O'Hearn, P.W.: BI as an assertion language for mutable data structures. In: POPL, January 2001, pp. 14–26 (2001)
28. Jones, C.B.: Tentative steps toward a development method for interfering programs. ACM Trans. Program. Lang. Syst. 5(4), 596–619 (1983)
29. Kernighan, B.W., Ritchie, D.M.: The C Programming Language, 2nd edn. Prentice Hall, Englewood Cliffs (1988)
30. Krishnaswami, N.R., Aldrich, J., Birkedal, L., Svendsen, K., Buisse, A.: Design patterns in separation logic. In: Proceedings of TLDI 2009, pp. 105–116 (2009)
31. Krishnaswami, N.R., Birkedal, L., Aldrich, J.: Verifying event-driven programs using ramified frame properties. In: TLDI, pp. 63–76 (2010)
32. Lamport, L.: A new solution of dijkstra's concurrent programming problem. Commun. ACM 17(8), 453–455 (1974)
33. Landin, P.J.: The next 700 programming languages. Commun. ACM 9(3), 157–166 (1966)
34. McCreight, A., Shao, Z., Lin, C., Li, L.: A general framework for certifying garbage collectors and their mutators. In: PLDI, pp. 468–479 (2007)
35. Mitchell, J.C., Plotkin, G.D.: Abstract types have existential type. ACM Trans. Program. Lang. Syst. 10(3), 470–502 (1988)
36. Nanevski, A., Ahmed, A., Morrisett, G., Birkedal, L.: Abstract predicates and mutable ADTs in Hoare type theory. In: De Nicola, R. (ed.) ESOP 2007. LNCS, vol. 4421, pp. 189–204. Springer, Heidelberg (2007)
37. Naumann, D.A., Banerjee, A.: Dynamic boundaries: Information hiding by second order framing with first order assertions. In: Gordon, A.D. (ed.) ESOP 2010. LNCS, vol. 6012, pp. 2–22. Springer, Heidelberg (2010)

38. O'Hearn, P.W.: Resources, concurrency and local reasoning. In: Gardner, P., Yoshida, N. (eds.) CONCUR 2004. LNCS, vol. 3170, pp. 49–67. Springer, Heidelberg (2004)
39. O'Hearn, P.W., Reynolds, J.C., Yang, H.: Local reasoning about programs that alter data structures. In: Fribourg, L. (ed.) CSL 2001 and EACSL 2001. LNCS, vol. 2142, pp. 1–19. Springer, Heidelberg (2001)
40. O'Hearn, P.W., Yang, H., Reynolds, J.C.: Separation and information hiding. In: Proc. 31th ACM Symp. on Principles of Prog. Lang., January 2004, pp. 268–280. ACM Press, New York (2004)
41. Owicki, S.S., Gries, D.: An axiomatic proof technique for parallel programs I. Acta Inf. 6, 319–340 (1976)
42. Parkinson, M.: Local Reasoning for Java. PhD thesis, University of Cambridge (November 2005)
43. Parkinson, M., Bierman, G.: Separation logic, abstraction and inheritance. In: ACM Symposium on Principles of Programming Languages (POPL 2008). ACM Press, New York (January 2008)
44. Parkinson, M.J., Bierman, G.M.: Separation logic and abstraction. In: POPL, pp. 247–258 (2005)
45. Parnas, D.L.: The secret history of information hiding, pp. 399–409. Springer, New York (2002)
46. Pottier, F.: Hiding local state in direct style: A higher-order anti-frame rule. In: LICS, pp. 331–340 (2008)
47. Reynolds, J.C.: Types, abstraction and parametric polymorphism. In: IFIP Congress, pp. 513–523 (1983)
48. Reynolds, J.C.: Separation logic: A logic for shared mutable data structures. In: LICS (2002)
49. Schwinghammer, J., Birkedal, L., Reus, B., Yang, H.: Nested hoare triples and frame rules for higher-order store. In: Grädel, E., Kahle, R. (eds.) CSL 2009. LNCS, vol. 5771, pp. 440–454. Springer, Heidelberg (2009)
50. Schwinghammer, J., Yang, H., Birkedal, L., Pottier, F., Reus, B.: A semantic foundation for hidden state. In: Ong, L. (ed.) FOSSACS 2010. LNCS, vol. 6014, pp. 2–17. Springer, Heidelberg (2010)
51. Torp-Smith, N., Birkedal, L., Reynolds, J.C.: Local reasoning about a copying garbage collector. ACM Trans. Program. Lang. Syst. 30(4) (2008)
52. Vafeiadis, V.: Modular Fine-Grained Concurrency Verification. PhD thesis, University of Cambridge (July 2007)
53. Vafeiadis, V., Parkinson, M.: A marriage of rely/guarantee and separation logic. In: Caires, L., Vasconcelos, V.T. (eds.) CONCUR 2007. LNCS, vol. 4703, pp. 256–271. Springer, Heidelberg (2007)
54. Villard, J., Lozes, É., Calcagno, C.: Proving copyless message passing. In: Hu, Z. (ed.) APLAS 2009. LNCS, vol. 5904, pp. 194–209. Springer, Heidelberg (2009)
55. Villard, J., Lozes, É., Calcagno, C.: Tracking heaps that hop with heap-hop. In: Esparza, J., Majumdar, R. (eds.) TACAS 2010. LNCS, vol. 6015, pp. 275–279. Springer, Heidelberg (2010)
56. Wickerson, J., Dodds, M., Parkinson, M.J.: Explicit stabilisation for modular rely-guarantee reasoning. In: ESOP, pp. 610–629 (2010)
57. Yang, H.: An example of local reasoning in BI pointer logic: the Schorr-Waite graph marking algorithm. In: Proceedings of the 1st Workshop on Semantics, Program Analysis, and Computing Environments for Memory Management (January 2001), http://www.dcs.qmul.ac.uk/~\hyang/paper/SchorrWaite.ps

Local Reasoning and Dynamic Framing for the Composite Pattern and Its Clients

Stan Rosenberg[1,*], Anindya Banerjee[2,**], and David A. Naumann[1,***]

[1] Stevens Institute of Technology, Hoboken NJ 07030, USA
[2] IMDEA Software Institute, Madrid, Spain

Abstract. The Composite design pattern is an exemplar of specification and verification challenges for sequential object-oriented programs. Region logic is a Hoare logic augmented with state dependent "modifies" specifications based on simple notations for object sets. Using ordinary first order logic assertions, it supports local reasoning and also the hiding of invariants on encapsulated state, in ways similar to separation logic but suited to off-the-shelf SMT solvers. This paper uses region logic to specify and verify a representative implementation of the Composite design pattern. To evaluate efficacy of the specification, it is used in verifications of several sample client programs including one with hiding. Verification is performed using a verifier for region logic built on top of an existing verification condition generator which serves as a front end to an SMT solver.

1 Introduction

The Composite pattern [7] captures a frequently encountered idiom in program design. The pattern centers on a collection of mutable data objects organized hierarchically, forming a rooted and possibly ordered tree. The operations include the addition and removal of subtrees anywhere in the tree. In contrast with the use of a tree as an encapsulated representation for an abstract set, this pattern exposes an interface that allows clients to directly access every node. The pattern was featured in a recent survey of challenges for reasoning about sequential object-oriented programs [11] and was the challenge problem of a workshop [18]. In this paper we present a novel solution aimed at current verification tools: indeed we machine-check the verification of the pattern and some sample clients using the Z3 SMT solver [6] via its Boogie 2 [14] front end.

The usual presentation of the Composite pattern involves two classes: class *Component* has subclass *Composite*, and the latter maintains a set of children of type *Component*. For brevity we sometimes refer to objects of type *Component* as *nodes*. Any particular use of the Composite pattern will involve application-specific operations, often supported by invariants that involve many or all of the nodes. The challenge problem [11,18] is an illustrative example. There is an operation, *getTotal*, that returns the number of descendants of a given node, counting the node itself. Method

* Partially supported by US NSF awards CNS-0627338, CRI-0708330.
** Partially supported by US NSF award CNS-0627448, CM Project S2009TIC-1465 Prometidos, MICINN Project TIN2009-14599-C03-02 Desafios, EU IST FET Project 231620 Hats.
*** Partially supported by US NSF awards CNS-0627338, CRI-0708330, CCF-0915611.

G.T. Leavens, P. O'Hearn, and S.K. Rajamani (Eds.): VSTTE 2010, LNCS 6217, pp. 183–198, 2010.
© Springer-Verlag Berlin Heidelberg 2010

getTotal is declared in *Component*, because one purpose of the pattern is to provide clients with a single interface for components, whether or not they are composite. If *getTotal* is invoked more often than adding and removing subtrees, it may be desirable to cache the result by declaring in *Component* an integer field, *total*, and to maintain the invariant that each node's *total* is the number of all descendants of the node. An invocation $n.add(p)$, which adds component p as child of composite n, increases the number of descendants of node n and of each of its ancestors. Method *add* must reestablish the ancestors' invariants and the challenge problem is how to streamline the specification and verification.

An attractive technique for reasoning about object-oriented programs is to focus on *object invariants*, declared in classes and pertaining to each instance individually. For an example, suppose *Composite* declares field *children* which is a sequence of objects. Consider the parameterized predicate $ok(o)$, defined at the top of Fig. 1, which says that the *total* at o is one plus the sum of *total* of all the children of o. This has the attractive feature of being "local" to node o and its children. Moreover, if every[1] o of type *Composite* satisfies $ok(o)$ then each $o.total$ is in fact the number of descendants.

The beauty of this formulation (stipulated in [11]) is that it does not involve recursion, which makes it more amenable to automated first-order reasoning. The notion of sequence sum, however, is inherently recursive. In other works this is avoided by treating composites as having exactly two children, as it is not the central issue of the challenge. Our work, however, alleviates reasoning about sequence sum by appealing to "local reasoning".

Because adding p as child of n falsifies *ok* for ancestors of n, class *Component* includes field *parent*: *Composite* (with "protected" visibility). Parent pointers can be traversed in order to fix the invariant at each ancestor. But what forces the implementation of *add* to fix the invariants of ancestor nodes? What lets us conclude that no other node's *total* needs to be updated? How can the specifications be formulated so that clients are neither able to break the invariant nor directly be responsible for maintaining it? We shall answer these questions without using specialized invariant disciplines or higher-order logic.

For some design patterns, reasoning about object invariants can be based on the idea that a client-visible object "owns" its *reps*, i.e., the objects that comprise its internal representation [19]. A discipline is imposed to ensure that the object invariant depends only on the reps and that clients cannot update the reps directly, so clients cannot falsify a candidate invariant. Thus the invariant may be *hidden* [8] in the sense that it is not mentioned in the public specification of a method like *add*. (While verifying the implementation of *add*, the invariant is assumed as the precondition and asserted as postcondition.) Ownership also supports reasoning that is "local" to the relevant part of the heap. A client can reason that the value of some query method invocation $o.m()$ is preserved over updates of some distinct object o', if $o.m()$ is known to depend only on the reps of o and moreover distinct objects have disjoint reps.

The Composite pattern was posed as a challenge problem because client access to internal nodes of a tree, rather than just the root, is incompatible with ownership disciplines. There are other design patterns, such as Observer and Iterator [7], that do not fit

---

[1] Quantification in region logic is bounded by a region expression.

well with ownership due to back and forth dependencies and reentrant callbacks. Proposed extensions of ownership that support hiding of invariants in these patterns [16,21] seem ad hoc. The difficulties led some researchers to abandon the traditional notion of hiding encapsulated invariants [8] in favor of making them explicit in contracts, abstracted in some way for information hiding [5]. We address the first posed question by using explicit invariants—each visible method's pre- and postconditions are conjoined with all the invariants; e.g., specification of *add* requires and ensures that the *total* is correct for each (allocated) node.

Procedure specifications are often phrased in terms of an *effect* (or "modifies") clause, separate from the designated postcondition ("ensures" clause), which lists the variables that may be written by the procedure. To deal with anonymous objects in the heap, and to hide effects on objects not supposed to be visible to clients, one technique is for the semantics of specifications to allow owned objects to be updated even when not explicitly mentioned in a write effect. Kassios [10] introduced a much more general technique, not for hiding but rather for abstracting from write effects. Auxiliary ("ghost") state is used in expressions that denote sets of locations[2]—for example, an object field *reps* may be used to hold the locations of the fields of all its rep objects— and such expressions are used in effect specifications. This is called *dynamic framing* because the locations on which an effect is allowed may be designated by an expression involving mutable ghost variables or fields of type "set of location". Others have explored this idea using pure methods that return sets of locations [26]. By specifying expressive (write) effects, we address the second question; i.e., effect specification of *add* allows us to conclude that the *total* field of any node other than an ancestor was not written.

In previous work [1], we formalized dynamic frames in *region logic*, a straightforward adaptation of Hoare logic that allows ghost fields/variables of type *region* in effect clauses. Regions are sets of object references. Our assertion language and effect clauses feature expressions of the form $G`f$ where $G$ is itself a region expression and $f$ a field name. As an r-value, $G`f$ is the set of values in f-fields of objects in G. Effect specifications refer to the l-value, i.e., the locations of those fields. As witnessed in our previous work [2], a judicious use of regions in effect specifications facilitates local reasoning (c.f. [22]) and its automation, which served as impetus for this work. We also find that regions support information hiding, without recourse to induction, higher-order logic, or method calls in specifications [26]. The solution to the last posed question is sketched in Sect. 5 where we show how to hide a conjunct from a client's view of the specification of *add*.

This paper. Using a simplified version of our specification of the Composite pattern, Sect. 2 reviews the basics of region logic. It also introduces our approach of using explicitly quantified invariants as opposed to hiding quantification via a built-in notion of object invariant. In Sect. 3 we discuss automated verification in our approach, i.e., using an automated prover for code annotated with loop invariants and other assertions.

---

[2] We are considering a Java-like state model, so the mutable locations are pairs (o, f) with o an object reference and f a field name.

A number of publications on reasoning about design patterns [4,9,24] focus on verifying the classes that make up the pattern. But the test of specifications is in their use by clients. Sect. 4 refines the specifications of Sect. 2 and shows their use in reasoning about nontrivial clients that manipulate several composites. Information hiding is sketched in Sect. 5. Sect. 6 discusses our experience and related work.

Contribution. We have successfully applied region logic to specify and verify the original challenge problem, and beyond, including well-chosen clients, which hints at the usability of our specification. We have implemented a verifier for region logic, VERL, built on top of the Boogie 2, Z3 tool chain. All of our code has been mechanically verified. It is available together with the verifier in [23].

2   Region Logic in a Composite Nutshell

In this section, we consider a simple illustrative implementation of the Composite pattern accompanied by specifications in region logic. Salient features of region logic are introduced as we explain the specifications.[3]

Implementation. Fig. 1 depicts a simple implementation (including all annotations) of the composite pattern. The pattern centers on a collection of mutable data objects organized as a tree. Class $Comp$ is used to represent leaf nodes as well as internal nodes of the tree. Field $parent$ contains an immediate ancestor (if any) of the current object (**self**) and field $total$ contains a count of all descendants including **self**. Field $children$ is a sequence of objects. We use a mathematical sequence for simplicity, to avoid the distraction of heap-allocated arrays. Addition of an element to a sequence is performed using the $+$ operation. Sequence membership is written as $o \in p.children$, which is a shorthand for $\exists i : \textbf{int} \mid 0 \le i < len(p.children) \land o = p.children[i]$. Note that the specifications in Fig. 1 are preliminary; later we refine them to provide more precise write effects suitable for clients and to illustrate hiding of some of the invariants.

Specification of add. Public method add inserts an existing composite into the children of **self** and then invokes private method $addToTotal$ which repairs the total of **self** and all of its ancestors (if any).

As usual, **requires** and **ensures** clauses express pre- and postconditions. The **effects** clause expresses write effects, that is, what variables and fields (of objects in add's *pre state*, i.e., state which satisfies the preconditions) may be written. We list write effects following keyword **wr**. A *region* is a set of references; region expressions, G, have type **rgn** and can occur in assertions and in effects. The region expression $\varnothing$ denotes the empty region, whereas $\{E\}$ (singleton region) denotes a singleton set containing the value, possibly null, denoted by expression E. Region expressions of the form $G`f$ (read "$G$'s image under $f$") when used for their r-values are restricted to fields $f$ of reference type or of type **rgn**. If $f$ is a field of reference type then the r-value of $G`f$ is

---

[3] For a more thorough exposition of region logic please refer to [1]. In the journal version (under preparation) we generalize and simplify some of the features of the logic, and those changes are also adopted herein.

$ok(o)$: $o.total = 1 + (\textbf{sum } i;\ 0 \leq i < len(o.children) \mid o.children[i].total)$

$I0$: $\forall o : Comp \mid o.total \geq 1$
$I1(r:\textbf{rgn})$: $\forall o : Comp \in \textbf{alloc} - r \mid ok(o)$
$I2$: $\forall p : Comp, o : Comp \mid o \in p.children \Leftrightarrow o.parent = p$
$I3$: $\forall o : Comp, i : \textbf{int}, j : \textbf{int} \mid 0 \leq i < j < len(o.children) \Rightarrow$
                                    $o.children[i] \neq o.children[j]$
$I(r:\textbf{rgn})$: $I0 \wedge I1(r) \wedge I2 \wedge I3$ and $I \mathrel{\hat{=}} I(\varnothing)$

```
public class Comp {
    seq<Comp> children; int total ; // initially total = 1 and children is empty sequence
    Comp parent; // initially parent = null
```

```
void add(Comp c)
    requires c ≠ null ∧ c.parent = null;
    requires self ≠ c ∧ I;
    ensures c.parent = self ∧ I;
    effects wr {c}ʻparent, {self}ʻchildren;
    effects wr allocʻtotal;
{
    assert c ∉ self.children;
    preserves I1({self}) {
        c.parent := self;
        self.children := [c] + self.children;
    }
    self.addToTotal(c.total);
}

int getTotal()
    requires I;
    ensures result = self.total ∧ I;
{
    result := self.total;
}
```

```
void addToTotal(int t)
    requires t ≥ 1;
    requires self.total + t =
        1 + sum i; 0 ≤ i < len(self.children) |
        self.children[i].total;
    requires I({self});
    ensures I;
    effects wr allocʻtotal;
{
    Comp p; int prv_total;
    p := self;
    while (p ≠ null)
        inv I({p})
        inv p ≠ null ⇒ p.total + t =
            1 + sum i; 0 ≤ i < len(p.children) |
            p.children[i].total;
    {
        assert p.parent ≠ null ⇒
            p ∈ p.parent.children;
        preserves I1({p} + {p.parent}) {
            prv_total := p.total;
            p.total := prv_total + t;
        }
        assert p ≠ p.parent ⇒ p ∉ p.children;
        p := p.parent;
    }
}
```

Fig. 1. Composite pattern: preliminary specifications and implementation. Complete code and annotations lifted from the VERL input file, `composite.rl`.

the set of v such that $v = o.f$ for some $o \in G$. However, if $f : \mathbf{rgn}$ then the r-value of $G\text{'}f$ denotes the union of the f-images (so we have no sets of sets). In effects, a use of $G\text{'}f$ refers to its l-value, and then f can have any type (c.f. $\mathbf{wr}\{c\}\text{'}parent$, $\mathbf{wr\,alloc'}total$ in Fig. 1).

The assertions $G \subseteq G'$ and $G \# G'$ say, respectively, that region G is a subset of G' and $G \cap G' \subseteq \{\mathsf{null}\}$. In particular, $G\text{'}f \subseteq G$ says that G is closed under f and $G\text{'}f \# G'$ says that G' is disjoint from G's f-image (but allows null in the intersection). The dual of write effects is read effects. Whereas write effects express a footprint of a command, read effects express a frame of an assertion, that is, variables and fields whose modification may cause a change in the assertion's denotation. A read effect $\mathbf{rd}\,G\text{'}f$ of an assertion says that the meaning of the assertion can vary with updates to f fields of G-objects, i.e., it depends on those fields.

In quantified assertions such as $I0$ (see Fig. 1), the bound variable ranges over allocated (thus non-null) references only. The default range is $\mathbf{alloc}$, i.e., the region of all allocated references,[4] but any smaller range can be specified as bound. Thus in $I2$, both p and o range over $\mathbf{alloc}$ whereas the o in $I1(r)$ ranges over all objects in the region $\mathbf{alloc} - r$. Here '$-$' denotes set subtraction. Write $I1$ for $I1(\varnothing)$ and I for $I(\varnothing)$.

Leaving aside condition I, the specification of add says: Given an initial state where c is an allocated component distinct from $\mathbf{self}$ and has no ancestors ($c.parent = \mathbf{null}$), a final state is one in which c's parent is $\mathbf{self}$. Furthermore the following updates (but no other) are licensed by the write effects: the $parent$ field of c, the $children$ field of $\mathbf{self}$, and the $total$ field of any allocated component. Condition I is intended to be invariant in the sense that it holds in all client-visible states; so it appears as both pre- and postcondition of add and $getTotal$. The conjunct $I0$ says every component's $total$ is positive; $I1(r)$ says every component except those in r has as $total$ one more than the sum of its children's $total$; $I2$ says that p is o's unique parent iff o is p's child; $I3$ says that $children$ does not contain any duplicates. In conjunction with the invariant, I, the specification of add says that c was added to $children$ of $\mathbf{self}$: initially, $c.parent = \mathbf{null}$ and $I2$ together entail $c \notin \mathbf{self}.children$; finally, $c.parent = \mathbf{self}$ and $I2$ together entail $c \in \mathbf{self}.children$. An astute reader will note that the specification is partially correct, but *not* totally correct. The reason is that the precondition of add does not preclude the creation of a multi-node cycle; e.g., consider $b.add(a)$ where $a \neq b$ and $a.parent = \mathbf{null}$ but $b.parent = a$. In such a case the call to add will diverge. Note, however, that the I-invariants entail[5] acyclicity. The strengthened preconditions in Sect. 4 prevent add from creating any cycle. (They should suffice to show *total* correctness of add.)

Last but not least, Fig. 1 contains the requisite annotations. Aside from the standard ones, i.e., loop invariants and $\mathbf{assert}$ statements, there appear $\mathbf{preserves}$ annotations. We shall explain them in Sect. 3 under the rubric of "Localized framing".

Proof system by example. The proof system of region logic features "local rules" empowered by the FRAME rule which we will see soon. The formal details can be gleaned from [1]; here we explain those informally. Let's consider proving a part of the

---

[4] The semantics is instrumented in that newly allocated objects are automatically added to $\mathbf{alloc}$. A command that allocates must report effect $\mathbf{wr\,alloc}$.

[5] The proof has not been mechanized but can be easily shown by induction.

specification needed in the proof of *add*, in particular, establishing the assertion $I1(\{\textbf{self}\})$ which is required, as a conjunct of $I(\{\textbf{self}\})$, immediately before the invocation of *addToTotal*. From the local specification ("small axiom") of *c.parent* := **self** we get $c \neq \textbf{null}$ as the precondition, *c.parent* = **self** as the postcondition, and $\textbf{wr}\{c\}\text{'}parent$ as the write effect which licenses the update. Observe locality at play: the rule refers only to the immediate state of the assignment at hand: $c, \textbf{self}$ and $\{c\}$ 'parent; the write effect specifies only the location which is pertinent to the field update. Intuitively, one can deduce that an assertion that does not "depend" on the write effect must be preserved by the field update: in this case, the truth of $I1$ is unaffected by the update of *c.parent* because $I1$ does not read the *parent* field of any object in **alloc**. Consequently, we can conjoin $I1$ to the pre- and postconditions. Then by the standard rule of CONSEQUENCE we can weaken the postcondition to obtain $I1(\{\textbf{self}\})$. For the next command that updates **self**.*children*, $I1(\{\textbf{self}\})$ holds in the pre-and postcondition because the write effect is $\{\textbf{self}\}\text{'}children$, whereas $I1(\{\textbf{self}\})$ reads the *children* field of all objects in **alloc** *except* **self**.

The above informal discourse is justified by the FRAME rule of region logic,

$$\text{FRAME}$$
$$\frac{\vdash \{P\}\ C\ \{P'\}\ [\overline{\varepsilon}] \qquad P \vdash \overline{\delta}\ \textbf{frm}\ Q \qquad P \Rightarrow \overline{\delta}\ \cdot/.\ \overline{\varepsilon}}{\vdash \{P \wedge Q\}\ C\ \{P' \wedge Q\}\ [\overline{\varepsilon}]}$$

read: Q is preserved by C under precondition P if $\overline{\varepsilon}$, the write effects of C, is separate from $\overline{\delta}$, the read effects of Q. The *frames judgement* $P \vdash \overline{\delta}\ \textbf{frm}\ Q$ asserts $\overline{\delta}$ are at least the read effects of Q. (We use syntax-driven analysis for read effects of atomic assertions, and an inductive definition of this judgement for all other formulas [1].) The antecedent $P \Rightarrow \overline{\delta}\ \cdot/.\ \overline{\varepsilon}$ asserts that the precondition may be assumed to prove that the read effects are separate from the write effects. We call $\overline{\delta}\ \cdot/.\ \overline{\varepsilon}$ a *separator*. The function $\cdot/.$ computes a conjunction R of disjointness formulas such that in R-states, writes allowed by $\overline{\varepsilon}$ cannot falsify a formula framed by $\overline{\delta}$. (Frames judgements in conjunction with separators formalize the notion of (in)dependence—whether or not an assertion may depend on write effects.)

Above, the read effects of $I1$ are $\textbf{rd alloc}, \textbf{alloc}\text{'}children, \textbf{alloc}\text{'}total$, which do not refer to *parent*, hence are separated from $\textbf{wr}\{c\}\text{'}parent$; thus $I1$ can be conjoined by FRAME. Read effects of $I1(\{\textbf{self}\})$ are $\textbf{rd alloc}, \textbf{self}, (\textbf{alloc} - \{\textbf{self}\})\text{'}children, (\textbf{alloc} - \{\textbf{self}\})\text{'}total$. These are separated from $\textbf{wr}\{\textbf{self}\}\text{'}children$ because $\textbf{alloc} - \{\textbf{self}\}$ is disjoint from $\{\textbf{self}\}$. So $I1(\{\textbf{self}\})$ can be conjoined by FRAME.

3   Region Logic Can Boogie: Automated Verification

We describe key steps in translating programs specified in region logic to Boogie 2 programs. We also share our experience with the translation and verification as it pertains to the Composite.

VERL. Our VErifier for Region Logic [23] translates a program specified in region logic to a Boogie 2 [14] program. We started with Dafny [13] and adapted its specification language while keeping its programming language mostly the same. Key features of VERL's specification language include the full generality of region assertions and effects as well as "localized framing"—code blocks annotated with formulas whose truth must be preserved by essentially appealing to FRAME. A distinguishing feature of VERL is an automatic (syntax-directed) computation[6] of read effects of formulas and expressions. For example, only the **sum** expression needed a read effect specification; read effects of all other formulas and invariants were inferred automatically.

Boogie. The Boogie 2 [14] verification platform consists of an intermediate procedural verification language Boogie [14], a verification condition generator (VCGen) and an SMT solver. Given a specified Boogie program, and a list of procedures to verify, VCGen computes the weakest precondition of each specified procedure relative to its implementation and specified loop invariants. These verification conditions (VCs) are handed off to a prover, such as Z3, together with the "background predicate" that axiomatizes the semantics of Boogie and any additional user-defined axioms (which typically encode the semantics of the source language).

A Boogie program may consist of logical declarations and definitions, procedures, as well as specifications thereof. The logical definitions may consist of variables, constants, function symbols and axioms. Procedure implementation can use ordinary assignment, control-flow commands such as **while**, typically annotated with loop invariants, **if-then-else**, **return** and **goto**, procedure call commands, as well as special (meta) commands: **assume, assert, havoc**. Procedure specifications consist of pre-/postconditions and write effects (of global variables). Specifications can be two-state, allowing a postcondition to refer to the pre state by way of **old**; e.g., $\text{old}(x) = x$ equates the values of x in the pre- and post states. Boogie comes equipped with some primitive types: **bool**, **int**, type constructors, as well as map types (corresponding to the theory of arrays). For example, given a type constructor **ref** we can define the map type **rgn** $\hat{=}$ **ref** $\rightarrow$ **bool** to encode regions as characteristic functions.

Encoding region logic. The encoding of the heap is similar to Dafny, except allocated objects are represented by the **alloc** region. Thus, the heap is essentially a pair consisting of the global variable *Heap*—a map indexed by (**ref**, **Field** α) pairs, where α ranges over any type [17], and the global region variable **alloc**; e.g., **in**(o, **alloc**) says that o is allocated, where **in** : **ref** $\times$ **rgn** $\rightarrow$ **bool**.

The translation of region assertions and hence pre- and postconditions is straightforward. To translate write effects, including for example **wr** $G^{'}f$, we conjoin the following postcondition in Boogie:

$$\forall \langle \alpha \rangle \ o : \textbf{ref}, g : \textbf{Field} \ \alpha \ | \ \textbf{in}(o, \textbf{old}(\textbf{alloc})) \Rightarrow$$
$$Heap[o, g] = H[o, g] \lor (\textbf{in}(o, [\![G]\!]_H) \land g = f)$$

where $H \ \hat{=} \ \textbf{old}(Heap)$, and $[\![\cdot]\!]_H$ is a translation function from VERL to Boogie, parameterized by the heap variable; e.g., $[\![x.f]\!]_H \ \hat{=} \ H[x, f]$. That is, for any object o, allocated in the pre state, and any field g, if the value $o.g$ has changed, then o must belong to G, evaluated in the pre state, and g must be f. There will be additional disjuncts if additional write effects are specified. When **wr alloc** is not specified in the

---

[6] Derived from frames judgements formalized in our earlier work [1].

write effects, we also conjoin the postcondition $\mathbf{old}(\mathbf{alloc}) = \mathbf{alloc}$ that asserts absence of allocation.

Localized framing. Local reasoning can aid the prover in two ways: firstly, by avoiding direct reasoning about complex formulas, and secondly by reducing the number of case splits performed when reasoning about heap updates. VERL supports code blocks annotated with **preserves** clauses as already witnessed in Fig. 1. For example, the **preserves** annotation in add instructs VERL to conjoin $I1(\{\mathbf{self}\})$ by essentially instantiating FRAME. In detail, **preserves** $P \{ C \}$ is encoded as

$$H := Heap; [\![C]\!]_{Heap}; \text{ assert } H, Heap \text{ agree on } \overline{\varepsilon}; \text{ assume } [\![P]\!]_H = [\![P]\!]_{Heap};$$

where $\vdash \overline{\varepsilon}$ **frm** P has been established, e.g., by a syntax-directed analysis. Prior to executing C we snapshot the heap into H. The assert statement ensures the heaps, before and after the execution of C, agree on the read effects $\overline{\varepsilon}$—roughly, for every o which was allocated before the execution of C, and for every $\mathbf{rd}$ $G'f$ in $\overline{\varepsilon}$, if $\mathbf{in}(o, [\![G]\!]_H)$, then $H[o,f] = Heap[o,f]$—thus we can assume P is preserved by C. The soundness of the above is a direct consequence of the frame agreement lemma [1, Lemma 4] that underlies soundness of the FRAME rule. Therefore, a **preserves** annotation establishes preservation of arbitrary formulas over the enclosed updates by merely appealing to the formulas' read effects as opposed to using the formulas' actual meaning. We call this "localized framing" to contrast with "framing axioms" [26,13].

Our experience. The sequence sum axiomatization draws on the axioms of Leino and Monahan [15]. We needed an additional axiom to express that the **sum** distributes over catenation. Our earlier verification efforts relied on framing axioms of [13] for all invariants. However, the prover exhibited difficulty (manifested by timeouts) in reasoning about the preservation of formulas containing **sum**. By switching to localized framing we were able to avoid timeouts and remove a significant number of **assert** annotations needed to guide the prover. By default, VERL does not generate framing axioms. However, a declaration of a function can be tagged to override the default. We used this feature to generate a single framing axiom for the function which encodes sequence sum. While the **preserves** annotations deal with the framing of $I1$, the generated framing axiom is used to reason about the preservation of **sum** expressions.

4   Refining Specifications: Smaller Footprints for Client Reasoning

The specifications in Fig. 1 are weak: they permit cycle creation (c.f. Sect. 2) and the effect $\mathbf{wr}\,\mathbf{alloc}'total$ is too imprecise for some client reasoning (as we see soon). This section refines the specification of add.

Consider a simple client program: $a.add(b)$, where $a, b : Comp$. By method call rule, we substitute actuals a and b for formals **self** and c resp. in the specification of add in Fig. 1, to obtain $\{ P \}$ $a.add(b)$ $\{ P' \}$ $[\overline{\varepsilon}]$, where $P \,\hat{=}\, b \neq \mathbf{null} \wedge b \neq a \wedge$ $b.parent = \mathbf{null}$, $P' \,\hat{=}\, b.parent = a$, $\overline{\varepsilon} \,\hat{=}\, \mathbf{wr}\{b\}'parent, \{a\}'children, \mathbf{alloc}'total$, and we elide the invariant I. A client could appeal to FRAME to show, e.g., $a.parent = x$ is preserved: the obligation is to show $P \Rightarrow (\mathbf{rd}\{a\}'parent, x) \cdot\!/\!. \overline{\varepsilon}$ which amounts to

$P \Rightarrow \{a\} \# \{b\}$. The disjointness evaluates to **true** using P. On the other hand, reasoning about *total* will not work because the effect, **wr alloc**'*total*, is too coarse. In detail, if the assertion to be preserved is $b.total = t$, then FRAME requires establishing the disjointness $\{b\} \# \textbf{alloc}$ — which is patently false.

We now consider clients that want to reason about *total* across calls to the *add* method. Our solution is based on exposing smaller, fine-grained footprints to the client. Consider composites $c0, \ldots, c4$ and the client code in Fig. 2. Here the composite tree

```
tBefore := c2.getTotal();
c0.add(c1); c1.add(c2); c0.add(c3); c3.add(c4);
tAfter := c2.getTotal();
assert tBefore = tAfter; // c2's total is preserved
```

Fig. 2. Client reasoning about the preservation of *total* across calls to *add*

at $c0$ is updated so that $c2$ is a child of $c1$ which in turn is a child of $c0$; similarly $c3$ is a child of $c0$ and $c4$ is a child of $c3$. To show the preservation of $c2$'s *total*, the key information that the client needs is disjointness: roughly, the trees need to have disjoint descendants and $c1, \ldots, c4$ must be roots (i.e., their parents are **null**). Furthermore, the effect specification of *add* must pin down the region whose *total* field is permitted to be written so that the client can deduce that $c2$ is not in this region. Consequently we need revised specifications for *add* and *addToTotal* — see Fig. 3. The figure also contains the definition of *ancestors* (in terms of *descendants*), and the supporting invariants J, K that capture sufficient "structural" information.

Specifications of add. We add ghost field $desc : \textbf{rgn}$ to keep track of the set of descendants of a node. We also add ghost field $root : Comp$ to point to the root of a composite tree. Note, by maintaining descendants and roots, we can express a common idiom: components with distinct roots have disjoint descendants. The set of ancestors is defined in terms of descendants by a means of a comprehension expression. (This saves us a ghost field declaration and corresponding updates.) Invariants $J0, J1$ constrain $desc$ to be a reflexive, transitive relation; $J2$ states that $root$ is always non-null, and that descendants of $o.root$ include those of o; $J3$ states that components with distinct roots have disjoint descendants; $J4, J5$ constrain every *parent* path to have the same root; $J6$ says that for any o which is a *proper* descendant of p, $o.parent.desc$ must be included in $p.desc$, whence by $J1$, $o.parent \in p.desc$. So $J6$ helps pin down that $desc$ contains only reachable components.

The above ghost fields and invariants were derived out of necessity to strengthen the specification of *add*. We are currently unaware of any general technique to derive the "right" set of essential annotations. However, we have some evidence to believe that the chosen invariants may be helpful in reasoning about other tree-like structures. For example, we can prove using induction on the length of a *parent* path, that $desc$ is the *smallest*, owing to $J6$ and acyclicity which follows, by induction, from the I invariants.

The postcondition of *add* is the same as before but with $J \wedge K$ conjoined. However, note that $c \in \textbf{self}.root.desc$ is entailed by the postcondition. (From $c.parent = \textbf{self}$ and

requires $c \neq$ **null** $\wedge\, c.parent =$ **null** $\wedge\, c.root \neq$ **self**.$root \wedge I \wedge J \wedge K$
ensures $c.parent =$ **self** $\wedge I \wedge J \wedge K$
effects wr $\{c\}$'$parent$, $ancestors(\text{\bf self})$'$(total, desc)$, $c.desc$'$root$, $\{\text{\bf self}\}$'$children$

$ancestors(o:Comp)$: $\{p \mid o \in p.desc\}$

$J0$: $\forall o:Comp \mid o.desc$'$desc \subseteq o.desc$
$J1$: $\forall o:Comp \mid o \in o.desc$
$J2$: $\forall o:Comp \mid o.root \neq$ **null** $\wedge\, o.desc \subseteq o.root.desc$
$J3$: $\forall o:Comp, p:Comp, q:Comp \mid o \in p.desc \wedge o \in q.desc \Rightarrow p.root = q.root$
$J4$: $\forall o:Comp \mid o.parent =$ **null** $\Rightarrow o.root = o$
$J5$: $\forall o:Comp \mid o.parent \neq$ **null** $\Rightarrow o.root = o.parent.root \wedge o \in o.parent.desc$
$J6$: $\forall o,p:Comp \mid o \in p.desc \wedge o \neq p \Rightarrow o.parent \neq$ **null** $\wedge\, o.parent.desc \subseteq p.desc$
I: $I0 \wedge I1 \wedge I2 \wedge I3$ (as in Fig. 1)
J: $J0 \wedge J1 \wedge J2 \wedge J3 \wedge J4 \wedge J5 \wedge J6$
K: $\forall o:Comp \mid \forall i:$**int** $\mid 0 \leq i < len(o.children) \Rightarrow o.children[i] \in o.desc$

Fig. 3. Strengthened specification of *add*, definition of *ancestors* and invariants. In $J0$, $o.desc$'$desc$ is a region expression whose r-value is the union of all $p.desc$ where p ranges over elements of the region $o.desc$.

$J5$, we obtain $c \in$ **self**.$desc$; $J2$ finishes the proof.) Finally, the most precise write effect for field *total* is **wr** $ancestors(\text{\bf self})$'$total$. It says that *add* may modify *total* of every ancestor of **self** (including **self**). Observe how cycles are precluded by the precondition $c.root \neq$ **self**.$root$, which, together with $J3$ entails that c's descendants are disjoint from **self**'s descendants.

Client verification. We have mechanically verified the client in Fig. 2 using *add*'s specification in Fig. 3. Note, the client code needs no annotations; Z3 proves the preservation of $c2$'s *total* automatically. For a lack of space, we do not sketch a decutive proof but note the key insight: **wr** $c.desc$'$root$ helps establish the requisite root disjointedness after each *add* which in turn with **wr** $ancestors(c)$'$total$ establishes that $c2.total$ was not written.

Implementation of add. We require two changes to Fig. 1: subsequent to the addition of c to **self**.$children$, we perform two bulk updates[7] of ghost fields *desc* and *root*. The *desc* field of all objects in $ancestors(\text{\bf self})$ is updated to contain c, and the *root* field of all objects in $c.desc$ is updated to point to **self**.$root$. See `composite.rl` in distribution; methods `add_simple`, `addToTotal_simple` correspond to Fig. 1 while `add`, `addToTotal` correspond to the strengthened version, i.e., this section.

5   Information Hiding

One dimension of the Composite challenge problem that we explore is information hiding. We argue that representation invariants—of which $I1$ is an example—should be

---

[7] Specification statements as embodied in Dafny and more generally in refinement calculus.

completely hidden from clients, to streamline the specifications and avoid unnecessary proof obligations on clients. The idea is very standard. The implementation of a method is verified with respect to a contract in which the invariant is an explicit pre- and post-condition, but the invariant does not appear in the contract used to reason about clients [8]. This mismatch is justified as follows: the invariant is supposed to depend only on the state that is encapsulated, and clients cannot write to that part of the state.

As a more general technique for hiding of internal invariants, we propose [20] that a module can declare a *dynamic boundary*, i.e., a read effect, in suitably abstract terms, that delimits its encapsulated state and frames the invariant to be hidden. (It is dynamic in that our effects are stateful, just like dynamic frames in method contracts.) Framing of the invariant involves nothing more than the framing judgement discussed in Sects. 2 and 3. For it to be sound to hide the invariant, client code must respect the dynamic boundary: it is subject to the proof obligation that it does not write within the dynamic boundary. In other words, intermediate steps in client code execution are required to respect the boundary, so that the write effects of the client are separate from the boundary. This notion can be captured by a second order rule of framing, as exemplified and formalized in [20].

In the sequel, we consider the clients from Sect. 4. Let us consider the invariants I and K. These can be framed by the effect **rd alloc**$'(desc, parent, children, root, total)$. For this to be a dynamic boundary, we require that clients never write any of these fields. In general, enforcement of a dynamic boundary may require reasoning about regions, but in this case it is entirely a matter of scope. Field $children$ should be private to class $Comp$. Because they are used in public contracts, the other fields need to be *private, spec-public* in the terminology of JML and similar formalisms. That is, they cannot be read or written in client code but are allowed in specifications visible to clients. Because it is impossible for the clients to write within the boundary, it is sound to hide I and K, i.e., omit them from the specifications with respect to which the clients are verified.

Invariant J is framed by **rd alloc**$'(desc, parent, root)$ and again for reasons of scope the clients respect the boundary **rd alloc**$'(desc, parent, children, root, total)$. Invariant J provides information needed for reasoning about clients as in Sect. 4. So J could be exported to the client as a public invariant [12]. That is, like I and K it is omitted from the public contracts, so clients are not responsible for establishing it. But it may be assumed at any point in client code. Boogie does not include this feature and instead of complicating our translation, we found it suffices to include J as explicit pre- and post-condition in the public specification of add. (In the distribution, the version with hidden invariants is in files `composite.rl`, `client.rl`; look for methods `addHidden`, `client_hiding`, resp.)

6   Discussion

On automating local reasoning about global invariants. In order to have a precise footprint for add we need to consider the ancestors of a node; ancestors are defined in terms of descendants. To reason about descendants we need universally quantified formulas with explicit ghost state (such as $desc, root$). There are two aspects to this reasoning: we need enough invariants—but not necessarily the minimal set—to get the inductive properties of interest (e.g., transitivity of descendants, and a limited form of reachability) and we need to tackle framing issues that arise because of universally quantified formulas.

The ubiquitous use of global invariants, as witnessed by the prevalence of universal quantifiers (often nested), ostensibly contradicts notions such as object-centric invariants, locality, or adherence to a particular programming methodology (see, e.g., the Composite verification in [27]). However, as we demonstrated, our approach is to use local reasoning in order to establish global invariants. In many cases, when updates are "shallow", the prover can automatically find the right instantiations without going astray. In more difficult cases, typically involving definitions inductive in flavor, we appeal to the user to add **preserves** annotations. Relying on such annotations is not all that different from relying on loop invariants; the user usually has some intuition about *what* invariants and *where* in the code. Arguably, we still achieve a high degree of automation in exchange for a reasonable request of user guidance.

Related work. We draw heavily on Kassios' [10] dynamic framing, which has been explored in a number of research efforts (e.g., [26]), as well as the frame rule and local reasoning in separation logic [22]. Because Kassios developed his ideas in a relational calculus of refinement, his effect specifications can be freely mixed with functional specifications, e.g., to express that a write effect takes place only under a certain condition. In contrast, our adoption of the popular "modifies clause" format fits with standard verification techniques. In recent work, Smans et. al. [25] avoid the need for a modifies clause somewhat in the manner of separation logic, but instead of a non-standard connective they use special "access predicates", acc, with a permission-based semantics and special program constructs. Every read/write of an expression $E.f$ is permitted by asserting $acc(E.f)$.

The most closely related works directly address the Composite challenge. Bierhoff and Aldrich [4] achieve fully automated checking of the add implementation using typestates (and no theorem proving at all) to express the $total$ invariant, our $I1$, in finite state form (i.e., the parity of each $total$). Permissions and data groups are used to track dependencies between typestates of different objects, to enforce separation and allow sharing (fractional permissions) where needed. The program needs to be instrumented with $pack/unpack$ notations, to an extent similar to the ghost assignments needed in our approach. The specification notations also use operators from linear type systems. Presumably, their types and permissions could be used for reasoning about clients at the level of precision we have considered.

Jacobs et al [9] present a specification of the Composite using separation logic with a number of inductive definitions, e.g., instead of the non-inductive $I1$ the main invariant uses an inductive definition of the descendant count to specify the value of $total$ at each node. The logic has been implemented in a tool that verifies the implementation of add as well as a client that constructs a tree with several nodes. A very interesting feature is that the specification describes a tree together with a focus node, to facilitate client access at any node. A "lemma function" is used in annotations to move the focus around, with the effect of folding and unfolding the inductive definition of a tree-with-focus. A dispose operation is included. Abstract predicates are used for hiding, as in [5].

Shaner et al [24] address invariant $I1$ and an implementation of add essentially like ours (which follows [11] but avoids arrays). The specification of add uses JML's model program feature which stipulates the implementation must call $addToTotal$ properly. The idea is to ensure preservation of a hidden invariant by specifying "mandatory calls" that must also be made in any override of a method like add. Framing for clients is not addressed in detail.

Summers and Drossopoulou [27] propose a methodology for (a) specifying object invariant semantics, i.e., which invariant(s) must hold and at what (program) location; (b) verifying preservation of invariants by computing an upper approximation on the set of objects for which an invariant may get invalidated and asserting the invariant holds for this set, thereby establishing that the invariant holds for all objects. The methodology is applied to the Composite problem by specifying and verifying an implementation of add which is nearly identical, (but weaker, e.g., no effects are specified and postcondition "forgets" that c was added) to our preliminary specification depicted in Fig. 1.

We expect that in future other automatic verification tools will address the Composite challenge as well. Rustan Leino has recently informed us of his specification and implementation of the Composite in Dafny (personal communication, May 2010).

Future work. While Sect. 5 shows how invariants I and K may be hidden, the full handling of abstraction is outside the scope of this paper. For that, one would need to verify that representations of internal heap-based data structures are such that client reasoning is unaffected: to wit, whether *children* is stored in an array or a list instead of a sequence, should not affect the behavior of add on client observable objects.

Automatically inferred **preserves** clauses could potentially relieve a number of required user annotations. A simple static analysis which computes the write effects of a command can be used to infer locations in code where relevant assertions must be preserved owing to separation (of reads from writes).

VERL currently uses quantified axioms to encode region assertions. Such an encoding does not constitute a decision procedure, yet we conjecture that an integrated decision procedure would improve reasoning about regions. A decision procedure for quantifier-free region assertions has been sketched in the first author's thesis proposal and will be implemented in an SMT solver.

Conclusion. Bierhoff and Aldrich [4] nicely summarize the challenge of the Composite pattern: "If nodes depend on invariants over their children then it becomes challenging to verify that adding a child to a node correctly notifies the node's parents of changes." We have used elementary and mostly familiar means to specify the Composite pattern and to mechanically verify its implementation and its clients. In our view, the specifications of the methods are fairly succinct and transparent. Their verification, and the verification of interesting client code, relies on a number of global invariants that capture inductive properties in non-inductive ways.

Acknowledgements. We thank Mike Barnett, Sophia Drossopoulou, Rustan Leino, Peter Müller, Shaz Qadeer, Jan Smans, and Alex Summers for helpful discussions. We thank the referees for their careful reading of the manuscript and for numerous suggestions on improving the presentation.

References

1. Banerjee, A., Naumann, D.A., Rosenberg, S.: Regional logic for local reasoning about global invariants. In: Vitek, J. (ed.) ECOOP 2008. LNCS, vol. 5142, pp. 387–411. Springer, Heidelberg (2008)

2. Barnett, M., Banerjee, A., Naumann, D.A.: Boogie meets regions: a verification experience report. In: Shankar, N., Woodcock, J. (eds.) VSTTE 2008. LNCS, vol. 5295, pp. 177–191. Springer, Heidelberg (2008)

3. Barnett, M., DeLine, R., Fähndrich, M., Jacobs, B., Leino, K.R.M., Schulte, W., Venter, H.: The Spec# programming system: Challenges and directions. In: Meyer, B., Woodcock, J. (eds.) VSTTE 2005. LNCS, vol. 4171, pp. 144–152. Springer, Heidelberg (2008)

4. Bierhoff, K., Aldrich, J.: Permissions to specify the composite design pattern. In: [18]

5. Bierman, G., Parkinson, M.: Separation logic and abstraction. In: POPL (2005)

6. de Moura, L.M., Bjørner, N.: Z3: An efficient SMT solver. In: Ramakrishnan, C.R., Rehof, J. (eds.) TACAS 2008. LNCS, vol. 4963, pp. 337–340. Springer, Heidelberg (2008)

7. Gamma, E., Helm, R., Johnson, R., Vlissides, J.: Design Patterns: Elements of Reusable Object-Oriented Software. Addison-Wesley, Reading (1995)

8. Hoare, C.A.R.: Proofs of correctness of data representations. Acta Inf. 1, 271–281 (1972)

9. Jacobs, B., Smans, J., Piessens, F.: Verifying the composite pattern using separation logic. In: [18]

10. Kassios, I.T.: Dynamic framing: Support for framing, dependencies and sharing without restriction. In: Misra, J., Nipkow, T., Sekerinski, E. (eds.) FM 2006. LNCS, vol. 4085, pp. 268–283. Springer, Heidelberg (2006)

11. Leavens, G.T., Leino, K.R.M., Müller, P.: Specification and verification challenges for sequential object-oriented programs. Formal Aspects of Computing 19(2), 159–189 (2007)

12. Leavens, G.T., Müller, P.: Information hiding and visibility in interface specifications. In: ICSE (2007)

13. Leino, K.R.M.: Dafny: An automatic program verifier for functional correctness. In: LPAR (2010)

14. Leino, K.R.M.: This is Boogie 2. Technical report, Microsoft Research (2010)

15. Leino, K.R.M., Monahan, R.: Reasoning about comprehensions with first-order SMT solvers. In: SAC (2009)

16. Leino, K.R.M., Müller, P.: Object invariants in dynamic contexts. In: Odersky, M. (ed.) ECOOP 2004. LNCS, vol. 3086, pp. 491–515. Springer, Heidelberg (2004)

17. Leino, K.R.M., Rümmer, P.: A polymorphic intermediate verification language: Design and logical encoding. In: Esparza, J., Majumdar, R. (eds.) TACAS 2010. LNCS, vol. 6015, pp. 312–327. Springer, Heidelberg (2010)

18. Robby et al: Proc. Seventh SAVCBS Workshop. Technical Report CS-TR-08-07, School of Electrical Engineering and Computer Science, University of Central Florida (2008)

19. Müller, P., Poetzsch-Heffter, A., Leavens, G.T.: Modular invariants for layered object structures. Sci. Comput. Programming 62(3), 253–286 (2006)

20. Naumann, D.A., Banerjee, A.: Dynamic boundaries: Information hiding by second order framing with first order assertions. In: Gordon, A.D. (ed.) ESOP 2010. LNCS, vol. 6012, pp. 2–22. Springer, Heidelberg (2010)

21. Naumann, D.A., Barnett, M.: Towards imperative modules: Reasoning about invariants and sharing of mutable state. Theoretical Comput. Sci. 365, 143–168 (2006)

22. O'Hearn, P.W., Reynolds, J.C., Yang, H.: Local reasoning about programs that alter data structures. In: Fribourg, L. (ed.) CSL 2001 and EACSL 2001. LNCS, vol. 2142, p. 1. Springer, Heidelberg (2001)

23. Rosenberg, S., Banerjee, A., Naumann, D.A.: Verifier for region logic (VERL),
    http://www.cs.stevens.edu/~naumann/pub/VERL/
24. Shaner, S.M., Rajan, H., Leavens, G.T.: Model programs for preserving composite invariants.
    In: [18]
25. Smans, J., Jacobs, B., Piessens, F.: Implicit dynamic frames: Combining dynamic frames and
    separation logic. In: Drossopoulou, S. (ed.) ECOOP 2009. LNCS, vol. 5653, pp. 148–172.
    Springer, Heidelberg (2009)
26. Smans, J., Jacobs, B., Piessens, F., Schulte, W.: An automatic verifier for Java-like programs
    based on dynamic frames. In: Fiadeiro, J.L., Inverardi, P. (eds.) FASE 2008. LNCS, vol. 4961,
    pp. 261–275. Springer, Heidelberg (2008)
27. Summers, A.J., Drossopoulou, S.: Considerate reasoning and the composite design pattern.
    In: Barthe, G., Hermenegildo, M. (eds.) VMCAI 2010. LNCS, vol. 5944, pp. 328–344.
    Springer, Heidelberg (2010)

Abstraction and Refinement for Local Reasoning

Thomas Dinsdale-Young, Philippa Gardner, and Mark Wheelhouse

Imperial College London
{td202,pg,mjw03}@ic.ac.uk

Abstract. Local reasoning has become a well-established technique in program verification, which has been shown to be useful at many different levels of abstraction. In separation logic, we use a low-level abstraction that is close to how the machine sees the program state. In context logic, we work with high-level abstractions that are close to how the clients of modules see the program state. We apply program refinement to local reasoning, demonstrating that high-level local reasoning is sound for module implementations. We consider two approaches: one that preserves the high-level locality at the low level; and one that breaks the high-level 'fiction' of locality.

1 Introduction

Traditional Hoare logic is an important tool for proving the correctness of programs. However, with heap programs, it is not possible to use this reasoning in a modular way. This is because it is necessary to account for the possibility of multiple references to the same data. For example, a proof that a program reverses a list cannot be used to establish that a second, disjoint list is unchanged; disjointness conditions must be explicitly added at every step in the proof.

Building on Hoare logic, O'Hearn, Reynolds and Yang addressed this problem by introducing separation logic [12] for reasoning *locally* about heap programs. The fundamental principle of local reasoning is that, if we know how a local computation behaves on some state, then we can infer the behaviour when the state is extended: it simply leaves the additional state unchanged. Separation logic achieves local reasoning by treating state as resource. A program is specified in terms of its *footprint* – the resource necessary for it to operate – and a *frame rule* is used to infer that any additional resource is indeed unchanged. For example, given a proof that a program reverses a list, the frame rule can directly establish that the program leaves a second, disjoint list alone. Consequently, separation logic enables modular reasoning about heap programs.

Abstraction and refinement are also essential for modular reasoning. Abstraction takes a concrete program and produces an abstract specification; refinement takes an abstract specification and produces a correct implementation. Both approaches result in a program that correctly implements an abstract specification. Such a result essential for modularity because it means that a program can be replaced by any other program that meets the same specification. Abstraction and refinement are well-established techniques in program verification, but have so far not been fully understood in the context of local reasoning.

G.T. Leavens, P. O'Hearn, and S.K. Rajamani (Eds.): VSTTE 2010, LNCS 6217, pp. 199–215, 2010.

Parkinson and Bierman have used abstract predicates to provide abstraction for separation logic [13]. An abstract predicate is, to the client, an opaque object that encapsulates the unknown representation of an abstract datatype. They inherit some of the benefits of locality from separation logic: an operation on one abstract predicate leaves others alone. However, the client cannot take advantage of local behaviour that is provided by the abstraction itself.

Consider a set module. The operation of removing, say, the value 3 from the set is local at the abstract level; it is independent of whether any other value is in the set. Yet, consider an implementation of the set as a sorted, singly-linked list in the heap, starting from address h. The operation of removing 3 from the set must traverse the list from h. The footprint therefore comprises the entire list segment from h up to the node with value 3. With abstract predicates, the abstract footprint corresponds to the concrete footprint and hence, in this case, includes all the elements of the set less than or equal to 3. Consequently, abstract predicates cannot be used to present a local abstract specification for removing 3.

Calcagno, Gardner and Zarfaty introduced context logic [2], a generalisation of separation logic, to provide such *abstract local reasoning* about structured data. Context logic has been used to reason about programs that manipulate e.g. sequences, multisets and trees [3]. In particular, it has been successfully applied to reason about the W3C DOM tree update library [8]. Thus far, context logic reasoning has always been justified with respect to an operational semantics defined at the same level of abstraction as the reasoning. In this paper, we combine abstract local reasoning about structured data with data refinement [10,5] in order to refine such abstract local specifications into correct implementations.

Mijajlović, Torp-Smith and O'Hearn previously combined data refinement with local operational reasoning [11] to demonstrate that module implementations are equivalent for well-behaved clients, specifically dealing with aliasing issues in the refinement setting. By contrast, we relate axiomatic abstract local reasoning about a module with axiomatic reasoning about its implementations.

The motivating example of this paper is the stepwise refinement of a tree module $\mathbb{T}$. The refinement is illustrated in Fig. 1. We show how the tree module $\mathbb{T}$ may be correctly implemented using the familiar separation-logic heap module $\mathbb{H}$ and an abstract list module $\mathbb{L}$. We then show how this list module $\mathbb{L}$ can be correctly implemented in terms of the heap module $\mathbb{H}$. Our approach is modular, so this refinement can be extended with a second instance of the heap module $\mathbb{H}$ (illustrated with a dotted arrow). Finally, we show that the double-heap module $\mathbb{H} + \mathbb{H}$ can be trivially implemented by the heap module $\mathbb{H}$, completing the refinement from the tree module $\mathbb{T}$ to the heap module $\mathbb{H}$. As a contrast, we also briefly consider a direct refinement of the tree module $\mathbb{T}$ using the heap module $\mathbb{H}$, although the details of this example are given in the full paper [7].

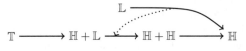

Fig. 1. Module Translations

Our development provides two general techniques for verifying module implementations with respect to their local specifications, using *locality-preserving* and *locality-breaking* translations. Locality-preserving translations, broadly speaking, relate locality at the abstract level with locality of the implementation. However, implementations typically operate on a larger state than the abstract footprint, for instance, by performing pointer surgery on the surrounding state. We introduce the notion of *crust* to capture this additional state. This crust intrudes on the context, and so breaks the disjointness that exists at the abstract level. We therefore relate abstract locality with implementation-level locality through a *fiction of disjointness*.

With locality-breaking translations, locality at the abstract level does not correspond to locality of the implementation. Even in this case, we can think about a locality-preserving translation using possibly the whole data structure as the crust. Instead, we prove soundness by establishing that the specifications of the module commands are preserved under translation in any abstract context, showing the soundness of the abstract frame rule. We thus establish a *fiction of locality* at the abstract level.

The full proofs of our results may be found in the full version of this paper [7].

2   Preliminaries

We begin by introducing two key concepts: the definition of a *context algebra* to model program state, and an *axiomatic semantics*, based on context algebras, to describe the behaviour of an imperative programming language.

2.1   State Models

We work with multiple data structures at multiple levels of abstraction. To handle these structures in a uniform way, we model our program states using context algebras. Context algebras are a generalisation of separation algebras [4] to more complex data structures. Whereas separation algebras are based on a commutative combination of resource, context algebras are based on non-commutative resource, which is necessary to handle structured data. We will see that many interesting state models fit the pattern of a context algebra.

Definition 1 (Context Algebra). *A* context algebra $\mathcal{A} = (\mathcal{C}, \mathcal{D}, \bullet, \circ, \mathbf{I}, \mathbf{0})$ *comprises:*

- *a non-empty set of state contexts, $\mathcal{C}$;*
- *a non-empty set of abstract states, $\mathcal{D}$;*
- *a partially-defined associative context composition function, $\bullet : \mathcal{C} \times \mathcal{C} \rightharpoonup \mathcal{C}$;*
- *a partially-defined context application function, $\circ : \mathcal{C} \times \mathcal{D} \rightharpoonup \mathcal{D}$,*
  with $c_1 \circ (c_2 \circ d) = (c_1 \bullet c_2) \circ d$ (undefined terms are considered equal);
- *a distinguished set of identity contexts, $\mathbf{I} \subseteq \mathcal{C}$; and*
- *a distinguished set of empty states, $\mathbf{0} \subseteq \mathcal{D}$;*

having the following properties: for all $c \in \mathcal{C}$, $d \in \mathcal{D}$, and $i' \in \mathbf{I}$

- *$i \circ d$ is defined for some $i \in \mathbf{I}$, and whenever $i' \circ d$ is defined, $i' \circ d = d$;*
- *the relation $\{(c, d) \mid \exists o \in \mathbf{0}. c \circ o = d\}$ is a total surjective function;*
- *$i \bullet c$ is defined for some $i \in \mathbf{I}$, and whenever $i' \bullet c$ is defined, $i' \bullet c = c$;*
- *$c \bullet i$ is defined for some $i \in \mathbf{I}$, and whenever $c \bullet i'$ is defined, $c \bullet i' = c$.*

Example 1. The following are examples of context algebras:

(a) *Heaps $h \in \mathrm{H}$ are defined as:*

$$h ::= \mathrm{emp} \mid n \mapsto v \mid h * h$$

where $n \in \mathbb{N}^+$ ranges over unique *heap addresses*, $v \in \mathrm{Val}$ ranges over *values*, and $*$ is associative and commutative with identity emp. (Heaps are thus finite partial functions from addresses to values.) Heaps form the *heap context algebra*, $\mathcal{H} = (\mathrm{H}, \mathrm{H}, *, *, \{\mathrm{emp}\}, \{\mathrm{emp}\})$. All separation algebras [4] can be viewed as context algebras in this way.

(b) *Variable stores $\sigma \in \Sigma$ are defined as:*

$$\sigma ::= \mathrm{emp} \mid x \Rightarrow v \mid \sigma * \sigma$$

where $x \in \mathrm{Var}$ ranges over unique *program variables*, $v \in \mathrm{Val}$ ranges over values, and $*$ is associative and commutative with identity emp. Variable stores form the *variable store context algebra*, $\mathcal{V} = (\Sigma, \Sigma, *, *, \{\mathrm{emp}\}, \{\mathrm{emp}\})$.

(c) *Trees $t \in \mathrm{T}$ and tree contexts $c \in \mathrm{C}$ are defined as:*

$$t ::= \varnothing \mid n[t] \mid t \otimes t$$
$$c ::= - \mid n[c] \mid t \otimes c \mid c \otimes t$$

where $n \in \mathbb{N}^+$ ranges over unique *node identifiers*, and $\otimes$ is associative with identity $\varnothing$. Context composition and application are standard (substituting a tree or context in the hole), and obviously non-commutative. Trees and tree contexts form the *tree context algebra*, $\mathcal{T} = (\mathrm{C}, \mathrm{T}, \bullet, \circ, \{-\}, \{\varnothing\})$.

(d) Given context algebras, $\mathcal{A}_1$ and $\mathcal{A}_2$, their product $\mathcal{A}_1 \times \mathcal{A}_2$ (defined as one would expect) is also a context algebra. For example, $\mathcal{H} \times \mathcal{V}$ and $\mathcal{T} \times \mathcal{V}$ combine, respectively, heaps and trees with variable stores.

2.2   Predicates

Predicates are either sets of abstract states (denoted p, q) or sets of state contexts (denoted f, g). We do not fix a particular assertion language, although we do use standard logical notation for conjunction, disjunction, negation and quantification. We lift operations on states and contexts to predicates: for instance, $x \mapsto v$ denotes the predicate $\{x \mapsto v\}$; $\exists v. x \mapsto v$ denotes $\{x \mapsto v \mid v \in \mathrm{Val}\}$; $p * q$ denotes $\{d_1 * d_2 \mid d_1 \in p \wedge d_2 \in q\}$; the separating application $f \circ p$ denotes $\{c \circ d \mid c \in f \wedge d \in p\}$; and so on. We also use $\prod^*$ to denote iterated $*$. We use set-theoretic notation for predicate membership ($\in$) and containment ($\subseteq$).

2.3   Language Syntax

Our programming language has a simple imperative core with standard constructs for variables, conditionals, iteration, and procedures. We tailor this language to different domains (heaps, trees, *etc.*) by choosing an appropriate set of basic commands for each domain.

Definition 2 (Programming Language). *Given a set of basic commands* Φ, *ranged over by* φ, *the language* $\mathcal{L}_\Phi$ *is defined by the following grammar:*

$$\mathbb{C} ::= \mathtt{skip} \mid \varphi \mid x := E \mid \mathbb{C}; \mathbb{C} \mid \mathtt{if}\ B\ \mathtt{then}\ \mathbb{C}\ \mathtt{else}\ \mathbb{C} \mid \mathtt{while}\ B\ \mathtt{do}\ \mathbb{C} \mid$$
$$\mathtt{procs}\ \overrightarrow{r}_1 := \mathtt{f}_1(\overrightarrow{x}_1)\{\mathbb{C}\},\ \cdots,\ \overrightarrow{r}_k := \mathtt{f}_k(\overrightarrow{x}_k)\{\mathbb{C}\}\ \mathtt{in}\ \mathbb{C} \mid$$
$$\mathtt{call}\ \overrightarrow{r} := \mathtt{f}(\overrightarrow{E}) \mid \mathtt{local}\ x\ \mathtt{in}\ \mathbb{C}$$

where $x, r, \ldots \in \mathrm{Var}$ *range over program variables,* $E, E_1, \ldots \in \mathrm{Exp}_{\mathrm{Val}}$ *range over value expressions,* $\overrightarrow{x}, \overrightarrow{E}, \ldots$ *represent vectors of program variables or expressions,* $B \in \mathrm{Exp}_{\mathrm{Bool}}$ *ranges over boolean expressions, and* $\mathtt{f}, \mathtt{f}_1, \ldots \in \mathrm{PName}$ *range over procedure names.*

2.4   Axiomatic Semantics

We give the semantics of the language $\mathcal{L}_\Phi$ as a program logic based on local Hoare reasoning. We model the state with the context algebra, $\mathcal{A} \times \mathcal{V}$, which combines two context algebras: the context algebra, $\mathcal{A}$, manipulated only by the commands of Φ; and the variable store context algebra, $\mathcal{V}$, used to interpret program variables. By treating variables as resource [1], we are able to avoid side-conditions in our proof rules. A set of axioms $\mathrm{Ax} \subseteq \mathcal{P}(\mathcal{D}_\mathcal{A} \times \Sigma) \times \Phi \times \mathcal{P}(\mathcal{D}_\mathcal{A} \times \Sigma)$ provides the semantics for the commands of Φ, where $\mathcal{D}_\mathcal{A}$ is the set of abstract states from $\mathcal{A}$ and Σ is the set of variable stores from $\mathcal{V}$.

The judgments of our proof system have the form $\Gamma \vdash \{p\}\ \mathbb{C}\ \{q\}$, where $p, q \in \mathcal{P}(\mathcal{D}_\mathcal{A} \times \Sigma)$ are predicates, $\mathbb{C} \in \mathcal{L}_\Phi$ is a program and Γ is a procedure specification environment. A *procedure specification environment* associates procedure names with pairs of pre- and postconditions (parameterised by the arguments and return values of the procedure respectively). The interpretation of judgments is that, in the presence of procedures satisfying Γ, when executed from a state satisfying p, the program $\mathbb{C}$ will either diverge or terminate in a state satisfying q.

The proof rules of the program logic are given in Fig. 2. The semantics of value expressions $[\![E]\!]_\sigma$ is the value of E in variable store σ. The variable store predicate ρ denotes an arbitrary variable store that evaluates all of the program variables that are read but not written in each command under consideration. We write $\mathrm{vars}(\rho)$ and $\mathrm{vars}(E)$ to denote the variables in ρ and E respectively.

The AXIOM rule allows us to use the given specifications of our basic commands and the FRAME rule is the natural generalisation of the frame rule for separation algebras to context algebras. The rules ASSGN, LOCAL, PDEF and PCALL are standard, adapted to our treatment of variables as resource. The

$$\frac{(p,\varphi,q) \in \text{Ax}}{\Gamma \vdash \{p\}\ \varphi\ \{q\}}\ \text{Axiom} \qquad \frac{\Gamma \vdash \{p\}\ \mathbb{C}\ \{q\}}{\Gamma \vdash \{f \circ p\}\ \mathbb{C}\ \{f \circ q\}}\ \text{Frame}$$

$$\frac{\text{vars}(\rho) = \text{vars}(E) - \{x\}}{\Gamma \vdash \{\mathbf{0}_A \times (x \Rightarrow v * \rho)\}\ x := E\ \{\mathbf{0}_A \times (x \Rightarrow [\![E]\!]_{(x \to v * \rho)} * \rho)\}}\ \text{Assgn}$$

$$\frac{\Gamma \vdash \{(\mathbf{I}_A \times x \Rightarrow -) \circ p\}\ \mathbb{C}\ \{(\mathbf{I}_A \times x \Rightarrow -) \circ q\} \quad (\mathbf{I}_A \times x \Rightarrow -) \circ p \neq \emptyset}{\Gamma \vdash \{p\}\ \texttt{local}\ x\ \texttt{in}\ \mathbb{C}\ \{q\}}\ \text{Local}$$

$$\frac{\forall (\mathtt{f}_i : P \to Q) \in \Gamma.\ \Gamma', \Gamma \vdash \begin{array}{c} \{\exists \overrightarrow{v}.\, P(\overrightarrow{v}) \times (\overrightarrow{x_i} \Rightarrow \overrightarrow{v} * \overrightarrow{r_i} \Rightarrow -)\} \\ \mathbb{C}_i \\ \{\exists \overrightarrow{w}.\, Q(\overrightarrow{w}) \times (\overrightarrow{x_i} \Rightarrow - * \overrightarrow{r_i} \Rightarrow \overrightarrow{w})\} \end{array} \qquad \forall (\mathtt{f} : P \to Q) \in \Gamma.\ \exists i.\, \mathtt{f} = \mathtt{f}_i \qquad \Gamma', \Gamma \vdash \{p\}\ \mathbb{C}\ \{q\}}{\Gamma' \vdash \{p\}\ \texttt{procs}\ \overrightarrow{r_1} := \mathtt{f}_1(\overrightarrow{x_1})\{\mathbb{C}_1\}, \ldots, \overrightarrow{r_k} := \mathtt{f}_k(\overrightarrow{x_k})\{\mathbb{C}_k\}\ \texttt{in}\ \mathbb{C}\ \{q\}}\ \text{PDef}$$

$$\frac{\text{vars}(\rho) = \text{vars}(E) - \{\overrightarrow{r}\}}{\Gamma, (\mathtt{f} : P \to Q) \vdash \begin{array}{c} \left\{ P([\![\overrightarrow{E}]\!]_{(\overrightarrow{r} \to \overrightarrow{v} * \rho)}) \times (\overrightarrow{r} \Rightarrow \overrightarrow{v} * \rho) \right\} \\ \texttt{call}\ \overrightarrow{r} := \mathtt{f}(\overrightarrow{E}) \\ \{\exists \overrightarrow{w}.\, Q(\overrightarrow{w}) \times (\overrightarrow{r} \Rightarrow \overrightarrow{w} * \rho)\} \end{array}}\ \text{PCall}$$

Fig. 2. Selected local Hoare logic rules for $\mathcal{L}_\Phi$

Assgn rule not only requires the resource $x \Rightarrow v$, but also the resource ρ containing the other variables used in E. For the Local rule, recall that the predicate p specifies a set of pairs consisting of resource from $\mathcal{D}_A$ and variable resource. The predicate $(\mathbf{I}_A \times x \Rightarrow -) \circ p$ therefore extends the variable component with variable x of indeterminate initial value. If a local variable block is used to re-declare a variable that is already in scope, the Frame rule must be used add the variable's outer scope after the Local rule is applied. For the PDef and PCall rules, the procedure $\mathtt{f}$ has parametrised predicates $P = \lambda \overrightarrow{x}.p$ and $Q = \lambda \overrightarrow{r}.q$ as its pre- and postcondition, with $P(\overrightarrow{v}) = p[\overrightarrow{v}/\overrightarrow{x}]$ and $Q(\overrightarrow{w}) = q[\overrightarrow{w}/\overrightarrow{r}]$; the parameters carry the call and return values of the procedure. We omit the Cons, Disj, Skip, Seq, If and While rules, which are standard. For all of our examples, the conjunction rule is admissible; in general, this is not the case.

3   Abstract Modules

The language given in §2 and its semantics are parameterised by a context algebra, a set of commands and a set of axioms. These parameters constitute an abstract description of a module. We shall use this notion of an *abstract module* to show how to correctly implement one module in terms of another.

Definition 3 (Abstract Module). *An* abstract module $\mathbb{A} = (\mathcal{A}_\mathbb{A}, \Phi_\mathbb{A}, \text{Ax}_\mathbb{A})$ *consists of a context algebra* $\mathcal{A}_\mathbb{A}$ *with abstract state set* $\mathcal{D}_\mathbb{A}$, *a set of commands* $\Phi_\mathbb{A}$ *and a set of axioms* $\text{Ax}_\mathbb{A} \subseteq \mathcal{P}(\mathcal{D}_\mathbb{A} \times \Sigma) \times \Phi_\mathbb{A} \times \mathcal{P}(\mathcal{D}_\mathbb{A} \times \Sigma)$.

Notation. We write $\mathcal{L}_\mathbb{A}$ for the language $\mathcal{L}_{\Phi_\mathbb{A}}$. We write $\vdash_\mathbb{A}$ for the proof judgment determined by the abstract module. When $\mathbb{A}$ can be inferred from context, we may simply write $\vdash$ instead of $\vdash_\mathbb{A}$.

3.1   Heap Module

The first and most familiar abstract module we consider is the abstract heap module, $\mathbb{H} = (\mathcal{H}, \Phi_\mathbb{H}, \mathrm{Ax}_\mathbb{H})$, which extends the core language with standard heap-update commands. The context algebra $\mathcal{H}$ was defined in Example 1. We give the heap update commands in Definition 4, and the axioms for describing the behaviour of these commands in Definition 5.

Definition 4 (Heap Update Commands). *The set of heap update commands* $\Phi_\mathbb{H}$ *comprises: allocation,* $n := \texttt{alloc}(E)$; *disposal,* $\texttt{dispose}(E, E')$; *mutation,* $[E] := E'$; *and lookup* $n := [E]$.

Definition 5 (Heap Axioms). *The set of heap axioms* $\mathrm{Ax}_\mathbb{H}$ *comprises:*

$$\left\{ \begin{array}{l} \mathrm{emp} \times n \Rrightarrow v * \rho \\ \wedge \, [\![E]\!]_{\rho * n \Rrightarrow v} \geq 1 \end{array} \right\} \quad n := \texttt{alloc}(E) \quad \left\{ \begin{array}{l} \exists x.\, x \mapsto - * \ldots \\ * \, x + [\![E]\!]_{\rho * n \Rrightarrow v} \mapsto - \\ \times \, n \Rrightarrow x * \rho \end{array} \right\}$$

$$\left\{ \begin{array}{l} [\![E]\!]_\rho \mapsto - * \ldots \\ * \, [\![E]\!]_\rho + [\![E']\!]_\rho \mapsto - \times \rho \end{array} \right\} \quad \texttt{dispose}(E, E') \quad \{\mathrm{emp} \times \rho\}$$

$$\{[\![E]\!]_\rho \mapsto - \times \rho\} \qquad [E] := E' \qquad \{[\![E]\!]_\rho \mapsto [\![E']\!]_\rho \times \rho\}$$

$$\{[\![E]\!]_{\rho * n \Rrightarrow v} \mapsto x \times n \Rrightarrow v * \rho\} \qquad n := [E] \qquad \{[\![E]\!]_{\rho * n \Rrightarrow v} \mapsto x \times n \Rrightarrow x * \rho\}$$

3.2   Tree Module

Another familiar abstract module that we consider is the abstract tree module, $\mathbb{T} = (\mathcal{T}, \Phi_\mathbb{T}, \mathrm{Ax}_\mathbb{T})$, which extends the core language with tree update commands acting on a single tree, similar to a document in DOM. The tree context algebra $\mathcal{T}$ was defined in Example 1. We give the tree update commands in Definition 6 and their corresponding axioms in Definition 7.

Definition 6 (Tree Update Commands). *The set of tree update commands* $\Phi_\mathbb{T}$ *comprises: relative traversal,* $\texttt{getUp}, \texttt{getLeft}, \texttt{getRight}, \texttt{getFirst}, \texttt{getLast}$; *node creation,* $\texttt{newNodeAfter}$; *and subtree deletion* $\texttt{deleteTree}$.

Definition 7 (Tree Axioms). *The set of tree update axioms* $\mathrm{Ax}_\mathbb{T}$ *includes:*

$$\left\{ \begin{array}{l} [\![E]\!]_{\rho * n \Rrightarrow n}[t] \otimes m[t'] \\ \times \, n \Rrightarrow n * \rho \end{array} \right\} \quad n := \texttt{getRight}(E) \quad \left\{ \begin{array}{l} [\![E]\!]_{\rho * n \Rrightarrow n}[t] \otimes m[t'] \\ \times \, n \Rrightarrow m * \rho \end{array} \right\}$$

$$\left\{ \begin{array}{l} m[t' \otimes [\![E]\!]_{\rho * n \Rrightarrow n}[t]] \\ \times \, n \Rrightarrow n * \rho \end{array} \right\} \quad n := \texttt{getRight}(E) \quad \left\{ \begin{array}{l} m[t' \otimes [\![E]\!]_{\rho * n \Rrightarrow n}[t]] \\ \times \, n \Rrightarrow \boldsymbol{null} * \rho \end{array} \right\}$$

$$\left\{ \begin{array}{l} [\![E]\!]_{\rho * n \Rrightarrow n}[t' \otimes m[t]] \\ \times \, n \Rrightarrow n * \rho \end{array} \right\} \quad n := \texttt{getLast}(E) \quad \left\{ \begin{array}{l} [\![E]\!]_{\rho * n \Rrightarrow n}[t' \otimes m[t]] \\ \times \, n \Rrightarrow m * \rho \end{array} \right\}$$

$$\left\{ \begin{array}{l} [\![E]\!]_{\rho * n \Rrightarrow n}[\varnothing] \\ \times \, n \Rrightarrow n * \rho \end{array} \right\} \quad n := \texttt{getLast}(E) \quad \left\{ \begin{array}{l} [\![E]\!]_{\rho * n \Rrightarrow n}[\varnothing] \\ \times \, n \Rrightarrow \boldsymbol{null} * \rho \end{array} \right\}$$

$$\{[\![E]\!]_\rho[t] \times \rho\} \ \texttt{newNodeAfter}(E) \ \{\exists m. \, [\![E]\!]_\rho[t] \otimes m[\varnothing] \times \rho\}$$
$$\{[\![E]\!]_\rho[t] \times \rho\} \ \texttt{deleteTree}(E) \ \{\varnothing \times \rho\}$$

The omitted axioms are analogous to those given above.

3.3 List Module

We will study an implementation of the tree module using lists of unique addresses. We therefore define an abstract module for manipulating lists whose elements are unique, $\mathbb{L} = (\mathcal{L}, \Phi_\mathbb{L}, \text{Ax}_\mathbb{L})$. The list context algebra $\mathcal{L}$ is given in Definition 10. The list update commands are given in Definition 11 and their corresponding axioms are given in Definition 12.

Superficially, our abstract list stores resemble heaps, in the sense that we have multiple lists each with a unique address. We write $(i \mapsto v_1 + v_2 + v_3) * (j \mapsto w_1 + v_1)$ to denote a list store consisting of two separate lists $v_1 + v_2 + v_3$ and $w_1 + v_1$, at different addresses i and j. However, unlike heaps, our list store contexts also allow us to consider separation within lists. For example, the same list store can be written as $(i \mapsto v_1 + \_ + v_3) \circ (i \mapsto v_2 * j \mapsto w_1 + v_1)$, describing a list context $v_1 + \_ + v_3$ at address i applied to the list store $i \mapsto v_2 * j \mapsto w_1 + v_1$: the application puts list v_2 at i into the context hole.

Furthermore, we make a distinction between lists $j \mapsto w_1 + v_1$ which can be extended by list contexts, and *completed* lists $j \mapsto [w_1 + v_1]$ which cannot be extended. The reason to work with completed lists is that sometimes we need to know which elements are the first or last elements in a list. For example, the command $\texttt{getHead}$ will return the first element of a list, so this element must be fully determined and not subject to change if a frame is applied. Completed lists may be separated into contexts and sublists, for example $j \mapsto [w_1 + \_] \circ j \mapsto v_1$ is defined, but may not be extended, for example $j \mapsto w_1 + \_ \circ j \mapsto [v_1]$ is undefined.

Definition 8 (List Stores and Contexts). Lists $l \in \text{L}$, list contexts $lc \in \text{LC}$, list stores $ls \in \text{Ls}$, *and* list store contexts $lsc \in \text{LSC}$ *are defined by:*

$$l ::= \varepsilon \mid v \mid l + l \qquad\qquad ls ::= \text{emp} \mid i \mapsto l \mid i \mapsto [l] \mid ls * ls$$
$$lc ::= \_ \mid lc + l \mid l + lc \qquad lsc ::= ls \mid i \mapsto lc \mid i \mapsto [lc] \mid lsc * lsc$$

where $v \in \text{Val}$ ranges over values, which are taken to occur uniquely in each list or list context, $i \in \text{LADDR}$ ranges over list addresses, which are taken to occur uniquely in each list store or list store context, $+$ is taken to be associative with identity ε, and $*$ is taken to be associative and commutative with identity emp.

Our context application $\circ$ actually subsumes our separating operator $*$, in that as well as extending existing lists, we can also add new lists to the store, for example $(j \mapsto w_1 + v_1) \circ (i \mapsto v_1 + v_2 + v_3) = (j \mapsto w_1 + v_1) * (i \mapsto v_1 + v_2 + v_3)$.

Definition 9 (Application and Composition). *The application of list store contexts to list stores* $\circ : \text{LSC} \times \text{LS} \rightharpoonup \text{LS}$ *is defined inductively by:*

$$\text{emp} \circ ls = ls$$
$$(lsc * i \mapsto l) \circ ls = (lsc \circ ls) * i \mapsto l$$
$$(lsc * i \mapsto [l]) \circ ls = (lsc \circ ls) * i \mapsto [l]$$

$$(lsc * i \mapsto lc) \circ (ls * i \mapsto l) = (lsc \circ ls) * i \mapsto lc_{[l/\_]}$$

$$(lsc * i \mapsto [lc]) \circ (ls * i \mapsto l) = (lsc \circ ls) * i \mapsto [lc_{[l/\_]}]$$

where $lc_{[l/\_]}$ denotes the standard replacement of the hole in lc by l. The result of the application is undefined when either the right-hand side is badly formed or no case applies. The composition $\bullet : \text{LSC} \times \text{LSC} \rightharpoonup \text{LSC}$ is defined similarly.

Definition 10 (List-Store Context Algebra). *The* list-store context alge-bra*, $\mathcal{L} = (\text{LSC}, \text{LS}, \bullet, \circ, \{\text{emp}\}, \{\text{emp}\})$ is given by the above definitions.*

Definition 11 (List Update Commands). *The set of list commands $\Phi_{\mathbb{L}}$ com-prises: lookup, getHead, getTail, getNext, getPrev; stack-style access, pop, push; value removal and insertion, remove, insert; and construction and de-struction, newList, deleteList.*

Definition 12 (List Axioms). *The set of list axioms $\text{Ax}_{\mathbb{L}}$ includes the follow-ing axioms: (the omitted axioms are analogous)*

$$\left\{ \begin{array}{l} [\![E]\!]_{\rho*v \to v} \mapsto [v'+l] \\ \times\, v \Rightarrow v * \rho \end{array} \right\} \quad v := E.\text{getHead}() \quad \left\{ \begin{array}{l} [\![E]\!]_{\rho*v \to v} \mapsto [v'+l] \\ \times\, v \Rightarrow v' * \rho \end{array} \right\}$$

$$\left\{ \begin{array}{l} [\![E]\!]_{\rho*v \to v} \mapsto [\varepsilon] \\ \times\, v \Rightarrow v * \rho \end{array} \right\} \quad v := E.\text{getHead}() \quad \left\{ \begin{array}{l} [\![E]\!]_{\rho*v \to v} \mapsto [\varepsilon] \\ \times\, v \Rightarrow \boldsymbol{null} * \rho \end{array} \right\}$$

$$\left\{ \begin{array}{l} [\![E]\!]_{\rho*v \to v} \mapsto [\![E']\!]_{\rho*v \to v}+u \\ \times\, v \Rightarrow v * \rho \end{array} \right\} \quad v := E.\text{getNext}(E') \quad \left\{ \begin{array}{l} [\![E]\!]_{\rho*v \to v} \mapsto [\![E']\!]_{\rho*v \to v}+u \\ \times\, v \Rightarrow u * \rho \end{array} \right\}$$

$$\left\{ \begin{array}{l} [\![E]\!]_{\rho*v \to v} \mapsto [l+[\![E']\!]_{\rho*v \to v}] \\ \times\, v \Rightarrow v * \rho \end{array} \right\} \quad v := E.\text{getNext}(E') \quad \left\{ \begin{array}{l} [\![E]\!]_{\rho*v \to v} \mapsto [l+[\![E']\!]_{\rho*v \to v}] \\ \times\, v \Rightarrow \boldsymbol{null} * \rho \end{array} \right\}$$

$$\{[\![E]\!]_{\rho} \mapsto [l] \times \rho \wedge ([\![E']\!]_{\rho} \notin l)\} \quad E.\text{push}(E') \quad \{[\![E]\!]_{\rho} \mapsto [[\![E']\!]_{\rho} + l] \times \rho\}$$

$$\{[\![E]\!]_{\rho} \mapsto [\![E']\!]_{\rho} \times \rho\} \quad E.\text{remove}(E') \quad \{[\![E]\!]_{\rho} \mapsto \varepsilon \times \rho\}$$

$$\left\{ \begin{array}{l} [\![E]\!]_{\rho} \mapsto [l+[\![E']\!]_{\rho}+l'] \times \rho \\ \wedge ([\![E'']\!]_{\rho} \notin l+[\![E']\!]_{\rho}+l') \end{array} \right\} \quad E.\text{insert}(E', E'') \quad \left\{ \begin{array}{l} [\![E]\!]_{\rho} \mapsto [l + [\![E']\!]_{\rho}+ \\ \qquad [\![E'']\!]_{\rho}+l'] \times \rho \end{array} \right\}$$

$$\{\emptyset \times i \Rightarrow i\} \quad i := \text{newList}() \quad \{\exists j.\, j \mapsto [\varepsilon] \times i \Rightarrow j\}$$

$$\{[\![E]\!]_{\rho} \mapsto [l] \times \rho\} \quad E.\text{deleteList}() \quad \{\emptyset \times \rho\}$$

3.4 Combining Abstract Modules

We provide a natural way of combining abstract modules that enables programs to be written that intermix commands from different modules. For example, we will use the heap and list module combination $\mathbb{H} + \mathbb{L}$ in §5.1 as the basis for implementing $\mathbb{T}$. The combination comprises both commands for manipulating lists and commands for manipulating heaps, defined so that they do not interfere with each other.

Definition 13 (Abstract Module Combination). *Given abstract modules $\mathbb{A}_1 = (\mathcal{A}_{\mathbb{A}_1}, \Phi_{\mathbb{A}_1}, \text{Ax}_{\mathbb{A}_1})$ and $\mathbb{A}_2 = (\mathcal{A}_{\mathbb{A}_2}, \Phi_{\mathbb{A}_2}, \text{Ax}_{\mathbb{A}_2})$, their combination $\mathbb{A}_1 + \mathbb{A}_2 = (\mathcal{A}_{\mathbb{A}_1} \times \mathcal{A}_{\mathbb{A}_2}, \Phi_{\mathbb{A}_1} \oplus \Phi_{\mathbb{A}_2}, \text{Ax}_{\mathbb{A}_1} + \text{Ax}_{\mathbb{A}_2})$ is defined by:*

– $\mathcal{A}_{\mathbb{A}_1} \times \mathcal{A}_{\mathbb{A}_2}$ *is the product of context algebras;*
– $\Phi_{\mathbb{A}_1} \oplus \Phi_{\mathbb{A}_2} = (\Phi_{\mathbb{A}_1} \times \{1\}) \cup (\Phi_{\mathbb{A}_2} \times \{2\})$ *is the disjoint union of command sets;*
– $\mathrm{Ax}_{\mathbb{A}_1} + \mathrm{Ax}_{\mathbb{A}_2}$ *is the lifting of the axiom sets* $\mathrm{Ax}_{\mathbb{A}_1}$ *and* $\mathrm{Ax}_{\mathbb{A}_2}$ *using the empty states from* $\mathrm{Ax}_{\mathbb{A}_2}$ *and* $\mathrm{Ax}_{\mathbb{A}_1}$: *formally,* $\mathrm{Ax}_{\mathbb{A}_1} + \mathrm{Ax}_{\mathbb{A}_2} =$
  $\{(\pi_1 p, (\varphi, 1), \pi_1 q) \mid (p, \varphi, q) \in \mathrm{Ax}_{\mathbb{A}_1}\} \cup \{(\pi_2 p, (\varphi, 2), \pi_2 q) \mid (p, \varphi, q) \in \mathrm{Ax}_{\mathbb{A}_1}\}$,
  where $\pi_1 p = \{(d, o, \sigma) \mid (d, \sigma) \in p, \ o \in \mathbf{0}_2\}$, $\pi_2 p = \{(o, d, \sigma) \mid (d, \sigma) \in p, \ o \in \mathbf{0}_1\}$.

When the command sets $\Phi_{\mathbb{A}_1}$ and $\Phi_{\mathbb{A}_2}$ are disjoint, we may drop the tags when referring to the commands in the combined abstract module. When we do use the tags, we indicate them with an appropriately placed subscript.

4   Module Translations

We define what it means to correctly implement one module in terms of another, using translations which are reminiscent of downward simulations in [9].

Definition 14 (Sound Module Translation). *A module translation* $\mathbb{A} \to \mathbb{B}$ *from abstract module* $\mathbb{A}$ *to abstract module* $\mathbb{B}$ *consists of*

– *a state translation function* $[\![-]\!] : \mathcal{D}_{\mathbb{A}} \to \mathcal{P}(\mathcal{D}_{\mathbb{B}})$, *and*
– *a substitutive implementation function* $[\![-]\!] : \mathcal{L}_{\mathbb{A}} \to \mathcal{L}_{\mathbb{B}}$ *obtained by substituting each basic command of* $\Phi_{\mathbb{A}}$ *with a call to a procedure written in* $\mathcal{L}_{\mathbb{B}}$.

A module translation is sound *if, for all* $p, q \in \mathcal{P}(\mathcal{D}_{\mathbb{A}} \times \Sigma)$ *and* $\mathbb{C} \in \mathcal{L}_{\mathbb{A}}$,

$$\vdash_{\mathbb{A}} \{p\} \ \mathbb{C} \ \{q\} \quad \Longrightarrow \quad \vdash_{\mathbb{B}} \{[\![p]\!]\} \ [\![\mathbb{C}]\!] \ \{[\![q]\!]\}.$$

where the predicate translation $[\![-]\!] : \mathcal{P}(\mathcal{D}_{\mathbb{A}} \times \Sigma) \to \mathcal{P}(\mathcal{D}_{\mathbb{B}} \times \Sigma)$ *is the natural lifting of the state translation given by* $[\![p]\!] = \bigvee_{(d,\sigma) \in p} [\![d]\!] \times \sigma$.

We will see that sometimes the module structure is preserved by the translations and sometimes it is not; also, sometimes the proof structure is preserved, sometimes not. Notice that, since we are only considering partial correctness, it is always acceptable for the implementation to diverge. In order to make termination guarantees, we could work with total correctness; our decision not to is for simplicity and based on prevailing trends in separation logic and context logic literature [12,4,2]. It is possible for our predicate translation to lose information. For instance, if all predicates were unsatisfiable under translation, it would be possible to implement every abstract command with `skip`; such an implementation is useless. It may be desirable to consider some injectivity condition which distinguishes states and predicates of interest. Our results do not rely on this.

Modularity. A translation $\mathbb{A}_1 \to \mathbb{A}_2$ can be naturally lifted to a translation $\mathbb{A}_1 + \mathbb{B} \to \mathbb{A}_2 + \mathbb{B}$, for any module $\mathbb{B}$. We would hope that the resulting translations would be sound, but it is not clear that this holds for all sound translations $\mathbb{A}_1 \to \mathbb{A}_2$. When it is does hold, we say that the translation $\mathbb{A}_1 \to \mathbb{A}_2$ is *modular*. The techniques we consider in this paper provide modular translations, because they inductively transform proofs from module $\mathbb{A}_1$ to proofs in module $\mathbb{A}_2$.

5   Locality-Preserving Translations

Sometimes there is a close correspondence between locality in an abstract module and locality in its implementation. We introduce locality-preserving module translations, and provide a general result that such translations are sound. Recall Fig. 1 of the introduction. We show that module translations $\mathbb{T} \to \mathbb{H} + \mathbb{L}$ and $\mathbb{H} + \mathbb{H} \to \mathbb{H}$ are locality preserving.

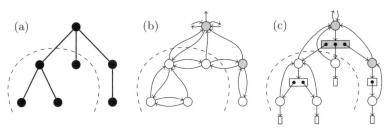

Fig. 3. An abstract tree from T (a), and its representations in H (b) and H × Ls (c)

Consider Fig. 3 which depicts a simple tree (a), and representations of it in the heap module $\mathbb{H}$ (b), and in the combined heap and list module $\mathbb{H} + \mathbb{L}$ (c). In (b), a node is represented by a memory block of four fields, recording the addresses of the left sibling, parent, right sibling and first child. In (c), a node is represented by a list of the child nodes (shown as boxes) and a block of two fields, recording the address of the parent and the child list. Just as the tree in (a) can be decomposed into a context and a disjoint subtree (as shown by the dashed lined), its representations can also be decomposed: the representations preserve context application. However, we must account for the pointers in the representations which cross the boundary between context and subtree. This means that the representation of a tree must be parameterised by an *interface* to the surrounding context. Similarly, contexts are parameterised by interfaces both to the inner subtree and outer context. We split the interface I into two components: the reference the surrounding context makes *in* to the subtree (the *in* part), and the reference the subtree makes *out* to the surrounding context (the *out* part).

Consider deleting the subtree indicated by the dashed lines in the figure. In the abstract tree, this deletion only operates on the subtree: the axiom for deletion has just the subtree as its precondition. In the implementations however, the deletion also operates on the representation of some of the surrounding context: in (b), this is the parent node and right sibling; in (c), the parent node and child list. We therefore introduce the idea of a *crust* predicate, m_I^F, that comprises the minimal additional state required by an implementation. The crust is parameterised by interface I and an additional crust parameter F that fully determine it. In the figure, the crusts for the subtree in (b) and (c) are shown shaded. (In the list-based representation, all the sibling nodes form part of the crust because they are required for node insertion.)

We define locality-preserving translations which incorporate three key properties: *application preservation, crust inclusion,* and *axiom correctness*. Application preservation, we have seen, requires that the low-level representations of abstract states can be decomposed in the same manner as the abstract states themselves. Crust inclusion requires that an abstract state's crust is subsumed by any context that is applied (together with the context's own crust). This allows us to frame on arbitrary contexts despite the crust already being present – we simply remove the state's crust from the context before applying it. (Since the crust represents an effective overlap between what represents a state and what represents its context, the abstract view that the two are disjoint is really a fiction of disjointness.) Finally, axiom correctness requires that the implementations of the basic commands meet the specifications given by the abstract module's axioms.

Definition 15 (Locality-Preserving Translation). *For interface set* $\mathcal{I} = \mathcal{I}_{\text{in}} \times \mathcal{I}_{\text{out}}$ *and crust parameter set* $\mathcal{F}$, *a locality-preserving translation* $\mathbb{A} \to \mathbb{B}$ *comprises:*

- *representation functions* $\langle\!\langle - \rangle\!\rangle^- : \mathcal{D}_\mathbb{A} \times \mathcal{I} \to \mathcal{P}(\mathcal{D}_\mathbb{B})$ *and* $\langle\!\langle - \rangle\!\rangle^-_- : \mathcal{C}_\mathbb{A} \times \mathcal{I} \times \mathcal{I} \to \mathcal{P}(\mathcal{C}_\mathbb{B})$;
- *a crust predicate* $\Cap_I^F$, *parameterised by* $I \in \mathcal{I}$ *and* $F \in \mathcal{F}$; *and*
- *a substitutive implementation function* $[\![-]\!] : \mathcal{L}_\mathbb{A} \to \mathcal{L}_\mathbb{B}$,

for which the following properties hold:

1. **application preservation:** *for all* $f \in \mathcal{P}(\mathcal{C}_\mathbb{A})$, $p \in \mathcal{P}(\mathcal{D}_\mathbb{A})$ *and* $I \in \mathcal{I}$,

$$\langle\!\langle f \circ_\mathbb{A} p \rangle\!\rangle^I \quad = \quad \exists I'. \, \langle\!\langle f \rangle\!\rangle^I_{I'} \circ_\mathbb{B} \langle\!\langle p \rangle\!\rangle^{I'} ;$$

2. **crust inclusion:** *for all* $\overrightarrow{out'}, \overrightarrow{out} \in \mathcal{I}_{\text{out}}$, $F \in \mathcal{F}$, $c \in \mathcal{C}_\mathbb{A}$, *there exist* $f \in \mathcal{P}(\mathcal{C}_\mathbb{B})$, $F' \in \mathcal{F}$ *such that, for all* $\overrightarrow{in} \in \mathcal{I}_{\text{in}}$,

$$\left(\exists \overrightarrow{in'}. \, \Cap^F_{\overrightarrow{in'},\overrightarrow{out'}} \bullet \langle\!\langle c \rangle\!\rangle^{\overrightarrow{in'},\overrightarrow{out'}}_{\overrightarrow{in},\overrightarrow{out}} \right) = f \bullet \Cap^{F'}_{\overrightarrow{in},\overrightarrow{out}}; \text{ and}$$

3. **axiom correctness:** *for all* $(p, \varphi, q) \in \text{Ax}_\mathbb{A}$, $\overrightarrow{out} \in \mathcal{I}_{\text{out}}$ *and* $F \in \mathcal{F}$,

$$\vdash_\mathbb{B} \left\{ (\!|p|\!)^{\overrightarrow{out},F} \right\} \, [\![\varphi]\!] \, \left\{ (\!|q|\!)^{\overrightarrow{out},F} \right\},$$

where $(\!|p|\!)^{\overrightarrow{out},F} = \bigvee_{(d,\sigma) \in p} (\exists \overrightarrow{in}. \, \Cap^F_{\overrightarrow{in},\overrightarrow{out}} \circ \langle\!\langle d \rangle\!\rangle^{\overrightarrow{in},\overrightarrow{out}}) \times \sigma.$

Notice that this locality-preserving translation is a module translation, with the state translation function $[\![-]\!] : \mathcal{D}_\mathbb{A} \to \mathcal{P}(\mathcal{D}_\mathbb{B})$ defined by $[\![d]\!] = \exists \overrightarrow{in}. \, \Cap^F_{\overrightarrow{in},\overrightarrow{out}} \circ \langle\!\langle d \rangle\!\rangle^{\overrightarrow{in},\overrightarrow{out}}$, for some choice of $\overrightarrow{out} \in \mathcal{I}_{\text{out}}$ and $F \in \mathcal{F}$.

Theorem 1. *A locality-preserving translation* $\mathbb{A} \to \mathbb{B}$ *is a sound translation.*

This theorem is proved by inductively transforming a high-level proof in $\mathbb{A}$ to the corresponding proof in $\mathbb{B}$, preserving the structure. Application preservation and crust inclusion allow us to transform a high-level frame into a low-level frame, and axiom correctness allows us to soundly replace the high-level commands with their implementations. The remaining proof rules transform naturally. If we chose to include the conjunction rule in our proof system, then we would need to additionally verify that our representation functions preserve conjunction and also that the crust predicate $\exists \overrightarrow{in}.\, \cap_{\substack{in,out}}^{F}$ is precise.

5.1 Module Translation: $\mathbb{T} \to \mathbb{H} + \mathbb{L}$

We study a list-based implementation of the tree module which uses a combination of the heap and list modules given in §3. We shall see that this implementation provides a locality-preserving translation of our abstract tree module. To define a locality-preserving translation we need to give a representation function, a crust predicate and a substitutive implementation function for the translation.

The representation functions for trees and tree contexts are given below. As we have seen, each node of the tree is represented by a list of addresses of the node's children and a memory block of two fields that record the addresses of the parent node and child list. The in part of the interface, $l \in (\mathbb{N}^+)^*$, is a list of the addresses of the top-level nodes of the subtree. The out part of the interface, $u \in \mathbb{N}^+$, is the address of the subtree's parent node. We use the notation $x \mapsto y,z$ to mean $x \mapsto y * x + 1 \mapsto z$ and also write $E_1 \doteq E_2$ to mean $emp \wedge (E_1 = E_2)$. We also abuse notation slightly, freely combining heaps and list stores with $*$.

$$\langle\!\langle \varnothing \rangle\!\rangle^{\varepsilon,u} ::= emp$$

$$\langle\!\langle n[t] \rangle\!\rangle^{n,u} ::= \exists i,l.\, n \mapsto u,i * i \mapsto [\,l\,] * \langle\!\langle t \rangle\!\rangle^{l,n}$$

$$\langle\!\langle t_1 \otimes t_2 \rangle\!\rangle^{l,u} ::= \exists l_1,l_2.\, (l \doteq l_1 + l_2) * \langle\!\langle t_1 \rangle\!\rangle^{l_1,u} * \langle\!\langle t_2 \rangle\!\rangle^{l_2,u}$$

$$\langle\!\langle - \rangle\!\rangle_{l',u'}^{l,u} ::= (l \doteq l') * (u \doteq u')$$

$$\langle\!\langle n[c] \rangle\!\rangle_{I'}^{n,u} ::= \exists i,l.\, n \mapsto u,i * i \mapsto [\,l\,] * \langle\!\langle c \rangle\!\rangle_{I'}^{l,n}$$

$$\langle\!\langle t \otimes c \rangle\!\rangle_{I'}^{l,u} ::= \exists l_1,l_2.\, (l \doteq l_1 + l_2) * \langle\!\langle t \rangle\!\rangle^{l_1,u} * \langle\!\langle c \rangle\!\rangle_{I'}^{l_2,u}$$

$$\langle\!\langle c \otimes t \rangle\!\rangle_{I'}^{l,u} ::= \exists l_1,l_2.\, (l \doteq l_1 + l_2) * \langle\!\langle c \rangle\!\rangle_{I'}^{l_1,u} * \langle\!\langle t \rangle\!\rangle^{l_2,u}$$

The crust, $\cap_I^F$, parameterised by interface $I = l,u$ and free logical variables $F = (l_1, l_2, u')$, is defined as follows:

$$\cap_{l,u}^{l_1,l_2,u'} ::= \exists i.\, u \mapsto u',i * i \mapsto [\,l_1 + l + l_2\,] * \left(\prod_{n \in l_1 + l_2}^{*} n \mapsto u \right)$$

This crust predicate captures the shaded part of the tree shown in Fig. 3(c) which includes the parent node u of the subtree and the list of u's children, including the top level nodes l of the subtree. These are needed by the implementations of commands that lookup siblings or parents, or delete a subtree. The crust also

```
n.parent ≜ n
n.children ≜ n + 1
n := newNode() ≜ n := alloc(2)
disposeNode(n) ≜ dispose(n, 2)

proc n′ := getLast(n){
  local x in
    x := [n.children] ;
    n′ := x.getTail()
}
```

```
proc n′ := getRight(n){
  local x, y in
    x := [n.parent] ;
    y := [x.children] ;
    n′ := y.getNext(n)
}
```

```
proc deleteTree(n){
  local x, y, z in
    x := [n.parent] ;
    y := [x.children] ;
    y.remove(n) ;
    y := [n.children] ;
    z := y.getHead() ;
    while z ≠ null do
      call deleteTree(z) ;
      z := y.getHead()
    disposeList(y) ;
    disposeNode(n)
}
```

Fig. 4. Selected procedures for the list-based implementation

includes the other sibling nodes as these are needed by the implementation of the node insertion command.

A selection of the procedures that constitute the substitutive implementation function is given in Fig. 4.

Theorem 2. *The representation function, crust predicate and substitutive implementation given above constitute a locality-preserving translation.*

5.2 Module Translation: $\mathbb{H} + \mathbb{H} \to \mathbb{H}$

Another example of a locality-preserving translation is given by implementing a pair of heap modules $\mathbb{H} + \mathbb{H}$ in a single heap $\mathbb{H}$, by simply treating the two heaps as disjoint portions of the same heap.

The representation function is the same both for states and for contexts: $\langle\!\langle (h_1, h_2) \rangle\!\rangle = \{h_1\} * \{h_2\}$. The interface set is trivial (just a single-element set). The crust parameter set is also trivial, and the crust predicate is simply emp. The substitutive implementation $[\![\mathbb{C}]\!]$ is defined to be the detagging of $\mathbb{C}$: that is, heap commands from both abstract modules are substituted with the corresponding command from the single abstract module. For example:

$$[\![n := \mathtt{alloc}_1(E)]\!] = n := \mathtt{alloc}(E) = [\![n := \mathtt{alloc}_2(E)]\!]$$

Theorem 3. *The representation function, crust predicate and substitutive implementation given above constitute a locality-preserving translation.*

(Note, the representation function in this case does not preserve conjunction.)

6 Locality-Breaking Translations

There is not always a close correspondence between locality in an abstract module and locality in its implementation. For example, consider an implementation of our list module that represents each list as a singly-linked list in the heap. In the abstract module, the footprint of removing a specific element from a list is just the element of the list. In the implementation however, the list is traversed from its head to reach the element, which is then deleted by modifying the pointer of its predecessor. The footprint is therefore the list fragment from the head of the list to the element, significantly more than the single list node holding the value to be removed. While we could treat this additional footprint as crust, in this case it seems appropriate to abandon the preservation of locality and instead give a locality-breaking translation that provides a fiction of locality.

Consider a translation from abstract module $\mathbb{A}$ to $\mathbb{B}$. With the exception of the frame rule and axioms, the proof rules for $\mathbb{A}$ can be mapped to the corresponding proof rules of $\mathbb{B}$: that is, from the translated premises we can directly deduce the translated conclusion. To deal with the frame rule, we remove it from proofs in $\mathbb{A}$ by 'pushing' applications of the frame rule to the leaves of the proof tree. In this way, we can transform any local proof to a non-local proof.

Lemma 1 (Frame-free Derivations). *Let $\mathbb{A}$ be an abstract module. If there is a derivation of $\vdash_{\mathbb{A}} \{p\} \; \mathbb{C} \; \{q\}$ then there is also a derivation that only uses the frame rule in the following ways:*

$$\frac{}{\dfrac{\Gamma \vdash \{p\} \; \mathbb{C} \; \{q\}}{\Gamma \vdash \{f \circ p\} \; \mathbb{C} \; \{f \circ q\}}} \; (\dagger) \qquad \frac{\vdots}{\dfrac{\Gamma \vdash \{p\} \; \mathbb{C} \; \{q\}}{\Gamma \vdash \{(\mathbf{I}_{\mathbb{A}} \times \sigma) \circ p\} \; \mathbb{C} \; \{(\mathbf{I}_{\mathbb{A}} \times \sigma) \circ q\}}}$$

where $(\dagger)$ *is either* AXIOM, SKIP *or* ASSGN.

By transforming a high-level proof of $\vdash_{\mathbb{A}} \{p\} \; \mathbb{C} \; \{q\}$ in this way, we can establish $\vdash_{\mathbb{B}} \{[\![p]\!]\} \; [\![\mathbb{C}]\!] \; \{[\![q]\!]\}$ provided that we can prove that the implementation of each command of $\varPhi_{\mathbb{A}}$ satisfies the translation of each of its axioms under every frame. (We can reduce considerations to *singleton* frames by considering any given frame as a disjunction of singletons and applying the DISJ rule.)

Definition 16 (Locality-breaking Translation). *A locality-breaking translation $\mathbb{A} \to \mathbb{B}$ is a module translation such that, for all $c \in \mathcal{C}_{\mathbb{A}}$ and $(p, \varphi, q) \in \mathrm{AX}_{\mathbb{A}}$, the judgment $\vdash_{\mathbb{B}} \{[\![\{c\} \circ p]\!]\} \; [\![\varphi]\!] \; \{[\![\{c\} \circ q]\!]\}$ holds.*

Theorem 4. *A locality-breaking translation is a sound translation.*

If we include the conjunction rule, then we must verify that every singleton context predicate is precise (i.e. the context algebra must be left-cancellative). Note that, whilst there is less to prove when working with locality-breaking translations than with locality-preserving translations, the actual proofs may be more difficult as we have to show that the axioms are preserved in *every* context. Our examples show that the two approaches are suited to different circumstances.

6.1 Module Translation: $\mathbb{L} \to \mathbb{H}$

We provide a locality-breaking translation $\mathbb{L} \to \mathbb{H}$, which implements abstract lists with singly-linked lists in the heap.

The state translation from list stores to heaps is defined inductively by:

$$[\![\emptyset]\!] ::= \mathrm{emp} \qquad\qquad [\![i \mapsto l * ls]\!] ::= \mathbf{False}$$
$$[\![i \mapsto [\,l\,] * ls]\!] ::= \exists x.\, i \mapsto x * \langle\!\langle l \rangle\!\rangle^{(x, \mathbf{null})} * [\![ls]\!]$$

where

$$\langle\!\langle \varepsilon \rangle\!\rangle^{(x,y)} ::= (x \doteq y) \qquad\qquad \langle\!\langle v \rangle\!\rangle^{(x,y)} ::= x \mapsto v,y$$
$$\langle\!\langle l + l' \rangle\!\rangle^{(x,y)} ::= \exists z.\, \langle\!\langle l \rangle\!\rangle^{(x,z)} * \langle\!\langle l' \rangle\!\rangle^{(z,y)}$$

Note that not all list stores are realised by heaps: only ones in which every list is complete. The intuition behind this is that partial lists are purely abstract notions that provide a useful means to our ultimate end, namely reasoning about complete lists. The abstract module itself does not provide operations for creating or destroying partial lists, and so we would not expect to give specifications for complete programs that concern partial lists. A selection of the procedures that constitute the substitutive implementation function is given in Fig. 5.

```
          x.value ≜ x                       then
          x.next ≜ x + 1                       [i] := y ;            proc v := i.getNext(v'){
    x := newNode() ≜ x := alloc(2)           disposeNode(x)           local x in
    disposeNode(x) ≜ dispose(x,2)         else                          x := [i] ;
                                             u := [y.value] ;            v := [x.value] ;
        proc  i.remove(v){                  while u ≠ v do             while v ≠ v' do
          local u, x, y, z in                 x := y ;                    x := [x.next] ;
          x := [i] ;                          y := [x.next] ;             v := [x.value]
          u := [x.value] ;                    u := [y.value]            x := [x.next] ;
          y := [x.next] ;                     z := [y.next] ;           if x = null then v := x
          if  u = v                           [x.next] := z ;           else v := [x.value]
                                              disposeNode(y)          }
        }
```

Fig. 5. Selected procedures for the linked-list implementation

Theorem 5. *The state translation and substitutive implementation given above constitute a locality-breaking translation.*

7   Conclusions

We have shown how to refine module specifications given by abstract local reasoning into correct implementations. We have identified two general approaches for proving correctness: locality-preserving and locality-breaking translations. Locality-preserving translations relate the abstract locality of a module with the low-level locality of its implementation. This is subtle since disjoint structures at the high-level are not quite disjoint at the low-level, because of the additional crust that is required to handle the pointer surgery. Locality-preserving translations thus establish a fiction of disjointness. Meanwhile, locality-breaking translations establish a fiction of locality, by justifying abstract locality even though this locality is not matched by the implementation.

This paper has focused on refinement for abstract local reasoning in the sequential setting. With Dodds, Parkinson and Vafeiadis, Dinsdale-Young and

Gardner have introduced concurrent abstract predicates [6] as a technique for verifying correct implementations of concurrent modules. They achieve local reasoning and disjoint concurrency at the abstract level, by abstracting from a low-level resource model with fine-grained permissions. Our next challenge is to extend our refinement techniques to the setting of disjoint concurrency.

Acknowledgments. Gardner acknowledges support of a Microsoft/RAEng Senior Research Fellowship. Dinsdale-Young and Wheelhouse acknowledge support of EPSRC DTA awards. We thank Mohammad Raza and Uri Zarfaty for detailed discussions of this work. In particular, some of the technical details in our locality-preserving translations come from an unpublished technical report *Reasoning about High-level Tree Update and its Low-level Implementation* written by Gardner and Zarfaty in 2008.

References

1. Bornat, R., Calcagno, C., Yang, H.: Variables as resource in separation logic. In: Proceedings of MFPS XXI. ENTCS, vol. 155, pp. 247–276. Elsevier, Amsterdam (2006)
2. Calcagno, C., Gardner, P., Zarfaty, U.: Context logic and tree update. In: POPL 2005. SIGPLAN Not., vol. 40, pp. 271–282. ACM, New York (2005)
3. Calcagno, C., Gardner, P., Zarfaty, U.: Local reasoning about data update. Electron. Notes Theor. Comput. Sci. 172, 133–175 (2007)
4. Calcagno, C., O'Hearn, P.W., Yang, H.: Local action and abstract separation logic. In: LICS 2007, Washington, DC, USA, pp. 366–378. IEEE Computer Society, Los Alamitos (2007)
5. DeRoever, W., Engelhardt, K.: Data Refinement: Model-Oriented Proof Methods and Their Comparison. Cambridge University Press, Cambridge (1999)
6. Dinsdale-Young, T., Dodds, M., Gardner, P., Parkinson, M., Vafeiadis, V.: Concurrent abstract predicates. In: D'Hondt, T. (ed.) ECOOP 2010. LNCS, vol. 6183, pp. 504–528. Springer, Heidelberg (2010)
7. Dinsdale-Young, T., Gardner, P., Wheelhouse, M.: Abstract local reasoning. Technical report, Imperial College London, London, UK (2010), http://www.doc.ic.ac.uk/~td202/papers/alrfull.pdf
8. Gardner, P.A., Smith, G.D., Wheelhouse, M.J., Zarfaty, U.D.: Local Hoare reasoning about DOM. In: PODS 2008, pp. 261–270. ACM, New York (2008)
9. He, J., Hoare, C.A.R., Sanders, J.W.: Data refinement refined. In: Robinet, B., Wilhelm, R. (eds.) ESOP 1986. LNCS, vol. 213, pp. 187–196. Springer, Heidelberg (1986)
10. Hoare, C.A.R.: Proof of correctness of data representations. Acta Inf. 1(4), 271–281 (1972)
11. Mijajlović, I., Torp-Smith, N., O'Hearn, P.W.: Refinement and separation contexts. In: Lodaya, K., Mahajan, M. (eds.) FSTTCS 2004. LNCS, vol. 3328, pp. 421–433. Springer, Heidelberg (2004)
12. O'Hearn, P.W., Reynolds, J., Yang, H.: Local reasoning about programs that alter data structures. In: Fribourg, L. (ed.) CSL 2001 and EACSL 2001. LNCS, vol. 2142, pp. 1–19. Springer, Heidelberg (2001)
13. Parkinson, M., Bierman, G.: Separation logic and abstraction. In: POPL 2005. SIGPLAN Not., vol. 40, pp. 247–258. ACM, New York (2005)

Author Index

Printing: Mercedes-Druck, Berlin
Binding: Stein+Lehmann, Berlin